Barnes & Noble Shakespeare

David Scott Kastan
Series Editor

BARNES & NOBLE SHAKESPEARE features newly edited texts of the plays prepared by the world's premiere Shakespeare scholars. Each edition provides new scholarship with an introduction, commentary, unusually full and informative notes, an account of the play as it would have been performed in Shakespeare's theaters, and an essay on how to read Shakespeare's language.

DAVID SCOTT KASTAN is the Old Dominion Foundation Professor in the Humanities at Columbia University and one of the world's leading authorities on Shakespeare.

Barnes & Noble Shakespeare
Published by Barnes & Noble
122 Fifth Avenue
New York, NY 10011
www.barnesandnoble.com/shakespeare

Image on p. 360
William Shakespeare, *Comedies, Histories, & Tragedies*, London, 1623, Bequest of Stephen Whitney Phoenix, Rare Book & Manuscript Library, Columbia University.

Library of Congress Cataloging-in-Publication Data

Shakespeare, William, 1564–1616.
  King Lear / William Shakespeare.
    p. cm. — (Barnes and Noble Shakespeare)
  Includes bibliographical references.
  ISBN-13: 978-1-4114-0079-5
  ISBN-10: 1-4114-0079-8
  1. Lear, King (Legendary character)—Drama. 2. Inheritance and succession—Drama. 3. Fathers and daughters—Drama. 4. Kings and rulers—Drama. 5. Aging parents—Drama. 6. Britons—Drama. I. Title.

  PR2819.A1 2006
  822.3'3—dc22
                        2006018627

Printed and bound in the United States.

     9 10

KING LEAR

William **SHAKESPEARE**

ANDREW HADFIELD
EDITOR

Barnes & Noble Shakespeare

Contents

Introduction to *King Lear*
by Andrew Hadfield

In the present case the public has decided. Cordelia from the time of Tate has always retired from the story with victory and felicity. And if my sensations could add anything to the general suffrage, I might relate that I was many years ago so shocked by Cordelia's death that I know not whether I ever endured to read again the last scenes of the play till I undertook to revise them as editor.

Samuel Johnson's words acknowledge the pain and bewilderment that many readers and audiences have felt when confronted by the brutal horror of the ending of Shakespeare's play. In fact, after the Restoration of the monarchy in 1660, when the theaters reopened, Nahum Tate radically altered Shakespeare's conclusion. Instead of Lear entering with the dead Cordelia in his arms, and the false hope that she might still be alive, Tate had Cordelia live, marry Edgar, and restore legitimate monarchy to Britain while her father retired to discuss the meaning of life with his friend Gloucester. Tate's revisions were often sneered at by commentators in the last century as a sentimental refusal to face the harsh reality of the human condition. But surely he has a point: *King Lear* is a relentlessly pessimistic play that was more often admired than enjoyed. Charles Lamb, writing in 1810, felt that *Lear* was "beyond all art" because it was "too hard and stony." Most tellingly he claimed, "*Lear* is essentially impossible to be represented on a stage." As with Samuel Johnson, it was the awful horror of the ending that so disturbed Lamb.

It is, however, important to realize that it was Shakespeare who altered the story of King Lear, not Tate. Tate actually restored it to its original form. Shakespeare's principal source was Geoffrey of Monmouth's *History of the Kings of Britain*, a twelfth-century chronicle that became one of the most influential works of British history. Geoffrey tells the story of the kings of Britain from the arrival of Brutus, a descendant of Aeneas, founder of Rome, to the flight of the Britons to Brittany when the Saxons overwhelm them. One of Geoffrey's principal achievements was to provide the first serious account of the reign of King Arthur, one of the central attractions of the book and something we should consider when thinking about the reasons for interest in stories such as that of King Lear. Geoffrey provided brief histories of all the reigns of the ancient British kings (one of these was Cymbeline, an account Shakespeare used later when he wrote one of his last plays about Cymbeline's reign).

Geoffrey describes Leir (Shakespeare's Lear) as a successful and powerful king, ruling before the invasion of the Romans for sixty years. He divides his kingdom among his three daughters when he recognizes that he is too old to rule effectively, giving each the chance to gain a larger share by stating exactly how much they love him. His plan is to give his favorite daughter, Cordelia, the chance to obtain the lion's share. Everything goes horribly wrong, however, when she refuses to play the game and her conniving elder sisters, Goneril and Regan, hoodwink their credulous father. Leir, furious with Cordelia, marries her off to Aganippus, King of the Franks, without a dowry. Goneril and Regan rule half of Britain with their husbands, the Dukes of Cornwall and Albany, while Leir rules the other half. Eventually Leir's people rebel, and Leir is reduced to staying with his two daughters, who cut down his retinue of knights until he is virtually alone.

Realizing his errors, Leir crosses the channel to Gaul and is restored to royal dignity by his truly loyal daughter. Together they invade Britain, defeat Goneril and Regan, and Leir is restored to his throne. After three years of peaceful rule, he dies, and Cordelia succeeds him. She rules successfully for some years but is eventually captured in a civil war fought with her sisters' sons. She commits suicide in prison.

From this outline it is clear how much of the historical story Shakespeare changed and how purposeful these changes were, especially when we note that a play on the same subject, *The Chronicle History of King Leir*, was performed at Philip Henslowe's Rose Theatre in 1594, which stuck largely to what Geoffrey had written. What we can conclude is that Shakespeare was deliberately altering a well-known story about Britain's past, suggesting that *King Lear*, even though it is described as a "history" in the Quarto of 1608, should not be read as a play of the same sort as the English histories he wrote in the 1590s. It is not an attempt merely to dramatize historical events. Shakespeare deliberately reshapes the history to make it into a powerful dramatic statement about both the human capacity for evil but also for love. Nahum Tate simply tried to return the story to its original form when he altered what Shakespeare had written. Shakespeare has written a much darker play than even the original history suggested, and Samuel Johnson and Charles Lamb were undoubtedly right to seize on that aspect.

King Lear starts off as the story that most of the audience would have recognized, and it is only as the plot unfolds that an audience would realize how much Shakespeare had changed the events. The changes that Shakespeare made can be summarized easily enough. First, he added the subplot of Gloucester, Edgar, and Edmund, based on Sir Philip Sidney's long romance, the *Arcadia*. Second, he condensed the action in the opening scenes so that the marriages take place immediately, and he made other changes to streamline the plot. Third, he added the characters of Kent and the Fool. Fourth, he invented the famous central scenes on the heath. Fifth, he developed Lear's anger into full-fledged madness. Sixth, the ending is dramatically altered so that Lear and Cordelia's forces lose the battle and she dies. These are substantial alterations that go well beyond the kinds of changes made in other plays based on historical sources.

We can, of course, never be entirely certain why Shakespeare made such changes and why he wrote *King Lear* in the way that he did, but the alterations suggest how bold and experimental Shakespeare could be. He endlessly tried out new forms, ideas, and styles in his work, eager to push the boundaries of what was possible on the London stage in Elizabethan and Jacobean England. Perhaps we should read *King Lear* mainly as a daring literary experiment rather than an existential statement about the nature of mankind. Shakespeare produced plays in clusters: in the 1590s he forged a new form of romantic comedy that was probably designed to rival the comedies of humors produced by his rivals at other playhouses. *Twelfth Night*, for example, seems designed to use the conventions of cross-dressing and the confusions such conventions create and push them to their limits. In the final phase of his career, he produced a series of romances, plays that did not fit into any of the recognized dramatic categories of history, tragedy, tragicomedy, or comedy. Shakespeare, especially once his position and status were secure, appears to have tried to see what he could do with the literary and cultural resources available to him, pushing them well beyond the formal and emotional limits other playwrights had established for them.

Critics of *King Lear* frequently note that the action constantly confounds our expectations. Edgar's disguise as Poor Tom, which might be thought to help Lear by showing him that there are those who are far worse off than he is, only serves to increase Lear's torment and madness. Later, Edgar tries to cure his father by making him think he has survived a fall from the tops of Dover cliffs. Just as Gloucester has accepted his fate and decided that he will "bear / Affliction till it do cry out itself / 'Enough, enough'" (4.5.75–77), Lear enters at his most insane, undercutting any progress toward restoration and harmony. As Lear moves toward an acceptance of his own fate and appears to be redeemed through the good offices of Cordelia, the allies lose the war, Cordelia is hanged, and Lear dies perhaps deluded that she might still live. The play almost perversely seems to frustrate any hope we have that it might result in a happy ending, confronting us with a bleak, desolate universe in which the gods are hostile to humanity rather than benign or simply indifferent to mankind's fate and in which the only mercy may be to die. Senecan tragedy, with its violent action and language, showing how the gods were immune to the pleas and actions of mankind, had enjoyed a considerable vogue on the Elizabethan stage and had influenced works such as *Hamlet*. *King Lear* suggests that Shakespeare, setting his play in the old, pagan world of ancient Britain, was deliberately outdoing Senecan writers and seeing how far he could test the limits of the form.

The play is replete with violence and brutality that seem ever more appropriate as the tragedy unfolds. Edgar's admission at the start of Act Four, "The worst is not / So long as we can say, 'This is the worst'" (4.1.27–28), is at one level a trite piece of homespun wisdom. But on another it is true, culminating in the horror of Lear's virtually unactable lines:

> Why should a dog, a horse, a rat have life,
> And thou no breath at all? Thou'lt come no more,
> Never, never, never, never, never! (5.3.281–283)

Or his agonized "Howl, howl, howl" (5.3.231). The play shows literally unspeakable suffering and makes us ask why such suffering exists. The answer the play gives may well be that in the old, pagan world there was no reason, and it was foolish to look for hope in a malign universe. Perhaps Lear is right to see it as a living Hell when he imagines himself "bound / Upon a wheel of fire, that mine own tears / Do scald like molten lead" (4.6.43–45). The images the characters invoke suggest that the world is a brutal place where only the fittest and the nastiest can hope to survive. The play makes numerous references to monsters and demons, who are dangerous and at times seem dominant. Albany calls Goneril a "devil," for example, but insists that "Proper deformity shows not in the fiend / So horrid as in woman" (4.2.35–37) making her even more monstrous than the devil himself.

Goneril is indeed fiend-like, capable, like her sister, of inhuman cruelty. Perhaps injustice is finally punished, as she commits suicide offstage after poisoning her sister. Albany indeed insists that the gods are proven just by the killing of Cornwall by his servant: "This shows you are above, / You justicers, that these our nether crimes / So speedily can venge" (4.2.46–48). But has the "wheel . . . come full circle" (5.3.165) as Edmund claims? And, if so, is this simply an arbitrary turn of the Wheel of Fortune rather than evidence of the action of a benign order in the universe? The fates of Lear and Cordelia might well suggest that the monsters of this world do really rule.

The critical history of *King Lear* would suggest that readings of the play have actually been remarkably consistent. If *Lear* was sidelined and transformed from the late seventeenth to the end of the nineteenth century because it disturbed and provoked readers so much that they could hardly bear to read it, to say nothing of watching it on stage, it was embraced in the twentieth century for precisely these reasons. A. C. Bradley's *Shakespearean Tragedy* (1904), probably the most influential book in the last 200 years of Shakespeare criticism, tried to make sense of Cordelia's death, the key problem for most readers. Bradley's starting point follows on from Samuel Johnson's question of why Cordelia needs to die: "I suppose no reader ever failed to ask that question, and to ask it with something more than pain,—to ask it, if only for a moment, in bewilderment or dismay, and even perhaps in tones of protest." Bradley tries to turn the question around rather than avoid it, embracing what he sees as a vital paradox that characterizes the greatest art. Bradley claims that we are moved by *King Lear* precisely because we witness the suffering and death of an innocent and wonderful human being, forcing us to think seriously about the nature of goodness:

> The force of the impression . . . depends on the very violence of the contrast between the outward and the inward, Cordelia's death and Cordelia's soul. The more unmotivated, unmerited, senseless, monstrous, her fate, the more do we feel that it does not concern her. The extremity of the disproportion between prosperity and goodness first shocks us, and then flashes on us the conviction that our whole attitude in asking or expecting that goodness should be prosperous is wrong[.]

Bradley sees *King Lear* as Shakespeare's most profound and sublime play, challenging received wisdom and laying bare the human condition. We become aware of the irreconcilable contrasts that define the nature of life, the contrast of suffering and goodness, "Sunshine and rain at once" (Appendix page 351, line 18).

Bradley's reading of *Lear* helped to inaugurate a revival of the play, so that it has come to be seen as Shakespeare's greatest work, eclipsing its rival *Hamlet*, which had been the play that had inspired the Romantics. Once *Lear* was performed in its unadulterated state, the leading role became one of the most challenging roles for any established stage actor to play. After the two World Wars, the bleak vision of the play was what made it seem especially relevant. In the 1960s, the flamboyant Polish critic Jan Kott argued that Shakespeare was indeed our contemporary in a best-selling book. Central to Kott's claims was the example of *King Lear*, which he compared to Samuel Beckett's plays *Waiting for Godot* and *Endgame*, in Kott's eyes, a grotesque vision of the sad absurdity of human existence. Kott argued that Shakespeare's work showed mankind as ridiculous and helpless in the face of the overwhelming and malign attention of the nameless gods. Like many twentieth-century readers of the play, he paid particular attention to the role of the Fool and saw his commentary as central to the meaning of the play. Just as the Fool, when pushed, defines himself as "Lear's shadow" (1.4.202), Kott suggested that "Everyone is just a shadow of himself; just a man," rather than rooted within a sustaining metaphysical order that creates meaning. *Lear* was taken to represent Shakespeare's most profound and complete statement of the pointlessness of existence in a world without values.

In an important sense, Kott's reading is a mirror image of that of Nahum Tate and Samuel Johnson. The latter two see the play as simply too gloomy to serve the proper tragic purpose of uplifting its audience after an emotionally draining experience so that the world is better understood. Kott sees *Lear* as a work that does make sense of the world in a century most notable for its appalling brutality and mass destruction. Kott undoubtedly had in mind Theodor Adorno's famous meditations on the possibility of producing art after Auschwitz in his *Negative Dialectics* (1966). Adorno argued against those who felt that art and literature were pointless after the Holocaust. On the contrary, it was vital that attention was paid to difficult and disturbing works of literature, art, and music, which would force audiences to confront the unbearable reality of the world. Adorno cited Beckett's *Endgame*, with its grim images of humans helpless in the face of an unbearable, unthinkable, and unknowable reality, as a consummate work of postwar literature that looked back directly to the atrocities of the concentration camps. Kott's attempt to link Shakespeare to Beckett, *King Lear* to *Endgame*, was a means of suggesting that both were our key contemporary writers as they alone were fearless enough to describe the nature of our nihilistic universe, proved by the experience of life in an inhuman, totalitarian world.

Kott's reading of *King Lear* has had a significant influence not just on subsequent readings of the play, but also on its role within contemporary culture as the most profound play by the world's pre-eminent author. Peter Brook's production of *Lear* in 1962, with Paul Schofield in the title role, was undoubtedly influenced by Kott's conception of Shakespeare. Brook represented the characters "stumbling about blindly in a hostile universe," as Reg Foakes put it, cutting any lines that might detract from a relentlessly pessimistic message, such as Edmund's last efforts to put right some of the wrongs he has perpetrated. Edward Bond's *Lear* (1971), a modern adaptation of Shakespeare's play, is an equally grim vision, concentrating less on a hostile universe and more on the inhuman behavior of men and women living in exploitative societies. Bond makes Cordelia a more central character than Shakespeare does and the wife of a carpenter, not the daughter of the king. She is raped at the start of the play and then returns to avenge the abuse she has suffered. Wresting the crown from Bodice and Fontanelle, Lear's daughters who have ousted their father, Cordelia becomes exactly like her predecessors once in power. The central image of Bond's play is a wall Lear builds to keep out the enemies of the state. He dies, having realized the futility of his life's work, when he is shot while trying to tear it down.

King Lear has also been made into two films that testify to the text's role as a modern parable of greed, violence, and despair. Peter Brook's 1962 stage production was adapted for film in 1971. The movie sets the story against the backdrop of a bleak winter landscape in Jutland, evoking the conflict and disruption of the heroic age of migrations after the Romans left Britain. The most significant traces that humans have left on the landscape are a series of primitive fortresses and dugouts, marking out a terrain geared toward warfare. Brook concentrates on the faces of the protagonists, either showing them looking blank and confused, unable to comprehend the horror that is taking place, or in the process of being violently disfigured (Gloucester has his eyes removed with a spoon, Edmund is decapitated). The film ends with a stark and haunting image— one of the best examples of the way in which *Lear* features in contemporary culture—of Lear carrying the dead Cordelia in his arms, striding along a deserted beach as the camera pans from his expressionless face to his body and up toward an empty gray sky. This *Lear* is indeed *Endgame*.

Akira Kurosawa's epic film adaptation *Ran* (1985) concentrates much more on the devastating political effects of Lear's actions than Brook's existential version. It is also an assault on the senses, a riot of color, whereas Brook's *Lear* is black and white. Kurosawa translates the story to medieval Japan, dominated by samurai warlords fighting to expand and protect their unstable dynasties. Hidetora (Lear) abdicates and divides his kingdom among his three sons, Taro (Goneril), Jiro (Regan), and Saburo (Cordelia). Hidetora explains that unity is strength, but he banishes Saburo, who warns him that it will not be long before internal division and the legacy of past actions destroy their fragile bonds. Saburo's prophecy is proved horribly apt as the past returns to overwhelm Hidetora. The victims of his past actions are everywhere, one of them being Lady Kaede, the wife of Taro, whose family was wiped out by Hidetora and who now dedicates her life to plotting his downfall. Eventually, of course, she succeeds.

Ran is a timely reminder that Shakespeare's tragedies were politically charged plays that made extensive reference to larger social forces than many productions of *King Lear* acknowledge. Hidetora pays for his past crimes with Kurosawa developing Lear's realization on the heath that he has been a less than ideal king:

> There thou mightst
> behold the great image of authority: a dog's obeyed
> in office.
> Thou rascal beadle, hold thy bloody hand!
> Why dost thou lash that whore? Strip thine own back;
> Thou hotly lusts to use her in that kind
> For which thou whipp'st her. The usurer hangs the cozener.
> Through tattered clothes great vices do appear;
> Robes and furred gowns hide all. Plate sin with gold,
> And the strong lance of justice hurtless breaks;
> Arm it in rags, a pygmy's straw does pierce it. (4.5.154–164)

The downfall of Shakespeare's Lear is only indirectly caused by his failure to govern properly, but Hidetora meets his fate because of his ruthless behavior when in power and his failure to realize that the present is determined by what has gone before, a modern parable as potent as that of *Endgame*.

Ran, even though it is an altered version of *Lear*, is faithful in many ways to the spirit of the original. Shakespeare's play had a distinct topical relevance, one rooted in contemporary arguments about kingship and the fear of the actions of the mighty. When James VI became James I in England in 1603 after Elizabeth died, he tried his hardest to bring about a formal union of England and Scotland. He failed to achieve this in 1604, when parliament rejected his plans, but he always styled himself *King of Britain* and tried to rule accordingly. Shakespeare wrote *King Lear* (circa 1605) in the wake of James's failed plans. As if to emphasize the link between his play and contemporary Britain, Shakespeare names the husbands of Goneril and Regan the Dukes of Cornwall and Albany, the titles of James's two sons, Henry and Charles, at the time the play was written.

While it is clear enough that there is a topical resonance in a play that represents a king of Britain immediately after the incumbent monarch granted himself the same title, the exact relationship between the Britain of *King Lear* and the Britain of King James, or between Lear and James as monarchs, is less easy to categorize. Was *Lear* a warning to James about the abuse of power and the dangers of autocratic rule? Was James a king like Lear who failed to listen to his advisors and so ruined himself and the lives of his subjects? Or does the play have a much more comforting message for the King and his supporters, working by way of contrast rather than comparison? It could be that Lear was an antitype of James, giving away his kingdom when he should have stuck to his guns and ruled with full power and majesty. In this reading, the problem the play is exposing is the lack of proper authority, not its abuse. Perhaps Shakespeare is arguing for a better, stronger monarchy, not its limitation or control. After all, this was a common feeling in the early years of James's reign, with many powerful men glad to have a king after years of what they saw as vacillating female rule. But for us the topical political meanings fade away in the brutal action that too easily recalls the murderousness of modern life and the deep need to find comfort, meaning, and value in the face of its constant threat.

Shakespeare and His England
by David Scott Kastan

hakespeare is a household name, one of those few that don't need a first name to be instantly recognized. His first name was, of course, William, and he (and it, in its Latin form, *Gulielmus*) first came to public notice on April 26, 1564, when his baptism was recorded in the parish church of Stratford-upon-Avon, a small market town about ninety miles northwest of London. It isn't known exactly when he was born, although traditionally his birthday is taken to be April 23rd. It is a convenient date (perhaps too convenient) because that was the date of his death in 1616, as well as the date of St. George's Day, the annual feast day of England's patron saint. It is possible Shakespeare was born on the 23rd; no doubt he was born within a day or two of that date. In a time of high rates of infant mortality, parents would not wait long after a baby's birth for the baptism. Twenty percent of all children would die before their first birthday.

Life in 1564, not just for infants, was conspicuously vulnerable. If one lived to age fifteen, one was likely to live into one's fifties, but probably no more than 60 percent of those born lived past their mid-teens. Whole towns could be ravaged by epidemic disease. In 1563, the year before Shakespeare was born, an outbreak of plague claimed over one third of the population of London. Fire, too, was a constant threat; the thatched roofs of many houses were highly flammable, as well as offering handy nesting places for insects and rats. Serious crop failures in several years of the decade of the 1560s created food shortages, severe enough in many cases to lead to the starvation of the elderly and the infirm, and lowering the resistances of many others so that between 1536 and 1560 influenza claimed over 200,000 lives.

Shakespeare's own family in many ways reflected these unsettling realities. He was one of eight children, two of whom did not survive their first year, one of whom died at age eight; one lived to twenty-seven, while the four surviving siblings died at ages ranging from Edmund's thirty-nine to William's own fifty-two years. William married at an unusually early age. He was only eighteen, though his wife was twenty-six, almost exactly the norm of the day for women, though men normally married also in their mid- to late twenties. Shakespeare's wife Anne was already pregnant at the time that the marriage was formally confirmed, and a daughter, Susanna, was born six months later, in May 1583. Two years later, she gave birth to twins, Hamnet and Judith. Hamnet would die in his eleventh year.

If life was always at risk from what Shakespeare would later call "the thousand natural shocks / That flesh is heir to" (*Hamlet*, 3.1.61–62), the incessant threats to peace were no less unnerving, if usually less immediately life threatening. There were almost daily rumors of foreign invasion and civil war as the Protestant Queen Elizabeth assumed the crown in 1558 upon the death of her Catholic half sister, Mary. Mary's reign had been marked by the public burnings of Protestant "heretics," by the seeming subordination of England to Spain, and by a commitment to a ruinous war with France, that, among its other effects, fueled inflation and encouraged a debasing of the currency. If, for many, Elizabeth represented the hopes for a peaceful and prosperous Protestant future, it seemed unlikely in the early days of her rule that the young monarch could hold her England together against the twin menace of the powerful Catholic monarchies of Europe and the significant part of her own population who were reluctant to give up their old faith. No wonder the Queen's principal secretary saw England in the early years of Elizabeth's rule as a land surrounded by "perils many, great and imminent."

In Stratford-upon-Avon, it might often have been easy to forget what threatened from without. The simple rural life, shared by about 90 percent of the English populace, had its reassuring natural rhythms and delights. Life was structured by the daily rising and setting of the sun, and by the change of seasons. Crops were planted and harvested; livestock was bred, its young delivered; sheep were sheared, some livestock slaughtered. Market days and fairs saw the produce and crafts of the town arrayed as people came to sell and shop—and be entertained by musicians, dancers, and troupes of actors. But even in Stratford, the lurking tensions and dangers could be daily sensed. A few months before Shakespeare was born, there had been a shocking "defacing" of images in the church, as workmen, not content merely to whitewash over the religious paintings decorating the interior as they were ordered, gouged large holes in those felt to be too "Catholic"; a few months after Shakespeare's birth, the register of the same church records another deadly outbreak of plague. The sleepy market town on the northern bank of the gently flowing river Avon was not immune from the menace of the world that surrounded it.

This was the world into which Shakespeare was born. England at his birth was still poor and backward, a fringe nation on the periphery of Europe. English itself was a minor language, hardly spoken outside of the country's borders. Religious tension was inescapable, as the old Catholic faith was trying determinedly to hold on, even as Protestantism was once again anxiously trying to establish itself as the national religion. The country knew itself vulnerable to serious threats both from without and from within. In 1562, the young Queen, upon whom so many people's hopes rested, almost fell victim to smallpox, and in 1569 a revolt of the Northern earls tried to remove her from power and restore Catholicism as the national religion. The following year, Pope

Pius V pronounced the excommunication of "Elizabeth, the pretended queen of England" and forbade Catholic subjects obedience to the monarch on pain of their own excommunication. "Now we are in an evil way and going to the devil," wrote one clergyman, "and have all nations in our necks."

It was a world of dearth, danger, and domestic unrest. Yet it would soon dramatically change, and Shakespeare's literary contribution would, for future generations, come to be seen as a significant measure of England's remarkable transformation. In the course of Shakespeare's life, England, hitherto an unsophisticated and under-developed backwater acting as a bit player in the momentous political dramas taking place on the European continent, became a confident, prosperous, global presence. But this new world was only accidentally, as it is often known today, "The Age of Shakespeare." To the degree that historical change rests in the hands of any individual, credit must be given to the Queen. This new world arguably was "The Age of Elizabeth," even if it was not the Elizabethan Golden Age, as it has often been portrayed.

The young Queen quickly imposed her personality upon the nation. She had talented councilors around her, all with strong ties to her of friendship or blood, but the direction of government was her own. She was strong willed and cautious, certain of her right to rule and convinced that stability was her greatest responsibility. The result may very well have been, as historians have often charged, that important issues facing England were never dealt with head-on and left to her successors to settle, but it meant also that she was able to keep her England unified and for the most part at peace.

Religion posed her greatest challenge, though it is important to keep in mind that in this period, as an official at Elizabeth's court said, "Religion and the commonwealth cannot be parted asunder." Faith then was not the largely voluntary commitment it is today, nor was there any idea of some separation of church and state. Religion was literally a matter of life and death, of salvation and damnation, and the Church was the Church of England. Obedience to it was not only a matter of conscience but also of law. It was the single issue on which the nation was most likely to be torn apart.

Elizabeth's great achievement was that she was successful in ensuring that the Church of England became formally a Protestant Church, but she did so without either driving most of her Catholic subjects to sedition or alienating the more radical Protestant community. The so-called "Elizabethan Settlement" forged a broad Christian community of what has been called prayer-book Protestantism, even as many of its practitioners retained, as a clergyman said, "still a smack and savor of popish principles." If there were forces on both sides who were uncomfortable with the Settlement—committed Protestants, who wanted to do away with all vestiges of the old faith, and convinced Catholics, who continued to swear their allegiance to Rome—the majority of the country, as she hoped, found ways to live comfortably both within the law and within their faith. In 1571, she wrote to the Duke of Anjou that the forms of worship she recommended would "not properly compel any man to alter his opinion in the great matters now in controversy in the Church." The official toleration of religious ambiguity, as well as the familiar experience of an official change of state religion accompanying the crowning of a new monarch, produced a world where the familiar labels of Protestant and Catholic failed to define the forms of faith that most English people practiced. But for Elizabeth, most matters of faith could be left to individuals, as long as the Church itself, and Elizabeth's position at its head, would remain unchallenged.

In international affairs, she was no less successful with her pragmatism and willingness to pursue limited goals. A complex mix of prudential concerns about religion, the economy, and national security drove her foreign policy. She did not have imperial ambitions; in the main, she wanted only to be sure there would be no invasion of England and to encourage English trade. In the event, both goals brought England into conflict with Spain, determining the increasingly anti-Catholic tendencies of English foreign policy and, almost accidentally, England's emergence as a world power. When Elizabeth came to the throne, England was in many ways a mere satellite nation to the Netherlands, which was part of the Hapsburg Empire that the Catholic Philip II (who had briefly and unhappily been married to her predecessor and half sister, Queen Mary) ruled from Spain; by the end of her reign England was Spain's most bitter rival.

The transformation of Spain from ally to enemy came in a series of small steps (or missteps), no one of which was intended to produce what in the end came to pass. A series of posturings and provocations on both sides led to the rupture. In 1568, things moved to their breaking point, as the English confiscated a large shipment of gold that the Spanish were sending to their troops in the Netherlands. The following year saw the revolt of the Catholic earls in Northern England, followed by the papal excommunication of the Queen in 1570, both of which were by many in England assumed to be at the initiative, or at very least with the tacit support, of Philip. In fact he was not involved, but England under Elizabeth would never again think of Spain as a loyal friend or reliable ally. Indeed, Spain quickly became its mortal enemy. Protestant Dutch rebels had been opposing the Spanish domination of the Netherlands since the early 1560s, but, other than periodic financial support, Elizabeth had done little to encourage them. But in 1585, she sent troops under the command of the Earl of Leicester to support the Dutch rebels against the Spanish. Philip decided then to launch a full-scale attack on England, with the aim of deposing Elizabeth and restoring the Catholic faith. An English assault on Cadiz in 1587 destroyed a number of Spanish ships, postponing Philip's plans, but in the summer of 1588 the mightiest navy in the world, Philip's grand armada, with 132 ships and 30,493 sailors and troops, sailed for England.

By all rights, it should have been a successful invasion, but a combination of questionable Spanish tactics and a fortunate shift of wind resulted in one of England's greatest victories. The English had twice failed to intercept the armada off the coast of Portugal, and the Spanish fleet made its way to England, almost catching the English ships resupplying in Plymouth. The English navy was on its heels, when conveniently the Spanish admiral decided to anchor in the English Channel off the French port of Calais to wait for additional troops coming from the Netherlands. The English attacked with fireships, sinking four Spanish galleons, and strong winds from the south prevented an effective counterattack from the Spanish. The Spanish fleet was pushed into the North Sea, where it regrouped and decided its safest course was to attempt the difficult voyage home around Scotland and Ireland, losing almost half its ships on the way. For many in England the improbable victory was a miracle, evidence of God's favor for Elizabeth and the Protestant nation. Though war with Spain would not end for another fifteen years, the victory over the armada turned England almost overnight into a major world power, buoyed by confidence that they were chosen by God and, more tangibly, by a navy that could compete for control of the seas.

From a backward and insignificant Hapsburg satellite, Elizabeth's England had become, almost by accident, the leader of Protestant Europe. But if the victory over the armada signaled England's new place in the world, it hardly marked the end of England's travails. The economy, which initially was fueled by the military buildup, in the early 1590s fell victim to inflation, heavy taxation to support the war with Spain, the inevitable wartime disruptions of trade, as well as crop failures and a general economic downturn in Europe. Ireland, over which England had been attempting to impose its rule since 1168, continued to be a source of trouble and great expense (in some years costing the crown nearly one fifth of its total revenues). Even when the most organized of the rebellions, begun in 1594 and led by Hugh O'Neill, Earl of Tyrone, formally ended in 1603, peace and stability had not been achieved.

But perhaps the greatest instability came from the uncertainty over the succession, an uncertainty that marked Elizabeth's reign from its beginning. Her near death from smallpox in 1562 reminded the nation that an unmarried queen could not insure the succession, and Elizabeth was under constant pressure to marry and produce an heir. She was always aware of and deeply resented the pressure, announcing as early as 1559: "this shall be for me sufficient that a marble stone shall declare that a queen, having reigned such a time, lived and died a virgin." If, however, it was for her "sufficient," it was not so for her advisors and for much of the nation, who hoped she would wed. Arguably Elizabeth was the wiser, knowing that her unmarried hand was a political advantage, allowing her to diffuse threats or create alliances with the seeming possibility of a match. But as with so much in her reign, the strategy bought temporary stability at the price of longer-term solutions.

By the mid 1590s, it was clear that she would die unmarried and without an heir, and various candidates were positioning themselves to succeed her. Enough anxiety was produced that all published debate about the succession was forbidden by law. There was no direct descendant of the English crown to claim rule, and all the claimants had to reach well back into their family history to find some legitimacy. The best genealogical claim belonged to King James VI of Scotland. His mother, Mary, Queen of Scots, was the granddaughter of James IV of Scotland and Margaret Tudor, sister to Elizabeth's father, Henry VIII. Though James had right on his side, he was, it must be remembered, a foreigner. Scotland shared the island with England but was a separate nation. Great Britain, the union of England and Scotland, would not exist formally until 1707, but with Elizabeth's death early in the morning of March 24, 1603, surprisingly uneventfully the thirty-seven-year-old James succeeded to the English throne. Two nations, one king: King James VI of Scotland, King James I of England.

Most of his English subjects initially greeted the announcement of their new monarch with delight, relieved that the crown had successfully been transferred without any major disruption and reassured that the new King was married with two living sons. However, quickly many became disenchanted with a foreign King who spoke English with a heavy accent, and dismayed even further by the influx of Scots in positions of power. Nonetheless, the new King's greatest political liability may well have been less a matter of nationality than of temperament: he had none of Elizabeth's skill and ease in publicly wooing her subjects. The Venetian ambassador wrote back to the doge that the new King was unwilling to "caress the people, nor make them that good cheer the late Queen did, whereby she won their loves."

He was aloof and largely uninterested in the daily activities of governing, but he was interested in political theory and strongly committed to the cause of peace. Although a steadfast Protestant, he lacked the reflexive anti-Catholicism of many of his subjects. In England, he achieved a broadly consensual community of Protestants. The so-called King James Bible, the famous translation published first in 1611, was the result of a widespread desire to have an English Bible that spoke to all the nation, transcending the religious divisions that had placed three different translations in the hands of his subjects. Internationally, he styled himself *Rex Pacificus* (the peace-loving king). In 1604, the Treaty of London brought Elizabeth's war with Spain formally to an end, and over the next decade he worked to bring about political marriages that might cement stable alliances. In 1613, he married his daughter to the leader of the German Protestants, while the following year he began discussions with Catholic Spain to marry his son to the Infanta Maria. After some ten years of negotiations, James's hopes for what was known as the Spanish match were finally abandoned, much to the delight of the nation, whose long-felt fear and hatred for Spain outweighed the subtle political logic behind the plan.

But if James sought stability and peace, and for the most part succeeded in his aims (at least until 1618, when the bitter religio-political conflicts on the European continent swirled well out of the King's control), he never really achieved concord and cohesion. He ruled over two kingdoms that did not know, like, or even want to understand one another, and his rule did little to bring them closer together. His England remained separate from his Scotland, even as he ruled over both. And even his England remained self divided, as in truth it always was under Elizabeth, ever more a nation of prosperity and influence but still one forged out of deep-rooted divisions of means, faiths, and allegiances that made the very nature of English identity a matter of confusion and concern. Arguably this is the very condition of great drama—sufficient peace and prosperity to support a theater industry and sufficient provocation in the troubling uncertainties about what the nation was and what fundamentally mattered to its people to inspire plays that would offer tentative solutions or at the very least make the troubling questions articulate and moving.

Nine years before James would die in 1625, Shakespeare died, having returned from London to the small market town in which he was born. If London, now a thriving modern metropolis of well over 200,000 people, had, like the nation itself, been transformed in the course of his life, the Warwickshire market town still was much the same. The house in which Shakespeare was born still stood, as did the church in which he was baptized and the school in which he learned to read and write. The river Avon still ran slowly along the town's southern limits. What had changed was that Shakespeare was now its most famous citizen, and, although it would take more than another 100 years to fully achieve this, he would in time become England's, for having turned the great ethical, social, and political issues of his own age into plays that would live forever.

William Shakespeare: A Chronology

1585 February 2: Twins, Hamnet and Judith, baptized (Shakespeare is 20)

1586 Babington Plot to dethrone Elizabeth and replace her with Mary, Queen of Scots

1587 February 8: Execution of Mary, Queen of Scots

1587 Rose Theatre built

1588 August: Defeat of the Spanish armada (Shakespeare is 24)

1588 September 4: Death of Robert Dudley, Earl of Leicester

1590 First three books of Spenser's *Faerie Queene* published; Marlowe's *Tamburlaine* published

1592 March 3: *Henry VI, Part One* performed at the Rose Theatre (Shakespeare is 27)

1593 February–November: Theaters closed because of plague

1593 Publication of *Venus and Adonis*

1594 Publication of *Titus Andronicus*, first play by Shakespeare to appear in print (though anonymously)

1594 Lord Chamberlain's Men formed

1595 March 15: Payment made to Shakespeare, Will Kemp, and Richard Burbage for performances at court in December, 1594

1595 Swan Theatre built

1596 Books 4–6 of *The Faerie Queene* published

1596 August 11: Burial of Shakespeare's son, Hamnet (Shakespeare is 32)

1596–1599 Shakespeare living in St. Helen's, Bishopsgate, London

1596 October 20: Grant of Arms to John Shakespeare

1597   May 4: Shakespeare purchases New Place, one of the two largest houses in Stratford (Shakespeare is 33)

1598   Publication of *Love's Labor's Lost*, first extant play with Shakespeare's name on the title page

1598   Publication of Francis Meres's *Palladis Tamia*, citing Shakespeare as "the best for Comedy and Tragedy" among English writers

1599   Opening of the Globe Theatre

1601   February 7: Lord Chamberlain's Men paid 40 shillings to play *Richard II* by supporters of the Earl of Essex, the day before his abortive rebellion

1601   February 17: Execution of Robert Devereaux, Earl of Essex

1601   September 8: Burial of John Shakespeare

1602   May 1: Shakespeare buys 107 acres of farmland in Stratford

1603   March 24: Queen Elizabeth dies; James VI of Scotland succeeds as James I of England (Shakespeare is 39)

1603   May 19: Lord Chamberlain's Men reformed as the King's Men

1604   Shakespeare living with the Mountjoys, a French Huguenot family, in Cripplegate, London

1604   First edition of Marlowe's *Dr. Faustus* published (written c. 1589)

1604   March 15: Shakespeare named among "players" given scarlet cloth to wear at royal procession of King James

1604   Publication of authorized version of *Hamlet* (Shakespeare is 40)

1605   Gunpowder Plot

1605   June 5: Marriage of Susanna Shakespeare to John Hall

1608   Publication of *King Lear* (Shakespeare is 44)

1608–1609   Acquisition of indoor Blackfriars Theatre by King's Men

1609   *Sonnets* published

1611   King James Bible published (Shakespeare is 47)

1612   November 6: Death of Henry, eldest son of King James

1613   February 14: Marriage of King James's daughter Elizabeth to Frederick, the Elector Palatine

1613   March 10: Shakespeare, with some associates, buys gatehouse in Blackfriars, London

1613   June 29: Fire burns the Globe Theatre

1614   Rebuilt Globe reopens

1616   February 10: Marriage of Judith Shakespeare to Thomas Quiney

1616   March 25: Shakespeare's will signed

1616   April 23: Shakespeare dies (age 52)

1616   April 23: Cervantes dies in Madrid

1616   April 25: Shakespeare buried in Holy Trinity Church in Stratford-upon-Avon

1623   August 6: Death of Anne Shakespeare

1623   October: Prince Charles, King James's son, returns from Madrid, having failed to arrange his marriage to Maria Anna, Infanta of Spain

1623   First Folio published with 36 plays (18 never previously published)

Words, Words, Words: Understanding Shakespeare's Language
by David Scott Kastan

I t is silly to pretend that it is easy to read Shakespeare. Reading Shakespeare isn't like picking up a copy of *USA Today* or *The New Yorker*, or even F. Scott Fitzgerald's *Great Gatsby* or Toni Morrison's *Beloved*. It is hard work, because the language is often unfamiliar to us and because it is more concentrated than we are used to. In the theater it is usually a bit easier. Actors can clarify meanings with gestures and actions, allowing us to get the general sense of what is going on, if not every nuance of the language that is spoken. "Action is eloquence," as Volumnia puts it in *Coriolanus*, "and the eyes of th' ignorant / More learnèd than the ears" (3.276–277). Yet the real greatness of Shakespeare rests not on "the general sense" of his plays but on the specificity and suggestiveness of the words in which they are written. It is through language that the plays' full dramatic power is realized, and it is that rich and robust language, often pushed by Shakespeare to the very limits of intelligibility, that we must learn to understand. But we can come to understand it (and enjoy it), and this essay is designed to help.

Even experienced readers and playgoers need help. They often find that his words are difficult to comprehend. Shakespeare sometimes uses words no longer current in English or with meanings that have changed. He regularly multiplies words where seemingly one might do as well or even better. He characteristically writes sentences that are syntactically complicated and imaginatively dense. And it isn't just we, removed by some 400 years from his world, who find him difficult to read; in his own time, his friends and fellow actors knew Shakespeare was hard. As two of them, John Hemings and Henry Condell, put it in their prefatory remarks to Shakespeare's First Folio in 1623, "read him, therefore, and again and again; and if then you do not like him, surely you are in some manifest danger not to understand him."

From the very beginning, then, it was obvious that the plays both deserve and demand not only careful reading but continued re-reading—and that not to read Shakespeare with all the attention a reader can bring to bear on the language is almost to guarantee that a reader will not "understand him" and remain among those who "do not like him." But Shakespeare's colleagues were nonetheless confident that the plays exerted an attraction strong enough to ensure and reward the concentration of their readers, confident, as they say, that in them "you will find enough, both to draw and hold you." The plays do exert a kind of magnetic pull, and have successfully drawn in and held readers for over 400 years.

Once we are drawn in, we confront a world of words that does not always immediately yield its delights; but it will—once we learn to see what is demanded of us. Words in Shakespeare do a lot, arguably more than anyone else has ever asked them to do. In part, it is because he needed his words to do many things at once. His stage had no sets and few props, so his words are all we have to enable us to imagine what his characters see. And they also allow us to see what the characters don't see, especially about themselves. The words are vivid and immediate, as well as complexly layered and psychologically suggestive. The difficulties they pose are not the "thee's" and "thou's" or "prithee's" and "doth's" that obviously mark the chronological distance between Shakespeare and us. When Gertrude says to Hamlet, "thou hast thy father much offended"

(3.4.8), we have no difficulty understanding her chiding, though we might miss that her use of the "thou" form of the pronoun expresses an intimacy that Hamlet pointedly refuses with his reply: "Mother, *you* have my father much offended" (3.4.9; italics mine).

Most deceptive are words that look the same as words we know but now mean something different. Words often change meanings over time. When Horatio and the soldiers try to stop Hamlet as he chases after the Ghost, Hamlet pushes past them and says, "I'll make a ghost of him that lets me" (1.4.85). It seems an odd thing to say. Why should he threaten someone who "lets" him do what he wants to do? But here "let" means "hinder," not, as it does today, "allow" (although the older meaning of the word still survives, for example, in tennis, where a "let serve" is one that is hindered by the net on its way across). There are many words that can, like this, mislead us: "his" sometimes means "its," "an" often means "if," "envy" means something more like "malice," "cousin" means more generally "kinsman," and there are others, though all are easily defined. The difficulty is that we may not stop to look thinking we already know what the word means, but in this edition a ° following the word alerts a reader that there is a gloss in the left margin, and quickly readers get used to these older meanings.

Then, of course, there is the intimidation factor—strange, polysyllabic, or Latinate words that not only are foreign to us but also must have sounded strange even to Shakespeare's audiences. When Macbeth wonders whether all the water in all the oceans of the world will be able to clean his bloody hands after the murder of Duncan, he concludes: "No; this my hand will rather / The multitudinous seas incarnadine, / Making the green one red" (2.2.64–66). Duncan's blood staining Macbeth's murderous hand is so offensive that, not merely does it resist being washed off in water, but it will "the multitudinous seas incarnadine": that is, turn the sea-green oceans blood-red. Notes will easily clarify the meaning of the two odd words, but it is worth observing that they would have been as odd to Shakespeare's readers as they are to us. The *Oxford English Dictionary* (*OED*) shows no use of "multitudinous" before this, and it records no use of "incarnadine" before 1591 (*Macbeth* was written about 1606). Both are new words, coined from the Latin, part of a process in Shakespeare's time where English adopted many Latinate words as a mark of its own emergence as an important vernacular language. Here they are used to express the magnitude of Macbeth's offense, a crime not only against the civil law but also against the cosmic order, and then the simple monosyllables of turning "the green one red" provide an immediate (and needed) paraphrase and register his own sickening awareness of the true hideousness of his deed.

As with "multitudinous" in *Macbeth*, Shakespeare is the source of a great many words in English. Sometimes he coined them himself, or, if he didn't invent them, he was the first person whose writing of them has survived. Some of these words have become part of our language, so common that it is hard to imagine they were not always part of it: for example, "assassination" (*Macbeth*, 1.7.2), "bedroom" (*A Midsummer Night's Dream*, 2.2.57), "countless" (*Titus Andronicus*, 5.3.59), "fashionable" (*Troilus and Cressida*, 3.3.165), "frugal" (*The Merry Wives of Windsor*, 2.1.28), "laughable" (*The Merchant of Venice*, 1.1.56), "lonely" (*Coriolanus*, 4.1.30), and "useful" (*King John*, 5.2.81). But other words that he originated were not as, to use yet another Shakespearean coinage, "successful" (*Titus Andronicus*, 1.1.66). Words like "crimeless" (*Henry VI, Part Two*, 2.4.63, meaning "innocent"), "facinorous" (*All's Well That Ends Well*, 2.3.30, meaning "extremely wicked"), and "recountment" (*As You Like It*, 4.3.141, meaning "narrative" or "account") have, without much resistance, slipped into oblivion. Clearly Shakespeare liked words, even unwieldy ones. His working vocabulary, about 18,000 words, is staggering, larger than almost any other English writer, and he seems to be the first person to use in print about 1,000 of these. Whether he coined the new words himself or was intrigued by the new words he heard in the streets of London doesn't really matter; the point is that he was remarkably alert to and engaged with a dynamic language that was expanding in response to England's own expanding contact with the world around it.

But it is neither new words nor old ones that are the source of the greatest difficulty of Shakespeare's language. The real difficulty (and the real delight) comes in trying to see how he uses the words, how he endows them with more than their denotative meanings. Why, for example, does Macbeth say that he hopes that the "sure and firm-set earth" (2.1.56) will not hear his steps as he goes forward to murder Duncan? Here "sure" and "firm-set" mean virtually the same thing: stable, secure, fixed. Why use two words? If this were a student paper, no doubt the teacher would circle one of them and write "redundant." But the redundancy is exactly what Shakespeare wants. One word would do if the purpose were to describe the solidity of the earth, but here the redundancy points to something different. It reveals something about Macbeth's mind, betraying through the doubling how deep is his awareness of the world of stable values that the terrible act he is about to commit must unsettle.

Shakespeare's words usually work this way: in part describing what the characters see and as often betraying what they feel. The example from *Macbeth* is a simple example of how this works. Shakespeare's words are carefully patterned. How one says something is every bit as important as what is said, and the conspicuous patterns that are created alert us to the fact that something more than the words' lexical sense has been put into play. Words can be coupled, as in the example above, or knit into even denser metaphorical constellations to reveal something about the speaker (which often the speaker does not know), as in Prince Hal's promise to his father that he will outdo the rebels' hero, Henry Percy (Hotspur):

Percy is but my factor, good my lord,

To engross up glorious deeds on my behalf.

And I will call him to so strict account

That he shall render every glory up,

Yea, even the slightest worship of his time,

Or I will tear the reckoning from his heart.

(Henry IV, Part One, 3.2.147–152)

The Prince expresses his confidence that he will defeat Hotspur, but revealingly in a reiterated language of commercial exchange ("factor," "engross," "account," "render," "reckoning") that tells us something important both about the Prince and the ways in which he understands his world. In a play filled with references to coins and counterfeiting, the speech demonstrates not only that Hal has committed himself to the business at hand, repudiating his earlier, irresponsible tavern self, but also that he knows it is a business rather than a glorious world of chivalric achievement; he inhabits a world in which value (political as well as economic) is not intrinsic but determined by what people are willing to invest, and he proves himself a master of producing desire for what he has to offer.

Or sometimes it is not the network of imagery but the very syntax that speaks, as when Claudius announces his marriage to Hamlet's mother:

Therefore our sometime sister, now our Queen,

Th' imperial jointress to this warlike state,

Have we—as 'twere with a defeated joy,

With an auspicious and a dropping eye,

With mirth in funeral and with dole in marriage,

In equal scale weighing delight and dole—

Taken to wife.   *(Hamlet, 1.2.8–14)*

All he really wants to say here is that he has married Gertrude, his former sister-in-law: "Therefore our sometime sister . . . Have we . . . Taken to wife." But the straightforward sentence gets interrupted and complicated, revealing his own discomfort with the announcement. His elaborations and intensifications of Gertrude's role ("sometime sister," "Queen," "imperial jointress"), the self-conscious rhetorical balancing of the middle three lines (indeed "in equal scale weighing delight and dole"), all declare by the all-too obvious artifice how desperate he is to hide the awkward facts behind a veneer of normalcy and propriety. The very unnaturalness of the sentence is what alerts us that we are meant to understand more than the simple relation of fact.

Why doesn't Shakespeare just say what he means? Well, he does—exactly what he means. In the example from *Hamlet* just above, Shakespeare shows us something about Claudius that Claudius doesn't know himself. Always Shakespeare's words will offer us an immediate sense of what is happening, allowing us to follow the action, but they also offer us a counterplot, pointing us to what might be behind the action, confirming or contradicting what the characters say. It is a language that shimmers with promise and possibility, opening the characters' hearts and minds to our view—and all we have to do is learn to pay attention to what is there before us.

Shakespeare's Verse

Another distinctive feature of Shakespeare's dramatic language is that much of it is in verse. Almost all of the plays mix poetry and prose, but the poetry dominates. *The Merry Wives of Windsor* has the lowest percentage (only about 13 percent verse), while *Richard II* and *King John* are written entirely in verse (the only examples, although *Henry VI, Part One* and *Part Three* have only a very few prose lines). In most of the plays, about 70 percent of the lines are written in verse.

Shakespeare's characteristic verse line is a non-rhyming iambic pentameter ("blank verse"), ten syllables with every second one stressed. In *A Midsummer Night's Dream*, Titania comes to her senses after a magic potion has led her to fall in love with an ass-headed Bottom: "Methought I was enamored of an ass" (4.1.76). Similarly, in *Romeo and Juliet*, Romeo gazes up at Juliet's window: "But soft, what light through yonder window breaks" (2.2.2). In both these examples, the line has ten syllables organized into five regular beats (each beat consisting of the stress on the second syllable of a pair, as in "But soft," the da-dum rhythm forming an "iamb"). Still, we don't hear these lines as jingles; they seem natural enough, in large part because this dominant pattern is varied in the surrounding lines.

The play of stresses indeed becomes another key to meaning, as Shakespeare alerts us to what is important. In *Measure for Measure*, Lucio urges Isabella to plead for her brother's life: "Oh, to him, to him, wench! He will relent" (2.2.129). The iambic norm (unstressed-stressed) tells us (and an actor) that the emphasis at the beginning of the line is on "to" not "him"—it is the action not the object that is being emphasized—and at the end of the line the stress falls on "will." Alternatively, the line can play against the established norm. In *Hamlet*, Claudius corrects Polonius's idea of what is bothering the Prince: "Love? His affections do not that way tend" (3.1.161). The iambic norm forces the emphasis onto "that" ("do not *that* way tend"), while the syntax forces an unexpected stress on the opening word, "Love." In the famous line, "The course of true love never did run smooth" (*A Midsummer Night's Dream*, 1.1.134), the iambic expectation is varied in both the middle and at the end of the line. Both "love" and the first syllable of "never" are stressed, as are both syllables at the end: "run smooth," creating a metrical foot in which both syllables are stressed (called a "spondee"). The point to notice is that the "da-dum, da-dum, da-dum, da-dum, da-dum" line is not inevitable; it merely sets an expectation against which many variations can be heard.

In fact, even the ten-syllable norm can be varied. Shakespeare sometimes writes lines with fewer or more syllables. Often there is an extra, unstressed syllable at the end of a line (a so-called "feminine ending"); sometimes there are verse lines with only nine. In *Henry IV, Part One*, King Henry replies incredulously to the rebel Worcester's claim that he hadn't "sought" the confrontation with the King: "You have not sought it. How comes it then?" (5.1.27). There are only nine syllables here (some earlier editors, seeking to "correct" the verse, added the word "sir" after the first question to regularize the line). But the pause where one expects a stressed syllable is dramatically effective, allowing the King's anger to be powerfully present in the silence.

As even these few examples show, Shakespeare's verse is unusually flexible, allowing a range of rhythmical effects. It should not be understood as a set of strict rules but as a flexible set of practices rooted in dramatic necessity. It is designed to highlight ideas and emotions, and it is based less upon rigid syllable counts than on an arrangement of stresses within an understood temporal norm, as one might expect from a poetry written to be heard in the theater rather than read on the page.

Here Follows Prose

Although the plays are dominated by verse, prose plays a significant role. Shakespeare's prose has its own rhythms, but it lacks the formal patterning of verse, and so is printed without line breaks and without the capitals that mark the beginning of a verse line. Like many of his fellow dramatists, Shakespeare tended to use prose for comic scenes, the shift from verse serving, especially in his early plays, as a social marker. Upper-class characters speak in verse; lower-class characters speak in prose. Thus, in *A Midsummer Night's Dream*, the Athenians of the court, as well as the fairies, all speak in verse, but the "rude mechanicals," Bottom and his artisan friends, all speak in prose, except for the comic verse they speak in their performance of "Pyramis and Thisbe."

As Shakespeare grew in experience, he became more flexible about the shifts from verse to prose, letting it, among other things, mark genre rather than class and measure various kinds of intensity. Prose becomes in the main the medium of comedy. The great comedies, like *Much Ado About Nothing, Twelfth Night,* and *As You Like It,* are all more than 50 percent prose. But even in comedy, shifts between verse and prose may be used to measure subtle emotional changes. In Act One, scene three of *The Merchant of Venice,* Shylock and Bassanio begin the scene speaking of matters of business in prose, but when Antonio enters and the deep conflict between the Christian and the Jew becomes evident, the scene shifts to verse. But prose may itself serve in moments of emotional intensity. Shylock's famous speech in Act Three, scene one, "Hath not a Jew eyes . . ." is all in prose, as is Hamlet's expression of disgust at the world ("I have of late— but wherefore I know not—lost all my mirth . . .") at 3.1.261–276. Shakespeare comes to use prose to vary the tone of a scene, as the shift from verse subtly alerts an audience or a reader to some new emotional register.

Prose becomes, as Shakespeare's art matures, not inevitably the mark of the lower classes but the mark of a salutary daily-ness. It is appropriately the medium in which letters are written, and it is the medium of a common sense that will at least challenge the potential self-deceptions of grandiloquent speech. When Rosalind mocks the excesses and artifice of Orlando's wooing in Act Four, scene one of *As You Like It,* it is in prose that she seeks something genuine in the expression of love:

> The poor world is almost six thousand years old, and in all this time there was not any man died in his own person, *videlicit* [i.e., namely], in a love cause. . . . Men have died from time to time, and worms have eaten them, but not for love.

Here the prose becomes the sound of common sense, an effective foil to the affectation of pinning poems to trees and thinking that it is real love.

It is not that prose is artless; Shakespeare's prose is no less self-conscious than his verse. The artfulness of his prose is different, of course. The seeming ordinariness of his prose is no less an effect of his artistry than is the more obvious patterning of his verse. Prose is no less serious, compressed, or indeed figurative. As with his verse, Shakespeare's prose performs numerous tasks and displays various, subtle formal qualities; and recognizing the possibilities of what it can achieve is still another way of seeing what Shakespeare puts right before us to show us what he has hidden.

Further Reading

N.F. Blake, *Shakespeare's Language: An Introduction* (New York: St. Martin's Press, 1983).

Jonathan Hope, *Shakespeare's Grammar* (London: Thomson, 2003).

Sister Miriam Joseph, *Shakespeare's Use of the Arts of Language* (New York: Columbia University Press, 1947).

M. M. Mahood, *Shakespeare's Wordplay* (London: Methuen, 1957).

Russ McDonald, *Shakespeare and the Arts of Language* (Oxford: Oxford University Press, 2001).

Brian Vickers, *The Artistry of Shakespeare's Prose* (London: Methuen, 1968).

George T. Wright, *Shakespeare's Metrical Art* (Berkeley: Univ. of California Press, 1991).

Key to the Play Text

Symbols

°   Indicates an explanation or definition in the
                 left-hand margin.

1   Indicates a gloss on the page facing the play text.

[ ]   Indicates something added or changed by the editors
                 (i.e., not in the early printed text that this edition
                 of the play is based on).

Terms

Q, Quarto   An edition of the play printed in 1608. *Quarto* refers to
                 a small, inexpensive format in which play books were
                 usually published.

F, Folio, or   The first collected edition of Shakespeare's plays,
First Folio   printed in 1623 and the basis for this edition (see
                 Editing *King Lear*, page 361).

King Lear

William Shakespeare

List of Roles

King Lear	*King of Britain*
Goneril	*his eldest daughter*
Regan	*his middle daughter*
Cordelia	*his youngest daughter*
Gloucester	*a nobleman*
Edgar	*his son, later disguised as Poor Tom*
Edmund	*a bastard son of Gloucester*
Kent	*a nobleman, later disguised as Caius*
Duke of Albany	*Goneril's husband*
Duke of Cornwall	*Regan's husband*
Fool	*Lear's jester*
King of **France**	
Duke of **Burgundy**	
Oswald	*Goneril's steward*
Curan	*a gentleman in Gloucester's household*
Old Man	*a tenant of Gloucester*
Knight	*in service to Lear*
Captains	
Gentlemen	
Servant	*in Cornwall's household*
Messengers	
Herald	

Knights, officers, soldiers, attendants, servants, and messengers

1   Gloucester

Pronounced "GLOS-ter," as it is
spelled in the 1608 Quarto.

2   *Albany than Cornwall*

The names are associated with
particular regions of Britain and
thus indicate how Lear is dividing
his kingdom (See LONGER NOTE on
page 357).

3   *division of the kingdom*

Gloucester's comments indicate
that he understands Lear to have
planned his actions in advance,
which means that the love test
is a sham. Lear intends all along
to give Cordelia the largest share
of his kingdom. These opening
comments give the audience an
ominous sense of Lear's autocratic
character, even if they show that
he understands his daughters'
true natures, something that is not
present in the sources and indicates the determined way in which
Shakespeare changed the story
that was available to him. They also
raise doubts about Lear's plan in
the absence of a son, though his
division is intended to stabilize the
country after his death (see lines
43–44).

**4   *equalities are so weighed that curiosity in
    neither can make choice of either's moiety***

The divisions (of Lear's kingdom)
are so equally balanced that careful
consideration reveals no reason to
prefer either's share

5   *breeding*

(See LONGER NOTE on page 357.)

6   *this young fellow's mother could*

Edmund's mother could *conceive*,
(i.e., bear a child), punning on
conceive meaning "understand," as
Kent uses it in line 11.

7   *by order of law*

I.e., legitimate

8   *some year elder than this*

Approximately a year older than
Edmund

9   *this knave came something saucily*

This boy came somewhat imperti-
nently (but also "wantonly")

Act 1, Scene 1

Enter **Kent**, **Gloucester**, [1] *and* **Edmund**.

Kent

favored   I thought the King had more affected° the Duke of
Albany than Cornwall. [2]

Gloucester

It did always seem so to us; but now, in the division
of the kingdom, [3] it appears not which of the dukes he
values most, for equalities are so weighed that curios-   5
ity in neither can make choice of either's moiety. [4]

Kent

Is not this your son, my lord?

Gloucester

care; expense   His breeding, [5] sir, hath been at my charge.° I have so
often blushed to acknowledge him that now I am
hardened   brazed° to 't.   10

Kent

understand   I cannot conceive° you.

Gloucester

Sir, this young fellow's mother could, [6] whereupon she
grew round-wombed and had indeed, sir, a son for her
before   cradle ere° she had a husband for her bed. Do you
sin; wrongdoing   smell a fault?°   15

Kent

offspring; outcome   I cannot wish the fault undone, the issue° of it being
handsome; fine   so proper.°

Gloucester

But I have a son, sir, by order of law, [7] some year elder
esteem   than this, [8] who yet is no dearer in my account.°
Though this knave came something saucily [9] to the   20
world before he was sent for, yet was his mother fair,
bastard   there was good sport at his making, and the whoreson°

1   *study deserving*

Work to merit (your favor)

2   Sennet

Trumpet fanfare (to denote a cer-
emonial entrance)

3   *we*

Here the royal plural by which monarchs express their mutuality with
their subjects

4   *map*

Either Kent or Gloucester must
carry the map (probably Gloucester, given his comments about
Lear's *division of the kingdom* in lines
3–4). The conspicuous prop allows
an audience to visualize Lear's
planned division and is also a sign
of the play's engagement with
issues current at the time it was
written, as numerous maps were
being commissioned in the early
years of James's reign in an attempt
to describe and assess the extent
and nature of the lands he ruled.
Map making could be a hazard-
ous experience, and a number of
surveyors were murdered as people
realized what was at stake in their
seemingly innocent actions.

must be acknowledged.—Do you know this noble
gentleman, Edmund?

Edmund

No, my lord.   25

Gloucester

My Lord of Kent—remember him hereafter as my
honorable friend.

Edmund

respects   My services° to your Lordship.

Kent

seek; ask   I must love you and sue° to know you better.

Edmund

Sir, I shall study deserving. [1]   30

Gloucester

out of the country   He hath been out° nine years, and away he shall again.
The King is coming.

Sennet. [2] *Enter* **King Lear**, **Cornwall**, **Albany**,
Goneril, **Regan**, **Cordelia**, *and attendants.*

Lear

i.e., Bring in   Attend° the Lords of France and Burgundy, Gloucester.

Gloucester

I shall, my lord.   *He exits [with* **Edmund**].

Lear

more hidden   Meantime we [3] shall express our darker° purpose.   35
Give me the map [4] there. Know that we have
    divided

firm   In three our kingdom, and 'tis our fast° intent

responsibility   To shake all cares and business° from our age,
Conferring them on younger strengths while we

1 *crawl toward death*

A line that makes Lear sound as if he is old and feeble, but his behavior in this scene suggests that he is still vigorous and keen to rule, and the line may be more self-pity (or merely disingenuous) than accurate description. The line perhaps is intended to recall the riddle of the sphinx, who tells Oedipus that man returns to an infantile state in old age when he can no longer walk on two legs. The allusion to Oedipus would suggest that Lear, like Oedipus, has yet to realize the full horror that his actions will cause.

2 *constant will to publish*

Firm resolve to make known

3 *several dowers*

Separate dowries

4 *That we our largest bounty may extend / Where nature doth with merit challenge*

I.e., so that I may bestow the largest portion of my generosity on that daughter who, by virtue of both my natural affection and her merit, deserves it. (See LONGER NOTE, page 358).

5 *found*

Discovered himself to be loved

6 *breath poor and speech unable*

Voice weak and words inadequate

7 *Beyond all manner of so much I love you*

I love you more than any possible way of saying "how much."

8 *With shadowy forests and with champains riched, / With plenteous rivers and wide-skirted meads*

With shady forests and rich open country, with abundant rivers and spacious meadows

son-in-law   Unburdened crawl toward death.¹ Our son° of Corn-
        wall,   40
    And you, our no less loving son of Albany,
    We have this hour a constant will to publish²
    Our daughters' several dowers,³ that future strife
    May be prevented now. The Princes, France and Burgundy,
    Great rivals in our youngest daughter's love,   45
    Long in our court have made their amorous sojourn
    And here are to be answered. Tell me, my daughters—
    Since now we will divest us both of rule,
Ownership   Interest° of territory, cares of state—
    Which of you shall we say doth love us most,   50
    That we our largest bounty may extend
    Where nature doth with merit challenge?⁴ Goneril,
    Our eldest born, speak first.

Goneril

express   Sir, I love you more than word can wield° the matter,
property   Dearer than eyesight, space,° and liberty,   55
    Beyond what can be valued, rich or rare,
    No less than life, with grace, health, beauty, honor;
    As much as child e'er loved or father found;⁵
    A love that makes breath poor and speech unable.⁶
    Beyond all manner of so much I love you.⁷   60

Cordelia

[*aside*] What shall Cordelia speak? Love and be silent.

Lear

[*indicating on map*] Of all these bounds, even from this
        line to this,
    With shadowy forests and with champains riched,
    With plenteous rivers and wide-skirted meads,⁸
heirs   We make thee lady. To thine and Albany's issues°   65
    Be this perpetual.—What says our second daughter,
    Our dearest Regan, wife of Cornwall?

1   *self mettle*

    (1) same spirit; (2) same substance
    (metal). As spelling had not yet
    been fixed, the two words, "mettle"
    and "metal," could be used inter-
    changeably for both meanings.

2   *prize me at her worth*

    Value myself no less than Goneril

3   *names my very deed of love*

    **Precisely articulates my love (for
    you)**

4   *square of sense*

    Sensitive part of our nature

5   *Strive to be interessed*

    Compete to claim their share

6   *Nothing*

    An important word in the play, as
    its repetition here (and at regular
    intervals throughout the play; see
    for example, 1.2.31–33; 1.4.119–123)
    suggests. *Nothing will come of nothing*
    (1.1.89) was a well-known proverb.
    The play's frequent references to
    nothingness beg the question of
    whether something exists beyond
    what we can see. In the hostile
    pre-Christian universe of *King Lear*,
    the characters have nothing to
    believe in beyond what they create
    themselves.

Regan

I am made of that self mettle[1] as my sister,
And prize me at her worth.[2] In my true heart
I find she names my very deed of love.[3]   70
in that Only she comes too short, that° I profess
Myself an enemy to all other joys
Which the most precious square of sense[4] possesses,
made happy And find I am alone felicitate°
In your dear Highness' love.

Cordelia

                                    [*aside*] Then poor Cordelia—   75
And yet not so, since I am sure my love's
substantial More ponderous° than my tongue.

Lear

To thee and thine hereditary ever
Remain this ample third of our fair kingdom,
value No less in space, validity,° and pleasure   80
Than that conferred on Goneril.—Now, our joy,
youngest Although our last and least,° to whose young love
vineyards/pastures The vines° of France and milk° of Burgundy
obtain Strive to be interested,[5] what can you say to draw°
A third more opulent than your sisters? Speak.   85

Cordelia

Nothing,[6] my lord.

Lear

Nothing?

Cordelia

Nothing.

Lear

Nothing will come of nothing. Speak again.

Cordelia

Unhappy that I am, I cannot heave   90
My heart into my mouth. I love your Majesty

1   *mysteries of Hecate*

    **Secret rites of Hecate (pagan god-
    dess of the underworld; affiliated
    with the night and witchcraft;
    pronounced HECK-it)**

2   *operation of the orbs / From whom we do
    exist and cease to be*

    **Influence of the planets, which
    determine our life and death**

3   *Propinquity, and property of blood*

    Close kinship and familial rights

4   *from this*

    **I.e., from this moment on (though
    possibly *this* refers to Lear's heart,
    toward which he might gesture)**

5   *Scythian*

    **Scythians were inhabitants of
    central Asia, whose name was
    synonymous with fierce cruelty.
    Herodotus describes them as sav-
    age cannibals, the opposite of all
    that civilized Greece stood for.**

natural affection; duty   According to my bond,° no more nor less.

Lear

How, how, Cordelia? Mend your speech a little,

Lest you may mar your fortunes.

Cordelia

                                        Good my lord,

raised; educated   You have begot me, bred° me, loved me. I   95

fitting   Return those duties back as are right fit,°

Obey you, love you, and most honor you.

Why have my sisters husbands if they say

exclusively / Perhaps   They love you all?° Haply° when I shall wed,

pledge (of love)   That lord whose hand must take my plight° shall carry   100

Half my love with him, half my care and duty.

Sure I shall never marry like my sisters.

Lear

But goes thy heart with this?

Cordelia

                                        Ay my good lord.

Lear

So young and so untender?

Cordelia

So young, my lord, and true.   105

Lear

dowry   Let it be so! Thy truth then be thy dower!°

For, by the sacred radiance of the sun,

The mysteries of Hecate [1] and the night,

By all the operation of the orbs

From whom we do exist and cease to be, [2]   110

Here I disclaim all my paternal care,

Propinquity, and property of blood, [3]

And as a stranger to my heart and me

Hold thee from this [4] forever. The barbarous Scythian, [5]

1   *he that makes his generation messes / To gorge his appetite*

    The cannibal who makes meals of his children and parents to satisfy his gluttony

2   *thought to set my rest / On her kind nursery*

    I.e., planned to entrust myself to her daughterly care. *Set my rest* may also mean "stake everything I have" (a term drawn from the card game primero).

3   *So be my grave my peace*

    I.e., may my death give me peace

4   *Who stirs?*

    Why is no one moving? (an impatient command)

5   *With my two daughters' dowers digest the third*

    Incorporate Cordelia's portion (of the kingdom) into Regan's and Goneril's shares

6   *marry her*

    Get her a husband (i.e., serve as her dowry)

7   *large effects / That troop with majesty*
    Splendid trappings of kingship

8   *With reservation of*
    Reserving the right to keep

9   *This coronet part between you*

    Lear gives Cornwall and Albany (significantly instead of his daughters) a *coronet* (small crown) as a token of Cordelia's portion of the kingdom.

Or he that makes his generation messes 115
To gorge his appetite,[1] shall to my bosom
treated Be as well neighbored,° pitied, and relieved
former As thou my sometime° daughter.
Kent

Good my liege—
Lear
Peace, Kent!
Come not between the dragon and his wrath. 120
I loved her most, and thought to set my rest
get out of On her kind nursery.[2] [*to* **Cordelia**] Hence, and avoid°
my sight!
remove —So be my grave my peace,[3] as here I give°
Her father's heart from her!—Call France. Who stirs?[4]
Call Burgundy. [*An attendant exits.*]
—Cornwall and Albany, 125
With my two daughters' dowers digest the third.[5]
plain speaking Let pride, which she calls plainness,° marry her.[6]
endow I do invest° you jointly with my power,
Preeminence, and all the large effects
Myself That troop with majesty.[7] Ourself,° by monthly course, 130
With reservation of[8] an hundred knights
paid for By you to be sustained,° shall our abode
Make with you by due turn. Only we shall retain
honors; privileges The name, and all th' addition° to a king.
authority The sway,° revenue, execution of the rest, 135
Belovèd sons, be yours, which to confirm,
small crown This coronet° part between you.[9]
Kent

Royal Lear,
always Whom I have ever° honored as my king,
Loved as my father, as my master followed,

1   *Make from the shaft.*

Avoid the arrow. The furious Lear has already *bent and drawn* the *bow* of his anger; he warns Kent to avoid having the wrath intended for Cordelia redirected at him.

2   *Think'st thou that duty shall have dread to speak / When power to flattery bows?*

Do you really believe that a man with a sense of duty would be afraid to speak out when he sees those in power succumbing to flattery?

3   *To plainness honor's bound*

Honor commands plain speaking. Kent's outburst is justified as a means of preventing the rightful king from behaving against his and the nation's interests. Political thought in the 16th and 17th centuries was largely conceived in terms of the rights and duties of subjects in relation to their rulers. Obedience was expected, but counselors were charged with offering advice, although monarchs were not bound to follow it—and unwelcome advice could land a counselor in trouble. Kent here feels that Lear has gone too far and that his loyalty demands that he speak out, whatever consequences he might suffer as a result.

4   *And in thy best consideration check*

And with careful scrutiny stop

5   *Answer my life my judgment*

I stake my life on my judgment

6   *Nor are those empty-hearted whose low sound / Reverb no hollowness*

A reversal of the proverbial expression, "Empty vessels produce the greatest sound." Kent implicitly compares Regan and Goneril to empty vessels, whose declarations of love merely represent insincere "reverberations" of Lear's own words. It is the elder sisters who are *empty-hearted* and *hollow*, not Cordelia.

7   *My life I never held but as a pawn / To wage against thine enemies*

I never thought of my life as anything other than your instrument to risk against your enemies.

8   *See better*

Kent's advice is designed to make Lear see his faults and so correct them. Sight is another theme running throughout the play.

9   *let me still remain / The true blank of thine eye*

I.e., continue to look to me for true guidance (the *blank* being the bullseye at the center of an archery target)

10   *Apollo*

God of the sun in classical mythology

As my great patron thought on in my prayers—   *140*
Lear
The bow is bent and drawn. Make from the shaft. ¹
Kent

strike / arrowhead   Let it fall° rather, though the fork° invade
The region of my heart. Be Kent unmannerly
When Lear is mad. What wouldst thou do, old man?
Think'st thou that duty shall have dread to speak   *145*
When power to flattery bows? ²
To plainness honor's bound ³

Retain / authority   When majesty falls to folly. Reserve° thy state,°
And in thy best consideration check ⁴
This hideous rashness. Answer my life my judgment: ⁵   *150*
Thy youngest daughter does not love thee least,
Nor are those empty-hearted whose low sounds
Reverb no hollowness. ⁶
Lear
                 Kent, on thy life, no more.
Kent
My life I never held but as a pawn
To wage against thine enemies, ⁷ nor fear to lose it,   *155*

my motivation   Thy safety being motive.°
Lear
                 Out of my sight!
Kent
See better, ⁸ Lear, and let me still remain
The true blank of thine eye. ⁹
Lear
Now, by Apollo ¹⁰—
Kent
Now, by Apollo, King,   *160*
Thou swear'st thy gods in vain.

1   *vent clamor*

     Cry out in protest

2   *To come betwixt our sentences and our*
     power, / Which nor our nature nor our
     place can bear

     **To come between my words and
     my deeds, which neither my
     personality nor my position (as
     king) can allow**

3   *Our potency made good*

     My power thus demonstrated

4   *your large speeches may your deeds*
     approve

     **May your actions live up to your
     generous declarations**

Lear

slave/Villain   Oh, vassal!° Miscreant!°   *[reaching for his sword]*

Albany, Cornwall

Dear sir, forbear.

Kent

Kill thy physician, and the fee bestow

Upon the foul disease. Revoke thy gift,   165

Or, whilst I can vent clamor¹ from my throat,

I'll tell thee thou dost evil.

Lear

traitor   Hear me, recreant;° on thine allegiance hear me!

Since   That° thou hast sought to make us break our vows,

dared/excessive   Which we durst° never yet, and with strained° pride   170

To come betwixt our sentences and our power,

neither   Which nor° our nature nor our place can bear,²

Our potency made good,³ take thy reward.

Five days we do allot thee for provision

To shield thee from disasters of the world,   175

And on the sixth to turn thy hated back

Upon our kingdom. If on the tenth day following

body   Thy banished trunk° be found in our dominions,

(king of the Roman gods)   The moment is thy death. Away! By Jupiter,°

This shall not be revoked.   180

Kent

Since   Fare thee well, King. Sith° thus thou wilt appear,

elsewhere   Freedom lives hence° and banishment is here.

[to **Cordelia***]* The gods to their dear shelter take thee,
    maid,

That justly think'st and hast most rightly said!

[to **Goneril** *and* **Regan***]* And your large speeches may
    your deeds approve,⁴   185

That good effects may spring from words of love.

1 *shape his old course*

**Follow his accustomed path (i.e.,
the path of honesty and integrity)**

2 Flourish

Trumpet fanfare

3 *What in the least / Will you require in
present dower with her / Or cease your
quest of love?*

**What is the lowest amount you
will now accept as a dowry for her,
before you abandon your pursuit of
her hand?**

4 *little-seeming substance*

**(1) one who is less than she seems;
(2) one so self-righteous that she
refuses to flatter**

5 *fitly like*

Appropriately please

6 *Dowered with our curse, and strangered
with our oath*

**With only the dowry of my curse,
and disowned by my oath**

Thus Kent, O Princes, bids you all adieu.

He'll shape his old course [1] in a country new.   *He exits.*

Flourish. [2] *Enter* **Gloucester**, *with* **France** *and*
Burgundy [*and*] *attendants.*

Gloucester

Here's France and Burgundy, my noble lord.

Lear

My Lord of Burgundy,   190

We first address toward° you, who with this King

Hath rivaled° for our daughter. What in the least

Will you require in present dower with her

Or cease your quest of love? [3]

Burgundy

Most royal Majesty,

I crave no more than hath your Highness offered,   195

Nor will you tender° less.

Lear

Right noble Burgundy,

When she was dear to us we did hold her so, °

But now her price is fallen. Sir, there she stands.

If aught° within that little-seeming substance, [4]

Or all of it, with our displeasure pieced, °   200

And nothing more, may fitly like [5] your Grace,

She's there, and she is yours.

Burgundy

I know no answer.

Lear

Will you, with those infirmities° she owes, °

Unfriended, new-adopted to our hate,

Dowered with our curse, and strangered with our oath, [6]   205

Take her or leave her?

(left margin glosses)

i.e., our words to — We first address toward

competed — Hath rivaled

offer — Nor will you tender

i.e., dear; valuable — we did hold her so

anything — If aught

added on — with our displeasure pieced

weaknesses / possesses — those infirmities she owes

1   *Election makes not up in such conditions.*

A choice is impossible to make under such conditions.

2   *tell you*

(1) advise you of; (2) count out for you

3   *make such a stray*

Stray so far

4   *Nature*

Lear now disinherits the daughter who, at the start of the scene, was his clear favorite. His appeal to *Nature*, however unnatural his response in fact is, is based on his conception that children naturally owe an unconditional loyalty to their parents and can never challenge them. Compare Edmund's conception of *Nature* in 1.2.1–22.

5   *Commit a thing so monstrous to dismantle / So many folds of favor*

Commit an act vile enough to strip her of the many protective layers of your *favor*. The King of France imagines Lear's affection for Cordelia as a rich garment, which Cordelia has now been denied.

6   *monsters it*

Makes it monstrous. In the early modern period, monsters were aberrations of nature whose existence challenged the regular order of God's universe. References to monsters appear at a number of key points in the play, drawing attention to the often unnatural acts of the play.

7   *or your forevouched affection / Fall into taint*

Or else your previous declarations of love must be questioned

8   *If for I want*

If (I have earned your hatred) because I lack

9   *and purpose not*

With no intention to do what I say

10 *vicious blot*

Mark of vice

11 *But even for want of that for which I am richer*

Merely for the lack of those very things I am better off without

Burgundy

> Pardon me, royal sir.
> Election makes not up in such conditions. [1]

Lear

> Then leave her, sir, for by the power that made me,
> *As for* I tell you [2] all her wealth. [*to* **France**] For° you, great King,
> I would not from your love make such a stray [3]   210
> *As to / to one whom* To° match you where° I hate; therefore beseech you
> *turn* T' avert° your liking a more worthier way
> Than on a wretch whom Nature [4] is ashamed
> Almost t' acknowledge hers.

France

> This is most strange,
> That she whom even but now was your best object,   215
> *subject* The argument° of your praise, balm of your age,
> *moment* The best, the dearest, should in this trice° of time
> *strip off* Commit a thing so monstrous to dismantle°
> *Certainly* So many folds of favor. [5] Sure° her offense
> Must be of such unnatural degree   220
> That monsters it, [6] or your forevouched affection
> Fall into taint, [7] which to believe of her
> Must be a faith that reason without miracle
> Should never plant in me.

Cordelia

> I yet beseech your Majesty—   225
> If for I want [8] that glib and oily art
> To speak and purpose not, [9] since what I well intend
> I'll do 't before I speak—that you make known
> *sinfulness* It is no vicious blot, [10] murder, or foulness,°
> *dishonorable* No unchaste action or dishonored° step   230
> That hath deprived me of your grace and favor,
> But even for want of that for which I am richer: [11]
> *constantly begging* A still-soliciting° eye and such a tongue

1   *Hath lost me in your liking*

    Has erased me from your love

2   *A tardiness in nature / Which often leaves*
    the history unspoke / That it intends to do

    An innate modesty, which often
    fails to make explicit everything it
    intends to do

3   *regards that stands / Aloof from th' entire*
    point

    Considerations that are irrelevant
    to the central matter

4   *Most choice forsaken, and most loved*
    despised

    Most favored (when you are) for-
    saken, and most loved (when you
    are) despised. Possibly an allusion
    to the paradoxes of 2 Corinthians:
    We are "as sorrowing, and yet
    always rejoicing; as poor, and yet
    make many rich; as having nothing,
    and yet possessing all things" (2 Cor
    6:10); "For you know the gracious
    act of our Lord Jesus Christ, that
    he being rich, yet for your sakes
    became poor, that ye through his
    poverty might be made rich"
    (2 Cor 8:9).

5   *Be it lawful*

    If it be lawful that

That I am glad I have not, though not to have it
Hath lost me in your liking. [1]

Lear

                                 Better thou   235
Hadst not been born than not t' have pleased me better.

France

only Is it but° this? A tardiness in nature
Which often leaves the history unspoke
That it intends to do? [2]—My Lord of Burgundy,
What say you to the lady? Love's not love   240
When it is mingled with regards that stands
Aloof from th' entire point. [3] Will you have her?
She is herself a dowry.

Burgundy

                          [*to* **Lear**] Royal King,
merely Give but° that portion which yourself proposed,
And here I take Cordelia by the hand,   245
Duchess of Burgundy.

Lear

Nothing. I have sworn. I am firm.

Burgundy

[*to* **Cordelia**] I am sorry, then, you have so lost a father
That you must lose a husband.

Cordelia

                          Peace be with Burgundy!
status Since that respect° and fortunes are his love,   250
I shall not be his wife.

France

Fairest Cordelia, that art most rich being poor,
Most choice forsaken, and most loved despised, [4]
Thee and thy virtues here I seize upon,
Be it lawful [5] I take up what's cast away.   255

                          [*He takes her hand.*]

1   *their*

The possessive pronoun may either
refer to Lear and Burgundy or to the
gods themselves.

2   *inflamed respect*

Passionate regard

3   *wat'rish*

(1) well-watered (i.e., full of rivers);
(2) watery, weak

4   *unprized*

The King of France's term simulta-
neously suggests both "unvalued"
(as Cordelia is by Lear and Burgundy) and "priceless" (as she is to
the King of France himself).

5   *jewels*

i.e., Goneril and Reagan

6   *like a sister*

Because I am your sister

7   *as they are named*

By their rightful names

8   *professèd bosoms*

I.e., declarations of love

9   *At Fortune's alms*

As one of Fortune's unpredictable
charitable gifts

10   *And well are worth the want that you have*
wanted

Goneril claims that Cordelia well
deserves the loss of that which she
wanted—*want* meaning both "to
desire" and "to lack." Goneril refers
to Cordelia's dowry and/or Lear's
love: two things that seemed to
be firmly in Cordelia's possession
at the beginning of this scene, but
which she now both lacks and,
presumably, desires.

Gods, gods! 'Tis strange that from their[1] cold'st neglect
My love should kindle to inflamed respect.[2]
—Thy dowerless daughter, King, thrown to my
fortune   chance,°
Is queen of us, of ours, and our fair France.
Not all the dukes of wat'rish[3] Burgundy   260
Can buy this unprized[4] precious maid of me.
though they are   —Bid them farewell, Cordelia, though° unkind.
this place / place   Thou losest here,° a better where° to find.

Lear

Thou hast her, France. Let her be thine, for we
Have no such daughter, nor shall ever see   265
That face of hers again. Therefore be gone
blessing   Without our grace, our love, our benison.°
Come, noble Burgundy.

Flourish. [All but **France**, **Cordelia**, **Goneril**, *and* **Regan**] *exit.*

France

Bid farewell to your sisters.

Cordelia

tearful   The jewels[5] of our father, with washed° eyes   270
Cordelia leaves you. I know you what you are,
And like a sister[6] am most loath to call
Your faults as they are named.[7] Love well our father.
To your professèd bosoms[8] I commit him.
But yet, alas, stood I within his grace,   275
recommend   I would prefer° him to a better place.
So, farewell to you both.

Regan

Prescribe not us our duty.

Goneril

aim   Let your study°
Be to content your lord, who hath received you
neglected   At Fortune's alms.[9] You have obedience scanted,°   280
And well are worth the want that you have wanted.[10]

1   *Time shall unfold what plighted cunning*
    hides; / Who covers faults, at last with
    shame derides.

    **Time will reveal what deceit hides;
    those who try to cover up their
    faults are ultimately exposed and
    scorned.**

2   *nearly appertains to*

    Closely concerns

3   *the observation we have made of it hath*
    not been little

    **I.e., we have often seen the
    evidence**

4   *The best and soundest of his time hath*
    been but rash.

    **Even in the prime of his life he was
    hasty and reckless.**

5   *Then must we look from his age to receive*
    not alone the imperfections of long-
    engrafted condition, but therewithal
    the unruly waywardness that infirm and
    choleric years bring with them.

    **Then, in his old age, we must expect
    to bear not only the long-standing
    imperfections of his character, but
    also the uncontrollable willfullness
    that the sickness and irritability of
    age will bring with them. (Accord-
    ing to the Elizabethan theory of
    humors, or bodily fluids, an excess
    of *choler* in the body resulted in an
    angry, hotheaded temperament.)**

6   *unconstant starts*

    Unexpected outbursts

Cordelia

enshrouded   Time shall unfold what plighted° cunning hides;
Who covers faults, at last with shame derides.[1]
Well may you prosper!

France

                  Come, my fair Cordelia.

                   France *and* **Cordelia** *exit.*

Goneril

Sister, it is not little I have to say of what most nearly   285
go   appertains to[2] us both. I think our father will hence°
tonight.

Regan

That's most certain, and with you; next month with us.

Goneril

inconstancy   You see how full of changes° his age is; the observation
we have made of it hath not been little.[3] He always   290
loved our sister most, and with what poor judgment
plainly   he hath now cast her off appears too grossly.°

Regan

'Tis the infirmity of his age, yet he hath ever but slen-
derly known himself.

Goneril

The best and soundest of his time hath been but rash.[4]   295
expect   Then must we look° from his age to receive not alone
the imperfections of long-engrafted condition, but
along with them   therewithal° the unruly waywardness that infirm and
choleric years bring with them.[5]

Regan

likely   Such unconstant starts[6] are we like° to have from him   300
as this of Kent's banishment.

Goneril

ceremony   There is further compliment° of leave-taking between
i.e., discuss this   France and him. Pray you, let us sit° together. If our

1   *If our father carry authority with such*
      disposition as he bears, this last surrender
      of his will but offend us.

      **If our father continues to wield
his power with his usual irrational
disposition, his abdication will only
do us harm.**

2   *i' th' heat*

      I.e., right now

father carry authority with such disposition as he
bears, this last surrender of his will but offend us. [1]   305

Regan

We shall further think of it.

Goneril

We must do something, and i' th' heat. [2]   *They exit.*

1   *Nature*

     In the state of *nature* (i.e., a world that lacks organized civilization), Edmund would not be disadvantaged by being a bastard son; it is social custom and religious and legal edict that keep him in his subordinate position. Edgar's idea of nature as a world of amoral appetite is in sharp contrast to Lear's sense of nature marked by order and obligation.

2   *Stand in the plague of custom*

     Be victimized by social conventions (that deny illegitimate children the right to inherit land)

3   *curiosity of nations*

     Nitpicking distinctions of national laws

4   *For that*

     Because

5   *Lag of*

     Younger than

6   *dimensions are as well compact*

     Body is as well formed

7   *honest madam's issue*

     The married woman's child (i.e., Edgar)

8   *Who in the lusty stealth of nature take / More composition and fierce quality / Than doth within a dull, stale, tired bed / Go to th' creating a whole tribe of fops / Got 'tween asleep and wake?*

     Edmund claims that illegitimate children are inherently stronger and more energetic than children born to lawful couples. According to Edmund, they *take more composition and fierce quality* (have a more perfect physical form and more aggressive temperament) from having been conceived *in the lusty stealth of nature* (in the stolen pleasures of vigorous lovemaking) than *a whole tribe of fops* (fools) can gain from the sexual activity conducted *within a dull, stale, tired bed* (i.e., the predictability of the marriage bed) during the nighttime hours.

9   *your land*

     I.e., the land that Edgar is to inherit as Gloucester's lawful heir

10   *Our father's love is to the bastard Edmund / As to th' legitimate.*

     Our father loves the bastard Edmund as much as he loves his legitimate son.

11   *this letter*

     Either Edmund enters with the letter visible or reveals it here.

12   *Prescribed his power; / Confined to exhibition?*

     His power limited; restricted to a (monetary) allowance?

Act 1, Scene 2

*Enter [**Edmund**, the]Bastard.*

Edmund

Thou, Nature, [1] art my goddess; to thy law
Why   My services are bound. Wherefore° should I
Stand in the plague of custom [2] and permit
The curiosity of nations [3] to deprive me,
months   For that [4] I am some twelve or fourteen moonshines°   5
Why / inferior   Lag of [5] a brother? Why bastard? Wherefore° base,
When my dimensions are as well compact, [6]
noble   My mind as generous,° and my shape as true
As honest madam's issue? [7] Why brand they us
With base? With baseness? Bastardy? Base, base,   10
Who in the lusty stealth of nature take
More composition and fierce quality
Than doth within a dull, stale, tired bed
fools   Go to th' creating a whole tribe of fops°
Begotten   Got° 'tween asleep and wake? [8] Well, then,   15
Legitimate Edgar, I must have your land. [9]
Our father's love is to the bastard Edmund
As to th' legitimate. [10] Fine word, "legitimate"!
succeed   Well, my legitimate, if this letter [11] speed°
plot   And my invention° thrive, Edmund the base   20
surpass   Shall top° th' legitimate. I grow; I prosper.
Now, gods, stand up for bastards!

*Enter **Gloucester**.*

Gloucester

anger/departed   Kent banished thus? And France in choler° parted?°
last night   And the King gone tonight?° Prescribed his power;
Confined to exhibition? [12] All this done   25

73

1   *Upon the gad*

    On an impulse (*gad* = goad)

2   *terrible dispatch*

    Panicky hiding

3   *essay or taste*

    Assay (trial) or test

4   *policy and reverence of age*

    Custom of revering (old) age

5   *bitter to the best of our times*

    The prime of our lives seem bitter

Upon the gad?[1] Edmund, how now? What news?

Edmund

So please your Lordship, none.   [*He hides the letter.*]

Gloucester

away Why so earnestly seek you to put up° that letter?

Edmund

I know no news, my lord.

Gloucester

What paper were you reading?   30

Edmund

Nothing, my lord.

Gloucester

No? What needed then that terrible dispatch[2] of it
character into your pocket? The quality° of nothing hath not
such need to hide itself. Let's see. Come, if it be
nothing I shall not need spectacles.

Edmund

I beseech you, sir, pardon me. It is a letter from my
brother that I have not all o'erread, and, for so much
inspection as I have perused, I find it not fit for your o'erlooking.°

Gloucester

Give me the letter, sir.

Edmund

withhold I shall offend either to detain° or give it. The contents,   40
blameworthy as in part I understand them, are too blame.°

Gloucester

Let's see; let's see.   [**Edmund** *hands over the letter.*]

Edmund

I hope for my brother's justification he wrote this but
as an essay or taste[3] of my virtue.

Gloucester

(*reads*) "This policy and reverence of age[4] makes the   45
world bitter to the best of our times,[5] keeps our

1   *idle and fond*

     Pointless and silly

2   *who sways not as it hath power but as it is*
     suffered

     Which rules not because it has
     power, but because we accept it

3   *in respect of that*

     I.e., considering the content

4   *sounded you*

     Tried to discover your feelings

5   *sons at perfect age and fathers declined*

     Sons in their prime of life and
     fathers old and infirm

6   *as ward to the son*

     Subject to the guardianship of the
     son

fortunes from us till our oldness cannot relish them. I
begin to find an idle and fond[1] bondage in the oppression of aged tyranny, who sways not as it hath power
but as it is suffered.[2] Come to me, that of this I may   50
speak more. If our father would sleep till I waked him,
you should enjoy half his revenue forever and live the
beloved of your brother, Edgar."
Hum! Conspiracy! "Sleep till I waked him, you should
enjoy half his revenue." My son Edgar! Had he a hand   55
to write this? A heart and brain to breed it in? When
came you to this? Who brought it?

Edmund

It was not brought me, my lord; there's the cunning of
it. I found it thrown in at the casement° of my closet.°

window / private chamber

Gloucester

You know the character° to be your brother's?   60

handwriting

Edmund

If the matter° were good, my lord, I durst° swear it were
his; but in respect of that[3] I would fain° think it were not.

content / would dare

gladly

Gloucester

It is his?

Edmund

It is his hand,° my lord, but I hope his heart is not in
the contents.   65

handwriting

Gloucester

Has he never before sounded you[4] in this business?

Edmund

Never, my lord. But I have heard him oft maintain it to
be fit° that, sons at perfect age and fathers declined,[5]
the father should be as ward to the son,[6] and the son
manage his revenue.   70

appropriate

1   *sirrah*

Term of address usually reserved
for a person of lower social standing, though here used affection-
ately

2   *run a certain course*

Proceed safely

3   *pawn down*

Put at risk; bet

4   *pretense of danger*

Dangerous purpose

5   *by an auricular assurance*

By hearing for yourself (what is
spoken)

6   *wind me into him*

Insinuate yourself into his
confidence (*me* is a colloquialism
calling attention to the interests of
the speaker).

7   *after your own wisdom*

As you see fit

8   *I would unstate myself to be in a due
resolution.*

I would give up all (my wealth and
status) to know the truth.

Gloucester

Oh, villain, villain! His very opinion in the letter!

Hateful / detestable   Abhorred° villain! Unnatural, detested,° brutish

villain! Worse than brutish! Go, sirrah;[1] seek him. I'll

apprehend him. Abominable villain! Where is he?

Edmund

I do not well know, my lord. If it shall please you to   75

suspend your indignation against my brother till you

can derive from him better testimony of his intent, you

whereas   should run a certain course;[2] where,° if you violently

proceed against him, mistaking his purpose, it would

make a great gap in your own honor and shake in pieces   80

the heart of his obedience. I dare pawn down[3] my life

test   for him that he hath writ this to feel° my affection to

your honor, and to no other pretense of danger.[4]

Gloucester

Think you so?

Edmund

fitting   If your honor judge it meet,° I will place you where you   85

shall hear us confer of this, and by an auricular

assurance[5] have your satisfaction, and that without

any further delay than this very evening.

Gloucester

He cannot be such a monster. Edmund, seek him out;

Devise   wind me into him,[6] I pray you. Frame° the business   90

after your own wisdom.[7] I would unstate myself to be

in a due resolution.[8]

Edmund

immediately / execute   I will seek him, sir, presently,° convey° the business as I

i.e., with the results   shall find means, and acquaint you withal.°

Gloucester

recent   These late° eclipses in the sun and moon portend no   95

study   good to us. Though the wisdom° of nature can reason

1   *Though the wisdom of nature can reason*
    it thus and thus, yet nature finds itself
    scourged by the sequent effects.

    **I.e., though science and philosophy
    can offer explanations for these
    strange occurrences, human nature
    nonetheless suffers the conse-
    quences.**

2   *comes under the prediction*

    **Corresponds with the predictions
    implied by the eclipses**

3   *surfeits of our own behavior*

    **Result of our own intemperate
    behavior**

4   *we make guilty of our disasters the sun,
    the moon, and stars*

    **We blame our misfortunes on
    astrological influences.**

5   *spherical predominance*

    **The influence of a particular planet
    (Ptolemaic astronomy held that the
    planets were carried around the
    earth in crystalline spheres)**

6   *divine thrusting on*

    Celestial insistence

7   *goatish*

    **Lustful. Goats were associated
    with lust (see, for example, *Othello*,
    3.3.407). Edmund points out that
    his father absolves himself of
    responsibility for his son's**

**character by blaming character
traits on the astrological conjunc-
tion of the stars instead of his own
lustful behavior in fathering a
bastard child.**

8   *My father compounded with my mother
    under the Dragon's tail, and my nativity
    was under Ursa Major*

    **I was conceived under *the Dragon's
    tail* (either the constellation Draco,
    or else referring to the descending
    point of the moon's orbit) and born
    under the constellation Ursa Major
    (also known as the Great Bear or Big
    Dipper).**

9   *Fut*

    **Contraction of the oath "by Christ's
    foot"**

Kingdom divided

it thus and thus, yet nature finds itself scourged by the
sequent effects.[1] Love cools, friendship falls off, brothers

riots divide; in cities mutinies;° in countries, discord; in pal-
aces, treason; and the bond cracked twixt son and father.   100
This villain of mine comes under the prediction:[2] there's

the tendency son against father. The King falls from bias° of nature:
there's father against child. We have seen the best of our

insincerity time. Machinations, hollowness,° treachery, and
all ruinous disorders follow us disquietly to our graves.   105
Find out this villain, Edmund; it shall lose thee noth-
ing. Do it carefully. And the noble and true-hearted Kent
banished! His offense, honesty! 'Tis strange.   *He exits.*

Edmund

foolishness This is the excellent foppery° of the world, that when
we are sick in fortune—often the surfeits of our own   110
behavior[3]—we make guilty of our disasters the sun,

by the moon, and stars,[4] as if we were villains on° necessity,
fools by heavenly compulsion, knaves, thieves, and

traitors treachers° by spherical predominance,[5] drunkards,

to liars, and adulterers by an enforced obedience of°   115
planetary influence, and all that we are evil in, by a
divine thrusting on.[6] An admirable evasion of whore-

lecherous master° man, to lay his goatish [7] disposition on the

copulated charge of a star! My father compounded° with my
mother under the Dragon's tail, and my nativity was   120
under Ursa Major,[8] so that it follows I am rough and

even if lecherous. Fut,[9] I should have been that I am, had° the

most chaste maidenliest° star in the firmament twinkled on my
bastardizing. Edgar—

Enter **Edgar.**

1 *catastrophe*

Resolution. Edmund compares
Edgar's timely entrance to the
arbitrary and contrived plot devices
found in an *old* (-fashioned) *comedy*.

2 *Tom o' Bedlam*

A generic name for a beggar, which
also suggested madness. Bethlehem Hospital, commonly known
as *Bedlam*, was the hospital for the
insane in London. Edmund's suggestion here provides the trigger
for his brother's disguise after he is
falsely disgraced.

3 *divisions*

Discord or disagreement, but also
"variations on a musical theme"
(thus prompting him to sing *Fa, sol,
la, mi*, a discordant sequence)

4 *with the mischief of your person it would*
   scarcely allay

If you suffered serious injury his
anger would scarcely be abated

on cue   and pat° he comes like the catastrophe [1] of the old   125
          comedy. My cue is villainous melancholy, with a sigh
          like Tom o' Bedlam. [2]—Oh, these eclipses do portend
          these divisions! [3] Fa, sol, la, mi.

Edgar

How now, brother Edmund, what serious contempla-
tion are you in?   130

Edmund

I am thinking, brother, of a prediction I read this
other day, what should follow these eclipses.

Edgar

Do you busy yourself with that?

Edmund

turn out   I promise you, the effects he writes of succeed° un-
           happily. When saw you my father last?   135

Edgar

The night gone by.

Edmund

Spake you with him?

Edgar

Ay, two hours together.

Edmund

Parted you in good terms? Found you no displeasure
appearance; behavior   in him by word nor countenance?°   140

Edgar

None at all.

Edmund

Recollect   Bethink° yourself wherein you may have offended him,
avoid   and, at my entreaty, forbear° his presence until some
moderated   little time hath qualified° the heat of his displeasure,
             which at this instant so rageth in him that with the   145
             mischief of your person it would scarcely allay. [4]

1   *have a continent forbearance*

**Patiently endure your absence
(from our father's presence)**

2   *but faintly, nothing like the image and
horror of it*

**But my limited description is
nothing like an accurate image of
its horror**

3   *All with me's meet that I can fashion fit.*

**Anything is justifiable to me if it
serves my purposes (*meet* meaning
"appropriate").**

Edgar

Some villain hath done me wrong.

Edmund

That's my fear. I pray you, have a continent forbearance[1] till the speed of his rage goes slower; and, as I say,

at a suitable time   retire with me to my lodging, from whence I will fitly°   150

i.e., Gloucester   bring you to hear my lord° speak. Pray ye, go! There's

outside   my key. [*He gives a key.*] If you do stir abroad,° go armed.

Edgar

Armed, brother?

Edmund

Brother, I advise you to the best. I am no honest man if

intention   there be any good meaning° toward you. I have told you   155

what I have seen and heard, but faintly, nothing like the
image and horror of it.[2] Pray you, away.

Edgar

soon   Shall I hear from you anon?°

Edmund

I do serve you in this business.   [**Edgar**] *exits.*

A credulous father and a brother noble,   160

Whose nature is so far from doing harms

decency   That he suspects none, on whose foolish honesty°

plots / way forward   My practices° ride easy. I see the business.°

intelligence   Let me, if not by birth, have lands by wit.°

All with me's meet that I can fashion fit.[3]   *He exits.*   165

1   steward

The steward was a pivotal figure
in the Renaissance household,
providing the link between the
owners and the servants. Stewards
had an intimate relationship with
their employers, who had to rely
on them to run the household
efficiently and economically, as the
relationship between Goneril and
Oswald demonstrates. Stewards
were often portrayed as men who
were keen to better themselves at
others' expense, often over-
reaching themselves in the process,
exactly as Oswald is represented
here. His name is, in fact, the Old
English word for *steward*.

2   *himself upbraids us / On every trifle*

He (Lear) reprimands us for every
little thing.

3   *come slack of former services*

I.e., serve him with less courtesy
and attentiveness than you used to

4   *come to question*

Become an issue

5   *let him to my sister*

Let him go to Regan's

6   *Whose mind and mine, I know, in that
are one*

Whose mind in this matter is of the
same opinion as I hold

7   *hold my course*

Behave in the same fashion

Act 1, Scene 3

Enter **Goneril** *and* [**Oswald**, *her*] *steward.* [1]

Goneril
Did my father strike my gentleman for chiding of his
fool?

Oswald – *chief servant*
Ay, madam.

Goneril
By day and night he wrongs me! Every hour

offense   He flashes into one gross crime° or other   5
That sets us all at odds. I'll not endure it.
His knights grow riotous, and himself upbraids us
On every trifle. [2] When he returns from hunting,
I will not speak with him. Say I am sick.
If you come slack of former services [3]   10

take responsibility for   You shall do well; the fault of it I'll answer.°

                                            [*Horns within.*]

Oswald
He's coming, madam. I hear him.

Goneril
Put on what weary negligence you please,

fellow servants   You and your fellows.° I'd have it come to question. [4]

dislike   If he distaste° it, let him to my sister, [5]   15
Whose mind and mine, I know, in that are one. [6]
Remember what I have said.

Oswald

Very well   Well,° madam.

Goneril
And let his knights have colder looks among you.
What grows of it, no matter. Advise your fellows so.

immediately   I'll write straight° to my sister to hold my course. [7]   20
Prepare for dinner.   *They exit.*

1   *If but as well I other accents borrow / That*
    can my speech diffuse, my good intent /
    May carry through itself to that full
    issue / For which I razed my likeness.

    If I can manage to disguise my voice
    as successfully as I have my ap-
    pearance, then my plan, for which
    I totally changed myself (*razed my***
    likeness), may succeed.**

2   *where thou dost stand condemned*

    I.e., in Lear's service

3   Horns within

    Hunting horns sound offstage (see
    1.3.11). In the Elizabethan amphi-
    theaters where *King Lear* **was first**
    performed, *within* **usually referred**
    to "within the tiring-house"—the
    enclosed structure, located behind
    the stage's back wall, where actors
    changed costumes and prepared
    for their entrances.

4   *What dost thou profess?*

    What is your profession? (Kent
    responds with a pun, taking *profess*
    to mean "claim")

5   *fear judgment*

    I.e., fear either secular or spiritual
    judgment, and therefore be com-
    pelled to act righteously

6   *cannot choose*

    Have no choice (but to fight)

7   *to eat no fish*

    The exact meaning of this phrase
    is unclear. Kent may imply, how-
    ever anachronistically, that he is a
    proper Protestant, since Catholics
    do not eat meat on Fridays; alterna-
    tively, he may be suggesting that,
    as a virile man, he eats meat rather
    than fish, or—relying on a crude
    insult—that he avoids sexual rela-
    tions with women.

Act 1, Scene 4

Enter **Kent** *[in disguise].*

Kent

If but as well I other accents borrow

i.e., disguise   That can my speech diffuse,° my good intent

May carry through itself to that full issue

For which I razed my likeness. [1] Now, banished Kent,

If thou canst serve where thou dost stand condemned, [2]   5

happen that   So may it come° thy master, whom thou lov'st,

useful services   Shall find thee full of labors. °

Horns within. [3] *Enter* **Lear**, *[knights,] and attendants.*

Lear

wait/bit   Let me not stay° a jot° for dinner. Go get it ready.

[An attendant exits.]

who   *[to* **Kent***]* How now, what° art thou?

Kent

A man, sir.   10

Lear

What dost thou profess? [4] What wouldst thou with us?

Kent

I do profess to be no less than I seem: to serve him truly

honorable   that will put me in trust, to love him that is honest,° to

converse with him that is wise and says little, to fear

judgment, [5] to fight when I cannot choose, [6] and to eat   15

no fish. [7]

Lear

What art thou?

Kent

A very honest-hearted fellow, and as poor as the King.

89

1   *You.*

Notice Kent's respectful use of *You*,
as opposed to Lear's use of "thou"
(e.g., line 34) appropriate for a king
speaking to a subject.

2   *keep honest counsel*

Keep secret honorable matters

3   *mar a curious tale in telling it*

Ruin an elaborate story when I
attempt to tell it (implying that he
is plainspoken)

Lear

If thou be'st as poor for a subject as he's for a king,
thou'rt poor enough. What wouldst thou?   20

Kent

Service.

Lear

Who wouldst thou serve?

Kent

You.[1]

Lear

Dost thou know me, fellow?

Kent

appearance; demeanor   No, sir, but you have that in your countenance° which   25
gladly   I would fain° call master.

Lear

What's that?

Kent

Authority.

Lear

What services canst thou do?

Kent

I can keep honest counsel,[2] ride, run, mar a curious   30
tale in telling it,[3] and deliver a plain message bluntly.
That which ordinary men are fit for I am qualified in,
and the best of me is diligence.

Lear

How old art thou?

Kent

as to   Not so young, sir, to° love a woman for singing, nor   35
so old to dote on her for anything. I have years on my
back forty-eight.

Lear

Follow me; thou shalt serve me, if I like thee no worse

after dinner. I will not part from thee yet.—Dinner,
boy ho, dinner! Where's my knave,° my fool? Go you and   40
call my fool hither.   [*An attendant exits.*]

Enter steward [**Oswald**].

You! You, sirrah, where's my daughter?
Oswald
So please you—   *He exits.*
Lear
blockhead (i.e., Oswald) What says the fellow there? Call the clodpoll° back.
[**Knight** *exits.*]
Where's my fool, ho? I think the world's asleep.   45

[*Enter* **Knight**.]

How now? Where's that mongrel?
Knight
He says, my lord, your daughter is not well.
Lear
Why came not the slave back to me when I called him?
Knight
bluntest; rudest Sir, he answered me in the roundest° manner, he
would not.   50
Lear
He would not?
Knight
My lord, I know not what the matter is, but to my
treated judgment your Highness is not entertained° with that
used to ceremonious affection as you were wont.° There's a
reduction great abatement° of kindness appears as well in the   55

1   *the general dependents*

    All the servants

2   *jealous curiosity*

    **Hypercritical concern (for proper
    protocol)**

3   *a very pretense*

    An actual intent

general dependents [1] as in the Duke himself also and
your daughter.

Lear
Ha? Say'st thou so?

Knight
I beseech you pardon me, my lord, if I be mistaken,
for my duty cannot be silent when I think your High-   60
ness wronged.

Lear
Thou but rememb'rest° me of mine own conception.° I   *remind / perception*
have perceived a most faint° neglect of late, which I   *lazy*
have rather blamed as mine own jealous curiosity [2]
than as a very pretense [3] and purpose of unkindness.   65
I will look further into 't. But where's my fool? I have
not seen him this two days.

Knight
Since my young lady's going into France, sir, the fool
hath much pined away.

Lear
No more of that. I have noted it well. Go you and tell   70
my daughter I would speak with her.   [**Knight** *exits*.]
—Go you, call hither my fool.   [*An attendant exits*.]

Enter steward [**Oswald**].

Oh, you, sir, you, come you hither, sir. Who am I, sir?

Oswald
My lady's father.

Lear
"My lady's father"? My lord's knave! You whoreson dog,   75
you slave, you cur!

1   *bandy looks*

Exchange glances (literally, to "hit glances back and forth," as in a tennis match). Lear takes offense at Oswald's behavior: as a servant, Oswald should avert his eyes when addressing the King.

2   *base football player*

Football (i.e., soccer) was considered a rough, unruly game, more appropriate for lower-class (*base*) men than gentlemen of good breeding.

3   *If you will measure your lubber's length again*

I.e., if you will be tripped by me again. Kent threatens to *measure* Oswald's *length* across the floor by tripping him and laying him out flat (a *lubber* is a clumsy oaf).

4   *Go to.*

An expression of impatience or derision

5   *earnest of thy service*

Payment in anticipation of future services

6   **Fool**

The relationship between the Fool and Lear is one of the most celebrated in the Shakespeare canon. Shakespeare's plays contain key roles for fools, licensed jesters whose words and actions were a mixture of insight and satire, verbal comedy and slapstick. The Fool in *King Lear* is by turns comic, pathetic, and insightful before he disappears in Act Three, perhaps for dramatic effect, perhaps because the actor doubled up to play another role (possibly Cordelia). More likely, the Fool would have been played by Robert Armin (1568–1616), who joined Shakespeare's acting company, the Lord Chamberlain's Men, around 1600 and who specialized in similarly edgy comic roles. The Fool in *Lear* has license to tell the truth in riddles that others need to heed, if they can understand them.

7   *pretty knave*

Good lad

Oswald

I am none of these, my lord, I beseech your pardon.

Lear

Do you bandy looks [1] with me, you rascal?

[*He strikes* **Oswald**.]

Oswald

hit   I'll not be strucken,° my lord.

Kent

Nor tripped neither, you base football player? [2]   80

[*He trips* **Oswald**.]

Lear

I thank thee, fellow. Thou serv'st me, and I'll love thee.

Kent

[*to* **Oswald**] Come, sir; arise; away! I'll teach you differ-

(in rank)   ences.° Away, away! If you will measure your lubber's
length again, [3] tarry; but away! Go to. [4] Have you
wisdom? [*shoves* **Oswald**] So.   [**Oswald** *exits*.]   85

Lear

servant   Now, my friendly knave,° I thank thee. There's earnest
of thy service. [5]   [*He gives* **Kent** *money*.]

Enter **Fool**. [6]

Fool

fool's cap   Let me hire him too. Here's my coxcomb.°

[*He offers* **Kent** *his cap*.]

Lear

How now, my pretty knave, [7] how dost thou?

Fool

had / fool's cap   [*to* **Kent**] Sirrah, you were° best take my coxcomb.°   90

Lear

Why, my boy?

1 *an thou canst not smile as the wind sits,*
   thou'lt catch cold shortly

   **I.e., if you can't please those in
   power, you'll find yourself in
   trouble.**

2 *banished*

   **The Fool speaks his characteristic
   idiom of inversion: Goneril and Regan have been given the kingdom
   to share but they are *banished*, while
   Cordelia, who literally has been
   banished, has been done a favor by
   allowing her to leave the increasingly savage Britain.**

3 *nuncle*

   **Contraction of "mine uncle," and
   the Fool's affectionate term for
   Lear**

4 *keep my coxcombs*

   **I.e., since such an act would prove
   him a fool**

5 *There's mine; beg another of thy
   daughters.*

   **Here's my coxcomb; ask your
   daughters to give you another one
   (i.e., your daughters have made you
   a fool).**

6 *Truth's a dog must to kennel. He must be
   whipped out, when Lady Brach may stand
   by th' fire and stink.*

   **I.e., those who speak the truth
   (Kent, Cordelia, the Fool) are
   punished, while those who flatter
   (Regan and Goneril) are given
   preference. *Brach* is a term for a
   female hound.**

7 *Have more than thou showest*

   Do not flaunt your wealth.

8 *Learn more than thou trowest*

   **Do not believe everything you hear
   (*trowest* meaning "believe").**

9 *Set less than thou throwest*

   **Do not risk all on one roll of the
   dice.**

Fool

i.e., Lear's Why? For taking one's° part that's out of favor.

if —Nay, an° thou canst not smile as the wind sits, thou'lt
catch cold shortly.[1] There, take my coxcomb. Why, this

of fellow has banished[2] two on°'s daughters and did the   95
third a blessing against his will. If thou follow him,
thou must needs wear my coxcomb.—How now,
nuncle?[3] Would I had two coxcombs and two daughters.

Lear

Why, my boy?

Fool

salary; property If I gave them all my living,° I'd keep my coxcombs[4]   100
myself. There's mine; beg another of thy daughters.[5]

Lear

Take heed, sirrah—the whip.

Fool

must be sent Truth's a dog must° to kennel. He must be whipped out,
when the Lady Brach may stand by th' fire and stink.[6]

Lear

irritation A pestilent gall° to me!   105

Fool

Sirrah, I'll teach thee a speech.

Lear

Do.

Fool

Mark it, nuncle:
　Have more than thou showest,[7]
　Speak less than thou knowest,   110
own 　Lend less than thou owest,°
walk 　Ride more than thou goest,°
　Learn more than thou trowest,[8]
　Set less than thou throwest;[9]
　Leave thy drink and thy whore,   115

1   *And thou shalt have more / Than two tens*
    to a score

    **You shall have more than two tens
    for every twenty (i.e., you will
    profit)**

2   *'tis like the breath of an unfeed lawyer*

    **It is like the speech of an unpaid
    lawyer (i.e., useless). In early mod-
    ern England, lawyers were proverbi-
    ally greedy, only giving worthwhile
    advice if well compensated for their
    efforts.**

3   *use of*

    Profit from

4   *so much the rent of his land comes to*

    **I.e., the income from Lear's land is
    nothing (since he has given it away).**

5   *bor'st thine ass on thy back o'er the dirt*

    **Bore the donkey on your back
    (rather than letting the donkey
    bear you)**

6   *If I speak like myself in this, let him be*
    whipped that first finds it so.

    **Although I speak in my role as a fool
    in this matter, let the first person
    who thinks it folly be whipped
    (rather than me).**

indoors And keep in-a-door, °
And thou shalt have more
Than two tens to a score. [1]

Kent

This is nothing, Fool.

Fool

Then 'tis like the breath of an unfeed lawyer; [2] you gave 120
me nothing for 't. Can you make no use of [3] nothing,
nuncle?

Lear

Why, no, boy. Nothing can be made out of nothing.

Fool

[to **Kent**] Prithee, tell him; so much the rent of his land
comes to. [4] He will not believe a fool. 125

Lear

disagreeable; harsh A bitter ° fool!

Fool

Dost thou know the difference, my boy, between a
bitter fool and a sweet one?

Lear

No, lad. Teach me.

Fool

Nuncle, give me an egg, and I'll give thee two crowns. 130

Lear

What two crowns shall they be?

Fool

Why, after I have cut the egg i' th' middle and eat up the
edible part / divided meat, ° the two crowns of the egg. When thou clovest °
thy crown i' th' middle and gav'st away both parts, thou
bor'st thine ass on thy back o'er the dirt. [5] Thou hadst little 135
head wit in thy bald crown ° when thou gav'st thy golden
one away. If I speak like myself in this, let him be
whipped that first finds it so. [6]

1   *Fools had ne'er less grace in a year, / For*
    wise men are grown foppish

    **(Professional) fools have never
    been less popular, now that wise
    men have grown so foolish them-
    selves.**

2   *And know not how their wits to wear, /*
    Their manners are so apish

    **And (the wise men) have forgotten
    how to use their intelligence, now
    that they merely imitate the fools.**

3   *used it*

    Made it a practice (to sing)

4   *What makes that frontlet on?*

    **What accounts for that frown? (A
    frontlet is literally a decorative band
    worn around the forehead.)**

[*sings*] Fools had ne'er less grace in a year,
For wise men are grown foppish ¹   140
display   And know not how their wits to wear,°
Their manners are so apish.²

Lear

When were you wont to be so full of songs, sirrah?

Fool

I have used it,³ nuncle, e'er since thou mad'st thy
daughters thy mothers; for when thou gav'st them the   145
rod and put'st down thine own breeches,
[*sings*] Then they for sudden joy did weep,
And I for sorrow sung,
peek-a-boo   That such a king should play bo-peep °
And go the fools among.   150
I pray you / employ   Prithee,° nuncle, keep° a schoolmaster that can teach
gladly   thy fool to lie. I would fain° learn to lie.

Lear

If   An° you lie, sirrah, we'll have you whipped.

Fool

i.e., similar creatures   I marvel what kin° thou and thy daughters are. They'll
have me whipped for speaking true, thou'lt have me   155
whipped for lying, and sometimes I am whipped for
holding my peace. I had rather be any kind o' thing
than a fool. And yet I would not be thee, nuncle. Thou
trimmed / intelligence   hast pared° thy wit° o' both sides and left nothing i'
th' middle. Here comes one o' th' parings.   160

Enter **Goneril**.

Lear

How now, daughter? What makes that frontlet on?⁴
You are too much of late i' th' frown.

1   *an O without a figure*

    **I.e., nothing; valueless, like a zero
    lacking an accompanying digit
    (*figure*)**

2   *He that keeps nor crust nor crumb, /
    Weary of all, shall want some*

    **I.e., he that gives all away will
    discover himself in need.**

3   *all-licensed*

    Authorized to do as he pleases

4   *which if you should, the fault / Would not
    scape censure, nor the redresses sleep /
    Which, in the tender of a wholesome
    weal, / Might in their working do you that
    offense / Which else were shame,
    that then necessity / Will call discreet
    proceeding*

    **I.e., if you should continue to
    allow the bad behavior of your
    attendants, I will be forced to
    remedy the situation out of con-
    cern for the common good, and,
    despite the shame it may cause you,
    my actions will be seen as prudent.**

5   *The hedge sparrow fed the cuckoo so
    long / That it's had it head bit off by it
    young.*

    **Cuckoos lay eggs in the nests of
    other birds, such as the hedge spar-
    row. As the baby cuckoo grows, it
    may kill its host parent in order to
    maintain its position in the nest.**

Fool

Thou wast a pretty fellow when thou hadst no need to
care for her frowning; now thou art an O without a figure.[1] I am better than thou art now: I am a fool; thou   165

truly   art nothing. [*to* **Goneril**] Yes, forsooth,° I will hold my
tongue; so your face bids me, though you say nothing.
　　[*sings*] Mum, mum,
　　　He that keeps nor crust nor crumb,
　　　Weary of all, shall want some.[2]   170

peapod   [*pointing to* **Lear**] That's a shelled peascod.°

Goneril

Not only, sir, this, your all-licensed[3] fool,
But other of your insolent retinue

find fault   Do hourly carp° and quarrel, breaking forth
numerous   In rank° and not-to-be-endurèd riots. Sir,   175
I had thought by making this well known unto you

certain/remedy   To have found a safe° redress,° but now grow fearful,
recently   By what yourself too late° have spoke and done,
encourage   That you protect this course and put° it on
acquiescence   By your allowance;° which if you should, the fault   180
Would not scape censure, nor the redresses sleep

care/country   Which, in the tender° of a wholesome weal,°
Might in their working do you that offense

otherwise/shameful   Which else° were shame,° that then necessity
Will call discreet proceeding.[4]   185

Fool

For you know, nuncle,
The hedge sparrow fed the cuckoo so long

has   That it's° had it head bit off by it young.[5]
in the dark   So out went the candle, and we were left darkling.°

Lear

[*to* **Goneril**] Are you our daughter?   190

1   *May not an ass know when the cart draws the horse?*

I.e., even a fool can see how backward everything is now.

2   *Jug*

A nickname for *Joan* (a generic term for a woman). Goneril may have directed an intimidating gesture at the Fool, thereby prompting him to lamely protest his affection.

3   *discernings / Are lethargied*

Powers of perception have grown weak

4   *Lear's shadow.*

The Fool may mean that Lear should ask himself, suggesting that Lear has become a faint image of his former self, or he may be referring to himself as *Lear's shadow* or "reflected image" (implying that Lear is a fool, too). In the 1608 Quarto, Lear speaks these words, meaning that Goneril casting him out of her house has reduced him to a shadow of the great king he used to be. The assignment of this speech to the Fool makes its meaning less transparent as it becomes one of the Fool's riddling remarks.

5   *much o' th' savor / Of other your new pranks*

Very similar to the rest of your recent behavior

6   *Epicurism*

Gluttony; taking intense pleasure in food and drink (appropriate to the *tavern*, as *lust* is to the *brothel*)

7   *disquantity your train*

Decrease the number of your entourage

8   *the remainders that shall still depend*

Those that continue in your service

Goneril

wish   I would° you would make use of your good wisdom,

well supplied   Whereof I know you are fraught,° and put away

moods   These dispositions° which of late transport you

From what you rightly are.

Fool

May not an ass know when the cart draws the horse?[1]   195

Whoop, Jug![2] I love thee.

Lear

Does any here know me? This is not Lear.

Does Lear walk thus, speak thus? Where are his eyes?

intellect   Either his notion° weakens, his discernings

Am I awake?   Are lethargied.[3] Ha! Waking?° 'Tis not so.   200

Who is it that can tell me who I am?

Fool

Lear's shadow.[4]

Lear

Your name, fair gentlewoman?

Goneril

(feigned) amazement   This admiration,° sir, is much o' th' savor

Of other your new pranks.[5] I do beseech you   205

To understand my purposes aright.

you should   As you are old and reverend, should° be wise.

Here do you keep a hundred knights and squires,

disorderly   Men so disordered,° so debauched and bold,

That this our court, infected with their manners,   210

Appears   Shows° like a riotous inn. Epicurism[6] and lust

Makes it more like a tavern or a brothel

dignified / ask   Than a graced° palace. The shame itself doth speak°

requested   For instant remedy. Be then desired,°

otherwise   By her, that else° will take the thing she begs,   215

A little to disquantity your train,[7]

And the remainders that shall still depend[8]

1   *Which know themselves and you*

     I.e., who know the proper behavior
     for both themselves and you

2   *Degenerate bastard*

     Not just an angry epithet, but Lear
     now declares his eldest daughter
     illegitimate, which, of course,
     invalidates his own marriage to his
     queen—who is only mentioned
     once in the play (2.4.127–128).
     Goneril is hereby equated with Ed-
     mund. In calling Goneril *degenerate,*
     Lear claims that she has deterior-
     ated from her human excellence to
     a more primitive and savage form
     of life, as if she were an unnatural
     aberration that it had been his
     misfortune to produce.

3   *thou show'st thee*

     You appear

4   *in the most exact regard, support / The*
     worships of their name

     With the most careful attention up-
     hold the honor of their reputation

5   *Which, like an engine, wrenched my*
     frame of nature / From the fixed place

     Which, like a pulley, tore my natural
     affection from its proper place

befit   To be such men as may besort° your age,
Which know themselves and you.[1]

Lear

                               Darkness and devils!

attendants   Saddle my horses! Call my train° together!   220

                          [*An attendant exits.*]

   —Degenerate bastard,[2] I'll not trouble thee.

Still   Yet° have I left a daughter.

Goneril

disorderly   You strike my people, and your disordered° rabble
Make servants of their betters.

                 Enter **Albany**.

Lear

to him that   Woe that° too late repents!   225
Is it your will? Speak, sir.—Prepare my horses.

                          [*An attendant exits.*]

   —Ingratitude, thou marble-hearted fiend,
More hideous when thou show'st thee[3] in a child
Than the sea monster!

Albany

Pray, sir, be patient.

Lear

(a bird of prey)   [*to* **Goneril**] Detested kite,° thou liest!   230

qualities   My train are men of choice and rarest parts,°
That all particulars of duty know
And, in the most exact regard, support
The worships of their name.[4] O most small fault,
How ugly didst thou in Cordelia show,   235
Which, like an engine, wrenched my frame of nature
From the fixed place,[5] drew from my heart all love,

bitterness   And added to the gall.° Oh, Lear, Lear, Lear!

1   *sterility*

Lear's horrifying curse follows from
his earlier comment that Goneril
was *degenerate*. He now unleashes
a furious tirade, wishing Goneril to
be prevented from procreating,
which, of course, would affect
his own dynastic line. His wish is
granted, as his family dies out without issue at the end of the play. The
curse on a woman to be childless
could recall Elizabeth I, who died
without children two or three years
before *King Lear* was written.

2   *thwart*

Perversely obstinate

3   *mother's pains and benefits*

Maternal cares and joys

Beat at this gate [*striking his head*] that let thy folly in

precious And thy dear° judgment out!—Go, go, my people. 240

[*Attendants exit.*]

Albany

My lord, I am guiltless as I am ignorant

Of what hath moved you.

Lear

It may be so, my lord.

—Hear, Nature, hear! Dear goddess, hear!

Suspend thy purpose if thou didst intend

i.e., Goneril To make this creature° fruitful! 245

Into her womb convey sterility, [1]

procreation Dry up in her the organs of increase,°

degenerate And from her derogate° body never spring

give birth A babe to honor her! If she must teem,°

malice; ill-nature Create her child of spleen,° that it may live 250

unnatural And be a thwart[2] disnatured° torment to her!

Let it stamp wrinkles in her brow of youth,

falling/engrave With cadent° tears fret° channels in her cheeks,

Turn all her mother's pains and benefits[3]

To laughter and contempt, that she may feel 255

How sharper than a serpent's tooth it is

To have a thankless child! Away, away!

He exits [with **Kent***, knights, and attendants*].

Albany

Now, gods that we adore, whereof comes this?

Goneril

bother Never afflict° yourself to know more of it,

mood But let his disposition° have that scope 260

his senility As dotage° gives it.

Enter **Lear***.*

1   *What? Fifty of my followers at a clap? /*
    Within a fortnight?

    **At line 216 Goneril has ordered Lear
    to reduce the number of knights in
    his retinue. Somehow the reduc-
    tion has been ordered (although
    Goneril has been on stage the en-
    tire time), and Lear, after an exit of
    only 4 lines, returns having learned
    that *at a clap* (in an instant) half of
    his hundred knights have been
    ordered to leave [*w*]*ithin a fortnight*
    (i.e., two weeks).**

2   *Blasts and fogs*

    Foul air carrying disease

3   *untented woundings*

    **Unattended and deep (and
    therefore more likely to become
    infected) wounds**

4   *Beweep this cause again, I'll pluck ye out /*
    And cast you, with the waters that you
    loose, / To temper clay

    **If you (i.e., his eyes) weep further
    for this cause (Goneril's treachery)
    again, I'll pluck you out of my head
    and throw you, along with the
    tears you shed, on the ground to
    mix with (or perhaps "soften") the
    earth.**

5   *kind*

    **Both "compassionate" and
    "natural"**

Lear

single stroke What? Fifty of my followers at a clap?°
Within a fortnight?[1]

Albany

What's the matter, sir?

Lear

I'll tell thee. [*to* **Goneril**] Life and death! I am ashamed
That thou hast power to shake my manhood thus,   265
unwillingly That these hot tears, which break from me perforce,°
Should make thee worth them. Blasts and fogs[2] upon
thee!
Th' untented woundings[3] of a father's curse
foolish Pierce every sense about thee! Old fond° eyes,
Beweep this cause again, I'll pluck ye out   270
And cast you, with the waters that you loose,
To temper clay.[4] Ha! Let it be so.
I have another daughter,
comforting Who, I am sure, is kind[5] and comfortable.°
When she shall hear this of thee, with her nails   275
face She'll flay thy wolvish visage.° Thou shalt find
(of king) That I'll resume the shape° which thou dost think
I have cast off for ever.   *He exits.*

Goneril

note [*to* **Albany**] Do you mark° that?

Albany

biased I cannot be so partial,° Goneril,   280
Because of To° the great love I bear you—

Goneril

be silent Pray you, content.° —What, Oswald, ho!
follow [*to* **Fool**] You, sir, more knave than fool, after° your
master.

1 *Should sure*

 Would surely be sent

2 *halter*

 (1) leash for an animal; (2) noose (to hang Goneril)

3 *politic*

 Prudent (spoken sarcastically)

4 *fear too far*

 Exaggerate the risk

5 *Not fear still to be taken*

 Rather than continually fear being in danger

Fool

Nuncle Lear, nuncle Lear! Tarry and take the fool with
    thee.

A fox, when one has caught her,   285

And such a daughter

Should sure¹ to the slaughter,

If my cap would buy a halter.²

So the fool follows after.   *He exits.*

Goneril

This man hath had good counsel. A hundred knights?   290

'Tis politic³ and safe to let him keep

arms/so that   At point° a hundred knights? Yes, that° on every
    dream,

rumor   Each buzz,° each fancy, each complaint, dislike,

protect   He may enguard° his dotage with their powers

his power   And hold our lives in mercy?°—Oswald, I say!   295

Albany

Well, you may fear too far.⁴

Goneril

Safer than trust too far.

always   Let me still° take away the harms I fear,

Not fear still to be taken.⁵ I know his heart.

What he hath uttered I have writ my sister.   300

If she sustain him and his hundred knights

When I have showed th' unfitness—

Enter steward [**Oswald**].

                                        How now, Oswald?

What, have you writ that letter to my sister?

Oswald

Ay, madam.

1   *away to horse*

    I.e., Ride to her

2   *under pardon*

    With your pardon (for saying so)

3   *Well, well, th' event.*

    I.e., time will tell

Goneril

Take you some company and away to horse.[1]   305

fully Inform her full° of my particular fear,

And thereto add such reasons of your own

confirm As may compact° it more. Get you gone,

And hasten your return.   [**Oswald** *exits.*]

           [*to* **Albany**] No, no, my lord,

effeminate / (of action) This milky° gentleness and course° of yours,   310

Though I condemn not, yet, under pardon,[2]

blamed / lack You're much more attasked° for want° of wisdom

Than praised for harmful mildness.

Albany

discern How far your eyes may pierce° I cannot tell.

Striving to better, oft we mar what's well.   315

Goneril

Nay, then—

Albany

Well, well, th' event.[3]   *They exit.*

1 *Gloucester*

Not the nobleman but the town of
the same name, in western England
on the eastern bank of the Severn
River

2 *demand out of*

Questions arising from

3 *were 't not in danger of kibes*

Wouldn't they be in danger of
chilblains (sores or swelling in the
feet caused by exposure to cold; a
specific form of frostbite)

4 *Thy wit shall not go slipshod.*

Your brain shall never wear slippers
(since you have no brain, as you
think you can rely on Regan's kindness, you clearly need no slippers
to protect it).

5 *kindly*

(1) with kindness; (2) according to
her nature

6 *she's as like this as a crab's like an apple*

Regan resembles Goneril the way
a crab apple resembles an apple
(perhaps suggesting that Regan is
smaller and more sour than Goneril
or merely that there is little difference between them).

Act 1, Scene 5

*Enter **Lear**, **Kent** [*in disguise*], and **Fool**.*

Lear

ahead [*giving a letter to* **Kent**] Go you before° to Gloucester [1]
with these letters. Acquaint my daughter no fur-
ther with anything you know than comes from her
demand out of [2] the letter. If your diligence be not
speedy, I shall be there afore you.   5

Kent

I will not sleep, my lord, till I have delivered your letter.

He exits.

Fool

his If a man's brains were in 's° heels, were 't not in
danger of kibes? [3]

Lear

Ay, boy.

Fool

Then, I prithee, be merry. Thy wit shall not go slipshod. [4]   10

Lear

Ha, ha, ha!

Fool

Thou shalt Shalt° see thy other daughter will use thee kindly, [5] for
i.e., Goneril though she's as like this° as a crab's like an apple, [6] yet I
can tell what I can tell.

Lear

What canst tell, boy?   15

Fool

She will taste as like this as a crab does to a crab. Thou
of canst tell why one's nose stands i' th' middle on° 's
face?

Lear

No.

1   *Why, to put 's head in, not to give it away*
     to his daughters and leave his horns
     without a case.

     **The ridiculous notion of a snail
     choosing to relinquish its protec-
     tive shell suggests how absurd and
     unnatural Lear's behavior seems
     to the Fool. The image may also
     suggest that Lear has suffered a
     kind of sexual defeat at the hands
     of his daughters, as exposed *horns*
     were the proverbial symbols of
     a cuckold (a man whose wife has
     been unfaithful).**

2   *the seven stars*

     **Probably a reference to the seven
     stars that make up the constella-
     tion Pleiades (also known as the
     Seven Sisters), or perhaps to the
     constellation Ursa Major, to which
     Edmund refers at 1.2.121.**

3   *To take 't again perforce!*

     **To take it back by force (apparently
     a reference to Lear's desire to take
     back his kingdom).**

Fool

on / of his   Why, to keep one's eyes of° either side 's° nose, that   20

what a man cannot smell out he may spy into.

Lear

i.e., Cordelia   I did her° wrong.

Fool

Canst tell how an oyster makes his shell?

Lear

No.

Fool

Nor I neither. But I can tell why a snail has a house.   25

Lear

Why?

Fool

Why, to put 's head in, not to give it away to his

daughters and leave his horns without a case. [1]

Lear

natural affection   I will forget my nature. ° So kind a father!—Be my

horses ready?   30

Fool

i.e., servants / to get   Thy asses° are gone about° 'em. The reason why the

seven stars[2] are no more than seven is a pretty reason.

Lear

Because they are not eight?

Fool

Yes, indeed. Thou wouldst make a good fool.

Lear

To take 't again perforce![3] Monster ingratitude!   35

Fool

If thou wert my fool, nuncle, I'd have thee beaten for

being old before thy time.

Lear

How's that?

1   *in temper*

Mentally stable; composed

2   *She that's a maid now and laughs at my*
     departure, / Shall not be a maid long,
     unless things be cut shorter.

**Addressed to the audience: She
that is a virgin and laughs at my
behavior cannot be wise enough to
keep her virginity for long, unless
(1) history stops now; (2) penises be
severed. The Fool bawdily warns
any spectators simple enough to
focus only on his comic antics that
they risk being caught unaware by
the impending tragedy.**

Fool

Thou shouldst not have been old till thou hadst been
wise.   40

Lear

Oh, let me not be mad, not mad, sweet Heaven!
Keep me in temper; [1] I would not be mad!

[*Enter* **Gentleman**.]

How now, are the horses ready?

Gentleman

Ready, my lord.

Lear

Come, boy.   45

Fool

She that's a maid now and laughs at my departure
Shall not be a maid long, unless things be cut shorter. [2]

They exit.

1   severally

    Separately

2   *ear-kissing arguments*

    **Softly spoken topics of conversa-
    tion**

3   *The better! Best!*

    **So much the better! Indeed the best
    (that could be)!**

4   *one thing of a queasy question*

    One task requiring delicate handling

Act 2, Scene 1

*Enter Bastard [**Edmund**] and **Curan**, severally.* [1]

Edmund

God save Save° thee, Curan.

Curan

And you, sir. I have been with your father and given
him notice that the Duke of Cornwall and Regan his
Duchess will be here with him this night.

Edmund

How comes that? 5

Curan

going around Nay, I know not. You have heard of the news abroad°—
i.e., rumors I mean the whispered ones,° for they are yet but ear-
kissing arguments? [2]

Edmund

Not I. Pray you, what are they?

Curan

impending Have you heard of no likely wars toward° twixt the 10
Dukes of Cornwall and Albany?

Edmund

Not a word.

Curan

i.e., hear You may do,° then, in time. Fare you well, sir. *He exits.*

Edmund

The Duke be here tonight? The better! Best! [3]
as a matter of course This weaves itself perforce° into my business. 15
arrest My father hath set guard to take° my brother,
And I have one thing of a queasy question [4]
Speed Which I must act. Briefness° and fortune, work!
—Brother, a word. Descend. Brother, I say!

*Enter **Edgar**.*

125

1   *watches*
    Is on the lookout (for you)

2   *Upon his party*
    In favor of him (Cornwall)

3   *Advise yourself.*
    Consider this carefully.

4   *In cunning*
    As a device (to fool Gloucester)

5   *quit you*
    Acquit yourself

6   *—Yield! Come before my father!—Light,*
    ho, here! / —Fly, brother.—Torches,
    torches! —So, farewell.
    Edmund creates the appearance of
    trying to detain Edgar.

7   *beget opinion / Of my more fierce*
    endeavor
    Create the impression that I fought
    fiercely

8   *stand auspicious mistress*
    Act as his benefactress

My father watches. ¹ Oh, sir, fly this place!   20
Information   Intelligence° is given where you are hid.
You have now the good advantage of the night.
Have you not spoken 'gainst the Duke of Cornwall?
He's coming hither, now, i' th' night, i' th' haste,
And Regan with him. Have you nothing said   25
Upon his party² 'gainst the Duke of Albany?
Advise yourself. ³

Edgar

of   I am sure on° 't; not a word.

Edmund

I hear my father coming. Pardon me;
In cunning⁴ I must draw my sword upon you.
Draw. Seem to defend yourself. Now, quit you⁵ well.   30
—Yield! Come before my father!—Light, ho, here!
—Fly, brother.—Torches, torches!—So, farewell. ⁶

                                  Edgar *exits.*

from   Some blood drawn on° me would beget opinion
Of my more fierce endeavor. ⁷ I have seen drunkards
jest   Do more than this in sport.° [*He wounds himself.*] Father,
    father!
Stop, stop! No help?   35

           Enter **Gloucester**, *and servants with torches.*

Gloucester

                    Now, Edmund, where's the villain?

Edmund

Here stood he in the dark, his sharp sword out,
Mumbling of wicked charms, conjuring the moon
To stand auspicious mistress. ⁸

Gloucester

                      But where is he?

1   *charges home / My unprovided body*

**Directly attacks my unprotected
body**

2   *latched mine arm*

**Wounded my arm (or maybe held
my arm)**

3   *my best alarumed spirits, / Bold in the
quarrel's right*

**My aroused courage, emboldened
by the righteousness of my cause**

4   *he which finds him*

He who apprehends Edgar

Edmund

Look, sir, I bleed.

Gloucester

Where is the villain, Edmund?   40

Edmund

Fled this way, sir, when by no means he could—

Gloucester

—Pursue him, ho! Go after.   [*Some servants exit.*]

By no means what?

Edmund

Persuade me to the murder of your Lordship.

when   But that° I told him the revenging gods

father-murderers/aim   'Gainst parricides° did all the thunder bend,°   45

about/multiple   Spoke with° how manifold° and strong a bond

summation   The child was bound to th' father, sir, in fine,°

opposed   Seeing how loathly opposite° I stood

fierce   To his unnatural purpose, in fell° motion

unsheathed   With his preparèd° sword he charges home   50

My unprovided body,[1] latched mine arm;[2]

And when he saw my best alarumed spirits,

Bold in the quarrel's right,[3] roused to th' encounter,

frightened   Or whether ghasted° by the noise I made,

Very   Full° suddenly he fled.

Gloucester

Let him fly far.   55

Not in this land shall he remain uncaught;

i.e., quickly executed   And found—dispatch.° The noble Duke my master,

lord   My worthy arch° and patron, comes tonight.

By his authority I will proclaim it

That he which finds him[4] shall deserve our thanks,   60

place of execution   Bringing the murderous coward to the stake;°

He that conceals him, death.

1   *unpossessing*

    **Landless (Edmund, as a bastard,
    could not legally inherit property)**

2   *If I would stand against thee, would the
    reposal / Of any trust, virtue, or worth in
    thee / Make thy words faithed*

    **If I spoke up against you, that
    anyone would place enough trust,
    virtue, or worth in you to believe
    your words (over mine)**

3   *character*

    **Handwriting, but inevitably with
    wider implications. Edmund's
    reported speech of what he falsely
    claims his legitimate brother said
    reverses their characters (i.e., their
    emotional and moral makeup), as if
    Edmund were the legitimate, loyal
    son and Edgar the false, illegit-
    imate one. Gloucester is too naïve
    to see through the subterfuge. Mis-
    placed and misleading letters are
    an important plot motif in *Lear*.**

4   *thou must make a dullard of the world / If
    they not thought the profits of my death /
    Were very pregnant and potential spirits /
    To make thee seek it*

    **You must suppose everyone in
    the world to be an imbecile if you
    think they don't see that you have
    compelling and powerful reasons
    to desire my death.**

5   Tucket within

    **A succession of trumpet notes
    played offstage**

6   *natural boy*

    **A richly complicated term. Most
    immediately, *natural* suggests
    "showing the natural affection of a
    son for his father" (i.e., a loving and
    reverent regard). It can also mean
    both "illegitimate" (a *natural* child
    being one born outside of wedlock)
    and "legitimate," in so far as what
    is *natural* is seen as inherently right,
    moral, and apt.**

Edmund

When I dissuaded him from his intent

determined/angry And found him pight° to do it, with curst° speech

expose I threatened to discover° him. He replied,   65

"Thou unpossessing[1] bastard, dost thou think,

placing If I would stand against thee, would the reposal°

Of any trust, virtue, or worth in thee

That which Make thy words faithed?[2] No. What° I should deny—

As this I would, ay, though thou didst produce   70

attribute My very character[3]—I'd turn° it all

scheming To thy suggestion, plot, and damnèd practice;°

And thou must make a dullard of the world

If they not thought the profits of my death

Were very pregnant and potential spirits   75

To make thee seek it."[4]

Gloucester

unnatural/confirmed   O strange° and fastened° villain!

Would he deny his letter, said he?   *Tucket within.*[5]

Hark, the Duke's trumpets! I know not why he comes.

seaports All ports° I'll bar; the villain shall not 'scape.

description The Duke must grant me that. Besides, his picture°   80

I will send far and near, that all the kingdom

May have due note of him; and of my land,

Loyal and natural boy,[6] I'll work the means

entitled to inherit To make thee capable.°

Enter **Cornwall**, **Regan**, *and attendants.*

Cornwall

How now, my noble friend? Since I came hither,   85

just Which I can call but° now, I have heard strange news.

1   *ill affected*

    Estranged; disloyal; ill disposed

2   *To have th' expense and waste of his*
    revenues

    In order to have access to his
    fortune

Regan

If it be true, all vengeance comes too short
Which can pursue th' offender. How dost, my lord?

Gloucester

Oh, madam, my old heart is cracked; it's cracked!

Regan

What, did my father's godson seek your life?   90
He whom my father named? Your Edgar?

Gloucester

Oh, lady, lady, shame would have it hid!

Regan

Was he not companion with the riotous knights
waited That tended° upon my father?

Gloucester

I know not, madam. 'Tis too bad, too bad.   95

Edmund

group; company Yes, madam, he was of that consort.°

Regan

if No marvel, then, though° he were ill affected.[1]
up to 'Tis they have put him on° the old man's death,
To have th' expense and waste of his revenues.[2]
I have this present evening from my sister   100
about Been well informed of° them, and with such cautions
That if they come to sojourn at my house
I'll not be there.

Cornwall

　　　　　　Nor I, assure thee, Regan.
Edmund, I hear that you have shown your father
properly filial A childlike° office.

Edmund

　　　　　　It was my duty, sir.   105

1   *bewray his practice*

     Expose his (i.e., Edgar's) plot

2   *Make your own purpose / How in my*
     strength you please.

     Freely use my power and resources
     as you need (to go after Edgar).

3   *however else*

     Above all

4   *Thus out of season*

     At an inconvenient time like this

5   *From hence attend dispatch*

     Are waiting to be sent (with replies)

Gloucester

[*to* **Cornwall**] He did bewray his practice,[1] and
   received

arrest This hurt you see striving to apprehend° him.

Cornwall

Is he pursued?

Gloucester

Ay, my good lord.

Cornwall

If he be taken, he shall never more   *110*

Be feared of doing harm. Make your own purpose

As for How in my strength you please.[2] For° you, Edmund,

Whose virtue and obedience doth this instant

So much commend itself, you shall be ours.

Natures of such deep trust we shall much need;   *115*

You we first seize on.

Edmund

               I shall serve you, sir,

Truly, however else.[3]

Gloucester

               For him I thank your Grace.

Cornwall

You know not why we came to visit you?

Regan

Thus out of season,[4] threading dark-eyed night?

importance Occasions, noble Gloucester, of some price,°   *120*

Wherein we must have use of your advice.

Our father he hath writ, so hath our sister,

quarrels Of differences,° which I best thought it fit

away from / various To answer from° our home. The several° messengers

From hence attend dispatch.[5] Our good old friend,   *125*

1   *the instant use*

Immediate attention

Lay comforts to your bosom and bestow

much needed   Your needful° counsel to our businesses,

Which craves the instant use.[1]

Gloucester

                  I serve you, madam.

Your Graces are right welcome.   *Flourish. They exit.*

1 severally
   Separately

2 *dawning*
   **Though the sun has not yet risen;
   see line 28.**

3 *if thou lov'st me*
   **I.e., if you'd be so kind (but Kent
   takes it literally)**

4 *in Lipsbury pinfold*
   **I.e., between my teeth. *Lipsbury* is
   an apparently invented place-
   name, equivalent to "lips-ville"; a
   pinfold is a pen for animals.**

5 *care for*
   Be concerned with (troubled by)

6 *eater of broken meats*
   **I.e., one who eats the leftovers
   after a feast. Kent implies (rightly)
   that Oswald is a sycophant who
   will do anything for his mistress
   and has reduced himself to the
   level of a household pet who is fed
   from the table scraps. In this scene,
   the loyal, good servant confronts
   the bad one. Numerous treatises
   on masters and servants warned
   against flatterers and sycophants
   and urged masters to employ
   people who would serve them hon-
   estly and offer good advice even if it
   was not what was easy to hear.**

7 *three-suited, hundred-pound*
   ***Three-suited* may be an insulting ref-
   erence to Oswald's menial position
   (three suits being a servant's total
   allotment of clothing for a year).
   A hundred pounds was the common price at which King James I of
   England would sell a knighthood,
   insulting Oswald's pretensions to
   be a gentleman.**

8 *worsted-stocking*
   **Woolen stockings, as opposed to
   the silk stockings normally worn by
   gentlemen**

9 *glass-gazing, superserviceable, finical*
   Vain, brown-nosing, affected

10 *one-trunk-inheriting*
   **Having only enough to fill a single
   trunk (i.e., very little)**

Act 2, Scene 2

Enter **Kent** *[in disguise] and steward [***Oswald***], severally.* [1]

Oswald

Good dawning [2] to thee, friend. Art of this house?

Kent

Ay.

Oswald

Where may we set our horses?

Kent

I' th' mire.

Oswald

Prithee, if thou lov'st me, [3] tell me.   5

Kent

I love thee not.

Oswald

Why then, I care not for thee.

Kent

If I had thee in Lipsbury pinfold, [4] I would make thee
care for [5] me.

Oswald

treat   Why dost thou use° me thus? I know thee not.   10

Kent

Fellow, I know thee.

Oswald

What dost thou know me for?

Kent

vile   A knave, a rascal, an eater of broken meats; [6] a base,°
proud, shallow, beggarly, three-suited, hundred-
cowardly   pound, [7] filthy worsted-stocking [8] knave; a lily-livered,°   15
litigious / bastard   action-taking,° whoreson,° glass-gazing, superserviceable, finical [9] rogue; one-trunk-inheriting [10] slave;

139

1   *wouldst be a bawd in way of good service*

Would be a pimp or pander if that is
what is required of him

2   *brazen-faced varlet*

Shameless knave

3   *make a sop o' th' moonshine of you*

Cut you full of holes so you soak up
the moonlight (a *sop* is a piece of
bread soaked in liquid)

4   *cullionly barbermonger*

Contemptible fop (*cullion* meaning
"testicle"; a *barbermonger* being
"one who frequents hairdressers")

5   *Vanity the puppet's part*

I.e., Goneril's part. Kent may
compare Goneril to the personifi-
cation of Vanity in a morality play
performed by puppets, or he may
be describing her as a vain woman
(*puppet* being a derisive term for a
woman made up with cosmetics)

6   *carbonado*

Slash (the term describes meat that
has been scored for grilling)

7   *Come your ways!*

I.e., come on

8   *Stand*

Defend yourself

one that wouldst be a bawd in way of good service,[1]

combination   and art nothing but the composition° of a knave, beggar, coward, pander, and the son and heir of a mongrel   20
bitch; one whom I will beat into clamorous whining if

attributes   thou deny'st the least syllable of thy addition.°

Oswald

Why, what a monstrous fellow art thou thus to rail on

by   one that is neither known of° thee nor knows thee!

Kent

What a brazen-faced varlet[2] art thou to deny thou   25
knowest me! Is it two days since I tripped up thy heels

i.e., Draw your sword   and beat thee before the King! Draw,° you rogue, for,
though it be night, yet the moon shines. I'll make a
sop o' th' moonshine of you,[3] you whoreson, cullionly
barbermonger.[4] Draw!   [*drawing his sword*]   30

Oswald

Away! I have nothing to do with thee.

Kent

Draw, you rascal! You come with letters against the
King, and take Vanity the puppet's part[5] against the
royalty of her father. Draw, you rogue, or I'll so
carbonado[6] your shanks—draw, you rascal! Come   35
your ways![7]

Oswald

Help, ho! Murder! Help!

Kent

foppish   Strike, you slave! Stand,[8] rogue; stand, you neat°
slave; strike!   [*He beats him.*]

Oswald

Help, ho! Murder! murder!   40

1   *With you*

    My quarrel (*matter*) is with you

2   *goodman*

    Term of address for a yeoman, or
    land-owning commoner (an insult
    when applied to Edmund, a gentle-
    man)

3   *flesh ye*

    Initiate you into the ways of combat
    by being the first to shed your
    blood (implying that Edmund is
    new to combat, a further insult)

4   *disclaims in thee*

    Disowns you; denies its hand in
    making you

5   *A tailor made thee.*

    Kent implies that Oswald is not a
    man at all, but merely a fancy suit
    of clothing.

6   *though they had been but two years o' th'*
    trade

    Even if they had practiced their
    trade for only two years (a full
    apprenticeship was for seven years)

7   *at suit of*

    Because of

Enter Bastard [**Edmund**, *with his rapier drawn*],
Cornwall, **Regan**, **Gloucester**, *servants*.

Edmund

How now, what's the matter? Part.

Kent

With you,[1] goodman[2] boy, if you please! Come,
I'll flesh ye.[3] Come on, young master.

Gloucester

Weapons? Arms? What's the matter here?

Cornwall

Keep peace, upon your lives!   45
He dies that strikes again. What is the matter?

Regan

The messengers from our sister and the King.

Cornwall

quarrel   What's your difference?° Speak.

Oswald

I am scarce in breath, my lord.

Kent

No marvel, you have so bestirred your valor. You   50
cowardly rascal, nature disclaims in thee.[4] A tailor
made thee.[5]

Cornwall

Thou art a strange fellow. A tailor make a man?

Kent

A tailor, sir. A stonecutter or a painter could not have
badly   made him so ill,° though they had been but two years   55
o' th' trade.[6]

Cornwall

Speak yet; how grew your quarrel?

Oswald

This ancient ruffian, sir, whose life I have spared at
suit of[7] his gray beard—

1   *zed*

The letter z. Z does not appear in
the Latin alphabet, and, since in
English it could usually be replaced
by an *s*, it was considered an
unnecessary letter.

2   *wagtail*

An insult implying impertinence,
derived from the name of a small,
sprightly bird of the Motacilla
family.

3   *oft bite the holy cords a-twain / Which are
too intrinse t' unloose*

I.e., often gnaw apart the bonds (of
family, of rank, of marriage, of society), that are too intricate to loosen
otherwise. Possibly a reference to
the legendary Gordian knot, which
was so intricate that it could not
be untied; it remained secure until
Alexander the Great sliced it apart
with his sword.

4   *smooth every passion*

Smooth may either suggest
"assuage" or, conversely,
"indulge." In either case, Kent
implies that sycophantic servants
like Oswald act according to their
masters' moods and whims, rather
than their own reason or good
judgment.

5   *halcyon beaks*

Suspended from a cord, the corpse
of a *halcyon* (Greek for the bird

known as the kingfisher) was used
as a weathervane, free to turn to
indicate the direction of the wind.
Like the dead kingfisher, Oswald
continually shifts his position to
match *every gale and vary* (every vari-
able whim) of his master's.

6   *gale and vary*

Varying wind; i.e., changing mood

7   *if I had you upon Sarum Plain, / I'd drive
ye cackling home to Camelot*

I.e., if I had my way, you cackling
goose, I would chase you out of
here. *Sarum* is the old name of
"Salisbury," and *Camelot* is the
legendary home of King Arthur,
sometimes thought to have been
not far from Salisbury, but the
intended connection between
these two places is unclear.

8   *How fell you out?*

How did you come to quarrel?

Kent

Thou whoreson zed![1] Thou unnecessary letter!—My   60

coarse; unsifted lord, if you will give me leave, I will tread this unbolted°

plaster / privy; outhouse villain into mortar and daub° the wall of a jakes° with

him.—Spare my gray beard, you wagtail?[2]

Cornwall

Peace, sirrah!

You beastly knave, know you no reverence?   65

Kent

i.e., to speak Yes, sir, but anger hath a privilege.°

Cornwall

Why art thou angry?

Kent

That such a slave as this should wear a sword,

Who wears no honesty. Such smiling rogues as these,

Like rats, oft bite the holy cords a-twain   70

Which are too intrinse t' unloose;[3] smooth every passion[4]

That in the natures of their lords rebel,

Being oil to fire, snow to the colder moods,

Deny Renege,° affirm, and turn their halcyon beaks[5]

With every gale and vary[6] of their masters,   75

Knowing naught, like dogs, but following.

distorted —A plague upon your epileptic° visage!

at my / as if Smile you my° speeches, as° I were a fool?

Goose, if I had you upon Sarum Plain,

I'd drive ye cackling home to Camelot.[7]   80

Cornwall

What, art thou mad, old fellow?

Gloucester

How fell you out?[8] Say that.

Kent

No contraries hold more antipathy

Than I and such a knave.

1   *doth affect / A saucy roughness and con-*
     strains the garb / Quite from his nature

     **Adopts a mode of insolent rude-
     ness and forces the style of plain
     speaking away from its normal use
     (i.e., to express the truth) into a
     mode of deception**

2   *twenty silly-ducking observants / That
     stretch their duties nicely*

     **Twenty absurdly obsequious
     attendants, who outdo themselves
     in meticulously performing their
     duties**

3   *Under th' allowance of your great aspect, /
     Whose influence, like the wreath of radi-
     ant fire / On flickering Phoebus' front—*

     **I.e., with the permission of your
     noble countenance, whose power,
     like the flickering crown of bright
     fire that Phoebus (the sun god)
     wears on his forehead. . . . Kent
     mockingly adopts the inflated
     flattering style of courtly speech,
     in response to Cornwall's cynical
     sneer at his usual plain speaking.**

4   *dialect*

     **Customary manner of speaking
     (i.e., plain speaking)**

Cornwall

Why dost thou call him knave? What is his fault?   *85*

Kent

pleases   His countenance likes° me not.

Cornwall

No more, perchance, does mine, nor his, nor hers.

Kent

habit/plainspoken   Sir, 'tis my occupation° to be plain:°

I have seen better faces in my time

Than stands on any shoulder that I see   *90*

Before me at this instant.

Cornwall

              This is some fellow,

Who, having been praised for bluntness, doth affect

A saucy roughness and constrains the garb

its   Quite from his° nature. [1] He cannot flatter, he;

An honest mind and plain, he must speak truth.   *95*

If/so be it   An° they will take 't, so;° if not, he's plain.

These kind of knaves I know, which in this plainness

Harbor more craft and more corrupter ends

foolishly bowing   Than twenty silly-ducking° observants

That stretch their duties nicely. [2]   *100*

Kent

truth   Sir, in good faith, in sincere verity,°

Under th' allowance of your great aspect,

Whose influence, like the wreath of radiant fire

On flickering Phoebus' front— [3]

Cornwall

              What mean'st by this?

Kent

disparage   To go out of my dialect, [4] which you discommend° so   *105*

much. I know, sir, I am no flatterer. He that beguiled

1   *He that beguiled you in a plain accent was*
    a plain knave, which for my part I will not
    be, though I should win your displeasure
    to entreat me to 't.

    I.e., whoever it was that once duped
    you with plain speech was clearly a
    villain—which I will never be, even
    if I could get you to put aside your
    scorn and ask me to be one.

2   *When he, compact and flattering his*
    displeasure

    I.e., when Kent, in league with Lear
    and pandering to his (Lear's) anger

3   *being down, insulted*

    When I was down, he (Kent) gloated
    over me

4   *put upon him such a deal of man / That*
    worthied him

    Acted with such a show of bravery
    that he seemed worthy

5   *got praises of the King / For him*
    attempting who was self-subdued

    Won praises from Lear for attacking
    someone who had already given up

6   *None of these rogues and cowards / But*
    Ajax is their fool.

    All such *rogues and cowards* just
    talk a good game (act as if Ajax, a
    legendary Greek hero, was merely
    their fool).

7   *stocks*

    A common instrument of punish-
    ment, comprised of a bench on
    which the offender sat and a
    wooden frame in front that
    imprisoned the ankles and often
    the wrists

---

you in a plain accent was a plain knave, which for my
part I will not be, though I should win your displeasure to entreat me to 't.[1]

Cornwall

[to **Oswald**] What was th' offense you gave him?   110

Oswald

I never gave him any.
It pleased the King his master very late°   *recently*
To strike at me upon his misconstruction;°   *misunderstanding*
When he,° compact and flattering his displeasure,[2]   *i.e., Kent*
Tripped me behind; being down, insulted,[3] railed,   115
And put upon him such a deal of man
That worthied him,[4] got praises of the King
For him attempting who was self-subdued,[5]
And, in the fleshment° of this dread exploit,   *excitement*
Drew on me here again.

Kent

                              None of these rogues and cowards   120
But Ajax is their fool.[6]

Cornwall

                              —Fetch forth the stocks![7]
—You stubborn, ancient knave, you reverend° braggart,   *old*
We'll teach you.

Kent

                   Sir, I am too old to learn.
Call not your stocks for me. I serve the King,
On whose employment I was sent to you.   125
You shall do small respects, show too bold malice
Against the grace° and person of my master,   *majesty*
Stocking his messenger.

Cornwall

—Fetch forth the stocks! As I have life and honor,
There shall he sit till noon.   130

1 *being his knave*

**Since you are his (i.e., her father's)
servant**

Regan

Till noon? Till night, my lord, and all night too.

Kent

Why, madam, if I were your father's dog

would You should° not use me so.

Regan

Sir, being his knave, ¹ I will.

Cornwall

character This is a fellow of the selfsame color°   135

sister-in-law / out Our sister° speaks of.—Come, bring away° the stocks!

Stocks brought out.

Gloucester

Let me beseech your Grace not to do so.

The King his master needs must take it ill

That he, so slightly valued in his messenger,

Should have him thus restrained.

Cornwall

take responsibility for   I'll answer° that.   140

Regan

My sister may receive it much more worse

To have her gentleman abused, assaulted,

For following her affairs. Put in his legs.

[**Kent** *is put in the stocks.*]

Cornwall

[*to **Gloucester***] Come, my lord, away.

[*All but **Gloucester** and **Kent***] *exit.*

Gloucester

I am sorry for thee, friend. 'Tis the Duke's pleasure,   145

Whose disposition, all the world well knows,

deflected Will not be rubbed° nor stopped. I'll entreat for thee.

Kent

gone without sleep Pray, do not, sir. I have watched° and traveled hard.

Some time I shall sleep out; the rest I'll whistle.

1 *grow out at heels*

I.e., turn bad

2 *that must approve the common saw*

That must confirm the old saying

3 *Thou out of Heaven's benediction com'st /
To the warm sun*

You fall from Heaven's bliss into the
hot sun; a proverbial expression
for a change of fortune from good
to bad.

4 *thou beacon to this under globe*

I.e., the sun

5 *Nothing almost sees miracles / But
misery.*

Virtually the only people who
experience miracles are those
who are truly miserable (because
to such wretched beings any amel-
ioration of their condition seems
miraculous)

6 *enormous state*

Dire situation

7 *o'erwatched*

Tired (from lack of sleep)

8 *turn thy wheel*

I.e., improve my situation. Fortune
was traditionally depicted as a
woman turning a wheel, which
carried some to great heights and
brought others low. Everyone was
aware that the wheel could turn
again at any minute. Fortune was
often dismissed as a pagan belief,
an explanation for the vicissitudes
of fate, though others thought
the changes brought about by
Fortune's wheel were not random
but God's rewards or punishments
for human actions. See 5.3.165.

A good man's fortune may grow out at heels.[1]   150
i.e., May God give   Give° you good morrow.

Gloucester

The Duke's to blame in this. 'Twill be ill taken.   *He exits.*

Kent

i.e., Lear   Good King,° that must approve the common saw,[2]
Thou out of Heaven's benediction com'st
To the warm sun![3]   [*He takes out a letter.*]   155
Approach, thou beacon to this under globe,[4]
comforting   That by thy comfortable° beams I may
Peruse this letter. Nothing almost sees miracles
But misery.[5] I know 'tis from Cordelia,
Who hath most fortunately been informed   160
disguised   Of my obscurèd° course, and shall find time
For this enormous state,[6] seeking to give
Losses their remedies. All weary and o'erwatched,[7]
advantage   Take vantage,° heavy eyes, not to behold
This shameful lodging.   165
Fortune, good night. Smile once more; turn thy
      wheel![8]   [*He sleeps.*]

1   *free*

Open (see 2.1.79, where Gloucester
orders the seaports guarded until
he is caught)

2   *attend my taking*

Seek to arrest me

3   *am bethought*

Have a plan

4   *That ever penury, in contempt of man, /
Brought near to beast*

That ever poverty, in its contempt
for mankind, has reduced to the
level of a beast

5   *Bedlam beggars*

Homeless beggars who claimed
to have escaped or been released
from Bedlam (Bethlehem hospital
in London; see 1.2.127 and note)

6   *numbed and mortifièd*

I.e., numbed from the cold and
deadened to pain

7   *Enforce their charity*

I.e., compel them to give the
beggars charitable donations (by
virtue of his repulsive appearance)

8   *Turlygod*

This is the only recorded appearance of this otherwise unknown
word that is apparently a name for
a *Bedlam beggar* (perhaps derived
from "Truly god").

9   *Poor Tom!*

Common name adopted by
beggars; see 1.2.127.

10 *Edgar I nothing am*

As Edgar I am nothing (or, I am in no
way Edgar)

Act 2, Scene 3

*Enter **Edgar**.*

Edgar

declared an outlaw	I heard myself proclaimed,°
fortunately placed	And by the happy° hollow of a tree
	Escaped the hunt. No port is free,[1] no place
In which	That° guard and most unusual vigilance
	Does not attend my taking.[2] Whiles I may 'scape 5
	I will preserve myself, and am bethought[3]
	To take the basest and most poorest shape
	That ever penury, in contempt of man,
darken	Brought near to beast.[4] My face I'll grime° with filth,
tangle; mat	Blanket my loins, elf° all my hairs in knots, 10
displayed / defy	And with presented° nakedness outface°
	The winds and persecutions of the sky.
example	The country gives me proof° and precedent
	Of Bedlam beggars,[5] who with roaring voices
Stick	Strike° in their numbed and mortifièd[6] arms 15
needles	Pins, wooden pricks,° nails, sprigs of rosemary;
spectacle / humble	And with this horrible object° from low° farms,
worthless	Poor pelting° villages, sheepcotes, and mills,
curses	Sometimes with lunatic bans,° sometimes with
	prayers,
	Enforce their charity.[7] Poor Turlygod![8] Poor Tom![9] 20
	That's something yet; Edgar I nothing am.[10] *He exits.*

1 *no purpose in them / Of this remove*

No intention to change residence

2 *cruel garters*

Painful garters (i.e., the stocks),
with a pun on *crewel*, a light wool
used in making stockings

3 *overlusty at legs*

(1) apt to wander (or run away); (2)
sexually overactive

Act 2, Scene 4

Enter **Lear**, **Fool**, *and* **Gentleman**. [**Kent** *asleep in the stocks.*]

Lear

Regan and Cornwall 'Tis strange that they° should so depart from home
And not send back my messenger.

Gentleman

As I learned,
The night before there was no purpose in them
Of this remove.¹

Kent

[*waking*] Hail to thee, noble master!

Lear

Ha!   5

amusement Mak'st thou this shame thy pastime?°

Kent

No, my lord.

Fool

Ha, ha, he wears cruel garters.² Horses are tied by the
heads, dogs and bears by th' neck, monkeys by th'
i.e., waist loins,° and men by th' legs. When a man's overlusty
stockings at legs,³ then he wears wooden netherstocks.°   10

Lear

Who's / rank What's° he that hath so much thy place° mistook
As to To° set thee here?

Kent

It is both he and she:
son-in-law Your son° and daughter.

Lear

No.

Kent

Yes.   15

157

1   *Juno*

    In Roman mythology, queen of the
    gods and wife of Jupiter

2   *upon respect*

    Either (1) deliberately; or (2) to
    someone owed respect

3   *Coming from us*

    Given that you were sent from me
    (*us* is the royal plural)

4   *Ere I was risen from the place that*
    showed / My duty kneeling

    Before I could rise from my respect-
    ful kneeling

5   *reeking post, / Stewed in his haste*

    A messenger (Oswald), hot and
    sweaty from his journey

6   *spite of intermission*

    Disregarding the fact that he had
    interrupted me

7   *which of late / Displayed so saucily*

    Who had recently behaved so
    insolently

Lear

No, I say.

Kent

I say yea.

Lear

By Jupiter, I swear no.

Kent

By Juno,[1] I swear ay.

Lear

They durst not do 't!
They could not, would not do 't. 'Tis worse than murder   20
To do upon respect[2] such violent outrage.

Inform / reasonable   Resolve° me with all modest° haste which way
treatment   Thou mightst deserve, or they impose, this usage,°
Coming from us.[3]

Kent

i.e., Regan and Cornwall's   My lord, when at their° home
deliver   I did commend° your Highness' letters to them,   25
Ere I was risen from the place that showed
messenger   My duty kneeling,[4] came there a reeking post,°
Stewed in his haste,[5] half breathless, panting forth
From Goneril his mistress salutations;
Delivered letters, spite of intermission,[6]   30
immediately   Which presently° they read; on those contents
servants / straightaway   They summoned up their meiny,° straight° took horse,
Commanded me to follow and attend
The leisure of their answer, gave me cold looks;
And meeting here the other messenger,   35
Whose welcome, I perceived, had poisoned mine—
Being the very fellow which of late
Displayed so saucily[7] against your Highness—

1   *more man than wit*

     More courage than sense

2   *Winter's not gone yet if the wild geese fly*
     that way.

     I.e., worse things are still to come.
     (Literally, "the winter hasn't arrived
     if birds are still flying south.")

3   *blind*

     Blind to the needs of their father

4   *Ne'er turns the key*

     I.e., never opens the door

5   *dolors*

     Griefs; sorrows; with a pun on
     dollars, the English term for German
     thalers (silver coins)

6   Hysterica Passio

     Hysterica Passio **was a disease**
     thought normally to afflict only
     women (and the disease was there-
     fore often known as the *mother*;
     see line 52). Its primary symptom
     was a severe swelling that travelled
     upward from the womb, passed
     through the stomach, and then
     choked the sufferer. It was believed
     that the womb itself (the *hystera*, **in**
     Greek) could wander at will through
     the woman's body, causing fits of
     hysteria. Lear's fear that he will lose
     control of his reason, as well as the
     particular image he chooses for it,
     suggests the overturning of values

in the play. Men were traditionally
thought to be more rational than
women and better able to govern
their passions.

7   *element's*

     Element **here means "proper**
     sphere" or "place."

i.e., drew my sword	Having more man than wit[1] about me, drew.°
	He raised the house with loud and coward cries. 40
wrongdoing	Your son and daughter found this trespass° worth
	The shame which here it suffers.

Fool

Winter's not gone yet if the wild geese fly that way.[2]
    Fathers that wear rags
    Do make their children blind,[3] 45

(of gold)	But fathers that bear bags°

    Shall see their children kind.

absolute	Fortune, that arrant° whore,

    Ne'er turns the key[4] to th' poor.

But, for all this, thou shalt have as many dolors[5] for 50

count	thy daughters as thou canst tell° in a year.

Lear

Oh, how this mother swells up toward my heart!
Hysterica Passio![6] Down, thou climbing sorrow!
Thy element's[7] below.—Where is this daughter?

Kent

With the Earl, sir, here within. 55

Lear

Follow me not. Stay here.   *He exits.*

Gentleman

Made you no more offense but what you speak of?

Kent

None.

does it happen that	How chance° the King comes with so small a number?

Fool

If	An° thou hadst been set i' th' stocks for that question, 60

thou'dst well deserved it.

Kent

Why, Fool?

1   *We'll set thee to school to an ant to teach*
    thee there's no laboring i' th' winter.

    I.e., we'll send you away to be edu-
    cated by an ant, who will teach you
    that you must grow and store your
    food before winter comes, recalling
    Aesop's fable about the ant and the
    grasshopper. Similarly, it's implied
    there is no profit in following Lear
    in the winter of his fortunes. The
    Fool offers worldly wisdom that his
    own actions belie.

2   *but can smell him that's stinking*

    I.e., that can tell when a man's
    fortunes have decayed

3   *draw thee after*

    Pull you up along with it

4   *give me mine again*

    Return my advice to me

5   *but for form*

    Only in appearance

6   *perdie*

    By God (from the French *par Dieu*)

7   *revolt and flying off*

    Disobedience and desertion

Fool

We'll set thee to school to an ant to teach thee there's
no laboring i' th' winter. [1] All that follow their noses

except   are led by their eyes but° blind men, and there's not a   65

i.e., twenty blindmen   nose among twenty° but can smell him that's stinking. [2] Let go thy hold when a great wheel runs down a
hill, lest it break thy neck with following; but the great
one that goes upward, let him draw thee after. [3] When
a wise man gives thee better counsel, give me mine   70
again. [4] I would have none but knaves follow it, since a
fool gives it.

man   That sir° which serves and seeks for gain,
     And follows but for form, [5]

depart   Will pack° when it begins to rain   75
     And leave thee in the storm.
     But I will tarry; the fool will stay,
     And let the wise man fly.

rogue   The knave° turns fool that runs away;
     The fool no knave, perdie. [6]   80

Enter **Lear** _and_ **Gloucester**.

Kent

Where learned you this, Fool?

Fool

Not i' th' stocks, fool.

Lear

Do they refuse   Deny° to speak with me? They are sick? They are weary?

excuses   They have traveled all the night? Mere fetches, °

signs   The images° of revolt and flying off. [7]   85
Fetch me a better answer.

Gloucester

              My dear lord,

1　*Infirmity doth still neglect all office /*
　Whereto our health is bound

**When ill we inevitably neglect
the duties that we would fulfill in
health.**

2　*And am fallen out with my more*
　headier will

And ignore my rasher impulses

3　*Death on my state!*

I.e., I curse my current situation!

4　*Give me my servant forth.*

**Release my servant (from the
stocks).**

disposition   You know the fiery quality° of the Duke,

steady   How unremovable° and fixed he is

     In his own course.

Lear

Destruction   Vengeance! Plague! Death! Confusion!°   90

     "Fiery"? What "quality"? Why Gloucester, Gloucester,

     I'd speak with the Duke of Cornwall and his wife.

Gloucester

     Well, my good lord, I have informed them so.

Lear

     Informed them? Dost thou understand me, man?

Gloucester

     Ay, my good lord.   95

Lear

     The King would speak with Cornwall. The dear father

awaits   Would with his daughter speak—commands, tends°

     service.

     Are they informed of this? My breath and blood!

     "Fiery"? The fiery Duke? Tell the hot Duke that—

     No, but not yet. Maybe he is not well.   100

always   Infirmity doth still° neglect all office

     Whereto our health is bound;[1] we are not ourselves

     When nature, being oppressed, commands the mind

be patient   To suffer with the body. I'll forbear,°

     And am fallen out with my more headier will,[2]   105

mistake   To take° the indisposed and sickly fit

     For the sound man. [*looking at* **Kent**] Death on my

Why   state![3] Wherefore°

     Should he sit here? This act persuades me

remoteness; neglect   That this remotion° of the Duke and her

trickery; deception   Is practice° only. Give me my servant forth.[4]   110

1   *Till it cry sleep to death*

     Till the noise ends their sleep

2   *nuncle*

     An affectionate form of "uncle"

3   *knapped 'em o' th' coxcombs*

     Hit them on the head

4   *'Twas her brother that, in pure kindness*
     to his horse, buttered his hay.

     Both the cockney and her brother
     made foolish mistakes *in pure kind-*
     ***ness*: one cooked eels alive in order**
     to avoid killing them, and the other
     buttered his horse's hay to make it
     more palatable, thereby making
     the hay unfit to eat. The Fool
     implies that Lear has been similarly
     misguided in his benevolence.

5   *I would divorce me from thy mother's*
     tomb, / Sepulch'ring an adultress

     I would refuse to be buried with
     your mother, since her tomb must
     hold the remains of an adulteress
     (i.e., if Regan is not happy to see her
     father, she must not be Lear's true
     daughter).

his   Go tell the Duke and 's° wife I'd speak with them—

Immediately   Now! Presently!° Bid them come forth and hear me,

Or at their chamber door I'll beat the drum

Till it cry sleep to death.[1]

Gloucester

I would have all well betwixt you.   *He exits.* 115

Lear

Oh, me, my heart, my rising heart! But down!

Fool

Londoner   Cry to it, nuncle,[2] as the cockney° did to the eels when

pastry   she put 'em i' th' paste° alive. She knapped 'em o' th'

rogues   coxcombs[3] with a stick and cried, "Down, wantons,°

down!" 'Twas her brother that, in pure kindness to his 120

horse, buttered his hay.[4]

Enter **Cornwall**, **Regan**, **Gloucester**, [*and*] *servants.*

Lear

Good morrow to you both.

Cornwall

Hail to your Grace!

Kent *here set at liberty.*

Regan

I am glad to see your Highness.

Lear

Regan, I think you are. I know what reason 125

I have to think so. If thou shouldst not be glad,

I would divorce me from thy mother's tomb,

Sepulch'ring an adultress.[5] [*to* **Kent**] Oh, are you free?

Some other time for that.—Belovèd Regan,

wicked; worthless   Thy sister's naught.° Oh, Regan, she hath tied 130

Sharp-toothed unkindness, like a vulture, here.

[*He gestures to his heart.*]

1   *I have hope / You less know how to value*
     her desert / Than she to scant her duty.

     **I think you are less likely to recog-
     nize her merit than she is to neglect
     her duty.**

2   *Nature in you stands on the very verge / Of*
     his confine.

     **I.e., you are almost at the end of
     your life.**

3   *some discretion that discerns your state*

     **Someone able to understand your
     condition**

4   *mark how this becomes the house*

     **See how well this suits the house-
     hold (sarcastic)**

5   *Age is*

     The elderly are

I can scarce speak to thee—thou 'lt not believe

manner   With how depraved a quality°—Oh, Regan!

Regan

I pray you, sir, take patience. I have hope

You less know how to value her desert   *135*

Than she to scant her duty.¹

Lear

                Say? How is that?

Regan

I cannot think my sister in the least

Would fail her obligation. If, sir, perchance

rowdy behavior   She have restrained the riots° of your followers,

'Tis on such ground and to such wholesome end   *140*

As clears her from all blame.

Lear

My curses on her!

Regan

Oh, sir, you are old.

Nature in you stands on the very verge

Of his confine.² You should be ruled and led   *145*

By some discretion that discerns your state³

Better than you yourself. Therefore, I pray you

That to our sister you do make return.

Say you have wronged her.

Lear

             Ask her forgiveness?

Do you but mark how this becomes the house:⁴   *150*

[*kneeling*] "Dear daughter, I confess that I am old;

Age is⁵ unnecessary. On my knees I beg

grant / clothing   That you'll vouchsafe° me raiment,° bed, and food."

Regan

unattractive   Good sir, no more. These are unsightly° tricks.

Return you to my sister.

1 *You fen-sucked fogs drawn by the power-*
   ful sun / To fall and blister

   You poisonous vapors, drawn up
   from the bogs by the heat of the sun
   so they may then rain down on her
   and raise blisters

2 *tender-hafted*

   I.e., gentle (literally, set in a
   delicate frame; *hafted* **comes from**
   "haft" meaning handle, particularly
   of a knife or other cutting instru-
   ment). Lear wants to say that Regan
   has a kinder disposition than her
   sister. However, he ignores the
   implicit comparison he has made
   between Regan and a knife blade,
   typical of his inability to recognize
   his daughters' true intentions.

3 *to scant my sizes*

   To shrink my allowances

4 *oppose the bolt*

   Lock the door

5 *offices of nature*

   Natural duties

6 *to th' purpose*

   (Get) to the point

Lear

       [*rising*] Never, Regan.   155

deprived She hath abated° me of half my train,

angrily / wounded Looked black° upon me, struck° me with her tongue

 Most serpentlike upon the very heart.

 All the stored vengeances of Heaven fall

head On her ingrateful top!° Strike her young bones, 160

infectious You taking° airs, with lameness!

Cornwall

        Fie, sir, fie!

Lear

lightning bolts You nimble lightnings,° dart your blinding flames

 Into her scornful eyes! Infect her beauty,

 You fen-sucked fogs drawn by the powerful sun

 To fall and blister!¹   165

Regan

This O the blessed gods! So° will you wish on me

 When the rash mood is on.

Lear

 No, Regan, thou shalt never have my curse.

 Thy tender-hafted² nature shall not give

 Thee o'er to harshness. Her eyes are fierce, but thine 170

 Do comfort and not burn. 'Tis not in thee

retinue To grudge my pleasures, to cut off my train,°

exchange To bandy° hasty words, to scant my sizes,³

 And, in conclusion, to oppose the bolt⁴

 Against my coming in. Thou better know'st 175

 The offices of nature,⁵ bond of childhood,

Actions Effects° of courtesy, dues of gratitude.

 Thy half o' th' kingdom hast thou not forgot,

 Wherein I thee endowed.

Regan

       Good sir, to th' purpose.⁶

1   Tucket within.

     See 2.1.77 and note.

2   *if your sweet sway / Allow obedience*

     **If your benevolent rule approves of
     obedience**

Lear

Who put my man i' th' stocks?   *Tucket within.*[1]

Cornwall

         What trumpet's that?   180

Regan

confirms   I know 't—my sister's. This approves° her letter,

That she would soon be here.

Enter steward [**Oswald**].

         Is your lady come?

Lear

easily feigned   This is a slave, whose easy-borrowed° pride

favor   Dwells in the fickle grace° of her he follows.

rogue   —Out, varlet,° from my sight!

Cornwall

         What means your Grace?   185

Lear

Who stocked my servant? Regan, I have good hope

of   Thou didst not know on° 't.

Enter **Goneril**.

         Who comes here? O heavens,

If you do love old men, if your sweet sway

Allow obedience,[2] if you yourselves are old,

Make it your cause; send down and take my part!   190

[*to* **Goneril**] Art not ashamed to look upon this beard?

         [**Goneril** *and* **Regan** *join hands.*]

Oh, Regan, will you take her by the hand?

Goneril

Why not by th' hand, sir? How have I offended?

1   *All's not offense that indiscretion finds /*
    And dotage terms so.

    Not everything that is thought to be
    offensive by those who lack judg-
    ment, or who have gone senile, is
    actually so.

2   *sides*

    The *sides* of his chest, which *yet hold*
    and do not break, despite the pain-
    ful swelling of his heart

3   *much less advancement*

    Cornwall sarcastically says that
    Kent in fact deserved much worse
    punishment.

4   *the expiration of your month*

    I.e., the end of your allotted month
    in Goneril's house

5   *enmity o' th' air*

    Harshness of the weather

6   *Necessity's sharp pinch*

    The sharp pains of poverty. The
    reduction of Lear's followers forces
    him to consider what is in fact nec-
    essary for human life, an issue that,
    as king, he has not had to consider
    previously. The question comes to
    the fore on the heath in the third
    act, when Lear learns about what
    [*u*]*naccommodated man* (3.4.102) truly
    needs.

7   *squirelike, pension beg / To keep base life*
    afoot

    Like a *squire* (vassal; attendant), beg
    a pension to keep my wretched life
    going

All's not offense that indiscretion finds
And dotage terms so. [1]

Lear

                O sides, [2] you are too tough!   195

still Will you yet° hold?—How came my man i' th' stocks?

Cornwall

I set him there, sir, but his own disorders
Deserved much less advancement. [3]

Lear

                    You? Did you?

Regan

I pray you, father, being weak, seem so.
If till the expiration of your month [4]   200

reside You will return and sojourn° with my sister,
followers Dismissing half your train,° come then to me.
away from my I am now from° home, and out of that provision
care Which shall be needful for your entertainment.°

Lear

Return to her? And fifty men dismissed?   205
No! Rather I abjure all roofs and choose
struggle To wage° against the enmity o' th' air, [5]
To be a comrade with the wolf and owl—
Necessity's sharp pinch. [6] Return with her?
Why, the hot-blooded France, that dowerless took   210
Our youngest born—I could as well be brought
kneel before To knee° his throne and, squirelike, pension beg
To keep base life afoot. [7] Return with her?
pack horse Persuade me rather to be slave and sumpter°
i.e., Oswald To this detested groom.°

Goneril

                At your choice, sir.   215

1 *mad*

   Both "angry" and "insane"

2 *embossèd carbuncle*

   Swollen tumor

3 *thunder-bearer*

   Jove (or Jupiter), king of the Roman
   gods, whose weapon was the
   thunderbolt

4 *looked not for you yet*

   Did not expect you yet

5 *mingle reason with your passion*

   Use reason to understand your
   outbursts

6 *or so many, sith that both charge and
   danger*

   Or even that many, since both
   expense and risk

7 *Hold amity*

   Reside peacefully together

Lear

I prithee, daughter, do not make me mad. [1]
I will not trouble thee, my child. Farewell.
We'll no more meet, no more see one another.
But yet thou art my flesh, my blood, my daughter—
Or rather a disease that's in my flesh,   220
Which I must needs call mine. Thou art a boil,
A plague-sore, or embossèd carbuncle [2]
In my corrupted blood. But I'll not chide thee;
Let shame come when it will, I do not call° it.   *summon*
I do not bid the thunder-bearer [3] shoot,   225
Nor tell tales of thee to high-judging° Jove.   *i.e., judging from above*
Mend° when thou canst; be better at thy leisure.   *Improve*
I can be patient. I can stay with Regan,
I and my hundred knights.

Regan

                                        Not altogether so.
I looked not for you yet, [4] nor am provided   230
For your fit welcome. Give ear, sir, to my sister;
For those that mingle reason with your passion [5]
Must be content to think you old, and so—
But she knows what she does.

Lear

                                        Is this well spoken?

Regan

I dare avouch° it, sir. What, fifty followers?   *vouch for*   235
Is it not well? What should you need of more?
Yea, or so many, sith° that both charge and danger [6]   *since*
Speak 'gainst so great a number? How in one house
Should many people under two commands
Hold amity? [7] 'Tis hard; almost impossible.   240

Goneril

Why might not you, my lord, receive attendance

1   *receive attendance from*
    Be served by

2   *But kept a reservation*
    Only reserved the right

3   *must I come to you / With five-and-*
    twenty?
    I.e., may I only have twenty-five
    attendants?

4   *Stands in some rank of praise*
    Deserves at least some measure
    of praise

From [1] those that she calls servants, or from mine?

Regan

Why not, my lord? If then they chanced to slack° ye,   *neglect*

We could control° them. If you will come to me—   *correct*

For now I spy a danger—I entreat you   245

To bring but five-and-twenty. To no more

Will I give place or notice.°   *recognition*

Lear

I gave you all—

Regan

And in good time you gave it.

Lear

Made you my guardians, my depositaries,°   *trustees*

But kept a reservation [2] to be followed   250

With such a number. What, must I come to you

With five-and-twenty? [3] Regan, said you so?

Regan

And speak 't again, my lord. No more with me.

Lear

Those wicked creatures yet do look well-favored°   *attractive*

When others are more wicked; not being the worst   255

Stands in some rank of praise. [4] [*to* **Goneril**] I'll go with
    thee.

Thy fifty yet doth double five-and-twenty,

And thou art twice her love.

Goneril

Hear me, my lord:

What need you five-and-twenty, ten, or five,

To follow° in a house where twice so many   *be your attendants*   260

Have a command to tend you?

Regan

What need one?

1   *reason not the need! Our basest beggars /*
     Are in the poorest thing superfluous.

     **Don't try to rationalize the need.
The most worthless item possessed
by the lowliest beggar is in some
sense unnecessary.**

2   *Allow not nature more than nature
needs, / Man's life is cheap as beast's.*

     **I.e., if you do not assume that we
have needs beyond what is necessary to survive, then human life is
of no greater value than *a beast*'s.**

3   *If only to go warm were gorgeous, / Why,
nature needs not what thou gorgeous
wear'st*

     **If clothing that kept you warm was
what was considered *gorgeous*, why,
you would never wear the *gorgeous*
clothes you now have on.**

4   *fool me not so much / To*

     Do not let me be such a fool as to

5   *Or ere*

     Before

6   *old man and 's people*

     Lear and his attendants

7   *'Tis his own blame hath put himself from
rest*

     **It is his own fault for not having (1) a
place to rest; (2) peace of mind**

Lear

Oh, reason not the need! Our basest beggars
Are in the poorest thing superfluous. [1]
Allow not nature more than nature needs,
Man's life is cheap as beast's. [2] Thou art a lady; 265
If only to go warm were gorgeous,
Why, nature needs not what thou gorgeous wear'st, [3]
Which scarcely keeps thee warm. But, for true need—
You heavens, give me that patience; patience I need!
You see me here, you gods, a poor old man, 270
As full of grief as age, wretched in both.
If it be you that stirs these daughters' hearts
Against their father, fool me not so much
To [4] bear it tamely; touch me with noble anger,
And let not women's weapons, water drops, 275
Stain my man's cheeks. No, you unnatural hags,
I will have such revenges on you both
That all the world shall—I will do such things—
What they are yet I know not, but they shall be
The terrors of the earth. You think I'll weep. 280
No, I'll not weep.   *Storm and tempest.*
I have full cause of weeping but this heart
fragments Shall break into a hundred thousand flaws°
Or ere [5] I'll weep. Oh, Fool, I shall go mad!
          [**Lear, Gloucester, Kent, Gentleman,** *and* **Fool**] *exit.*

Cornwall

Let us withdraw. 'Twill be a storm. 285

Regan

This house is little. The old man and 's people [6]
housed Cannot be well bestowed. °

Goneril

'Tis his own blame hath put himself from rest, [7]

1   *For his particular*

    On his own

2   *So am I purposed.*

    That is also what I intend.

3   *to horse*

    To be brought his horse

4   *'Tis best to give him way; he leads*
    himself.

    It is best to let him do what he
    wants; he listens to no one.

5   *with a desperate train*

    By a violent group of attendants

experience And must needs taste° his folly.

Regan

For his particular, ¹ I'll receive him gladly,   290
But not one follower.

Goneril

So am I purposed. ² Where is my Lord of Gloucester?

Cornwall

Followed the old man forth.

Enter **Gloucester**.

                                        He is returned.

Gloucester

The King is in high rage.

Cornwall

                            Whither is he going?

Gloucester

will go He calls to horse,³ but will° I know not whither.   295

Cornwall

'Tis best to give him way; he leads himself.⁴

Goneril

[*to* **Gloucester**] My lord, entreat him by no means to
    stay.

Gloucester

Alack, the night comes on, and the high winds
bluster Do sorely ruffle.° For many miles about
There's scarce a bush.

Regan

obstinate   Oh, sir, to wilful° men   300
The injuries that they themselves procure
Must be their schoolmasters. Shut up your doors.
He is attended with a desperate train,⁵

1   *being apt / To have his ear abused*
    Since he is easily misled

2   *wisdom bids fear*
    Prudence demands we take
    precautions.

incite   And what they may incense° him to, being apt
To have his ear abused,¹ wisdom bids fear.²   305
Cornwall
Shut up your doors, my lord; 'tis a wild night.
My Regan counsels well: come out o' th' storm.

They exit.

1 Storm still.

Storm continually (i.e., through-out the scene). The storm on the heath, when Lear has to confront the nature of his humanity, is one of the most famous episodes in Shakespeare. The scene has always demanded special effects, and when the play was first performed in the Globe, the noise of thunder was probably made by rolling can-nonballs on a metal sheet, while lightning was provided by a form of fireworks. (It is worth noting that the early stage directions make no actual reference to a "heath." The word was introduced in 1709 in the edition of Shakespeare edited by Nicholas Rowe. Nonetheless, the bare, flat tract of land has assumed great importance as the play has been imagined on stage, in criti-cism, and in painting.)

2 severally

From different directions

3 *Contending with the fretful elements*

Both "struggling with" and "com-peting against" the violent weather

4 *heart-struck injuries*

Injuries that wound to the heart

5 *upon the warrant of my note*

Based on what I have observed

6 *Commend a dear thing to you*

Entrust you with an important matter

7 *that their great stars / Throned and set high*

Who have been raised by fate to such greatness

8 *servants, who seem no less*

Servants, who appear to be simply that

9 *Intelligent of*

Supplying information about

10 *snuffs and packings*

Offenses and plots

Act 3, Scene 1

Storm still. [1] *Enter* **Kent** [*in disguise*] *and a*
Gentleman, *severally.* [2]

Kent

Who's there, besides foul weather?

Gentleman

of a mind   One minded° like the weather, most unquietly.

Kent

I know you. Where's the King?

Gentleman

Contending with the fretful elements; [3]

He bids   Bids° the winds blow the earth into the sea   5

mainland   Or swell the curlèd waters 'bove the main,°

i.e., everything   That things° might change or cease.

Kent

But who is with him?

Gentleman

alleviate by joking   None but the fool, who labors to outjest°

i.e., Lear's   His° heart-struck injuries. [4]

Kent

Sir, I do know you,

And dare upon the warrant of my note [5]   10

Commend a dear thing to you. [6] There is division,

Although as yet the face of it is covered

With mutual cunning, 'twixt Albany and Cornwall,

Who have—as who have not, that their great stars

Throned and set high? [7]—servants, who seem no less, [8]   15

observers   Which are to France the spies and speculations°

Intelligent of [9] our state: what hath been seen,

Either in snuffs and packings [10] of the Dukes,

1　　*Or the hard rein which both of them hath*
　　　borne / Against the old kind King

　　　I.e., or the cruel way they have treat-
　　　ed Lear. Albany and Cornwall have
　　　restrained Lear as one might *rein* in
　　　a horse (with a pun on "reign").

2　　*fear not but*

　　　Be assured that

3　　*to effect*

　　　In their importance

4　　*in which your pain / That way, I'll this*

　　　You focus your effort in that
　　　direction, while I go in this

Or the hard rein which both of them hath borne
Against the old kind King, [1] or something deeper,   20
superficial aspects Whereof perchance these are but furnishings.°

Gentleman

I will talk further with you.

Kent

                     No, do not.
For confirmation that I am much more
appearance Than my outwall,° open this purse and take
What it contains. [*He hands him a purse and a ring.*] If you
    shall see Cordelia—   25
As fear not but [2] you shall—show her this ring,
And she will tell you who that fellow is
That yet you do not know. Fie on this storm!
I will go seek the King.

Gentleman

Give me your hand. Have you no more to say?   30

Kent

Few words, but, to effect, [3] more than all yet:
That when we have found the King—in which your
    pain
That way, I'll this [4]—he that first lights on him
Call for Holla° the other.   *They exit [separately].*

1   *crack your cheeks*

I.e., howl. Renaissance maps were
often adorned with depictions
of the winds, portrayed as cloudy
faces with puffed-out cheeks.

2   *cataracts and hurricanoes*

Torrential rain and waterspouts

3   *cocks*

Weathervanes (located on top of
the *steeples*)

4   *sulf'rous and thought-executing fires*

I.e., lightning. Lear may describe
the lightning as *thought-executing*
since it "flashes more quickly as
thought," or perhaps since it "de-
stroys thought."

5   *Strike flat the thick rotundity o' th' world*

Flatten out the solid roundness
of the world. This is an image of
Doomsday. *King Lear* is set in a
remote and prehistoric past, but
parts of the play look forward to
the very end of time when all will be
destroyed

6   *Crack nature's molds; all germens spill*

Break nature's patterns (from
which all forms of life are created);
destroy all seeds.

7   *court holy water*

A proverbial expression for the flattery necessary to prosper at *court*

8   *ask thy daughters blessing*

Ask your daughters for their blessing (thereby accepting their authority over you).

9   *Nor rain, wind, thunder, fire are my
daughters.*

It is all right if the weather is fierce,
since it is not related to me (unlike
my daughters, who are and should
be gentle)

10 *unkindness*

(1) unnaturalness; (2) lack of
affection

11 *high-engendered battles*

Armies bred in the heavens (i.e., the
violent storm)

12 *headpiece*

(1) cover for one's head; (2) brain

Act 3, Scene 2

Storm still. Enter **Lear** *and* **Fool**.

Lear

Blow, winds, and crack your cheeks![1] Rage, blow!
You cataracts and hurricanoes[2] spout
Till you have drenched our steeples, drowned the cocks![3]
You sulf'rous and thought-executing fires,[4]

Forerunners Vaunt-couriers° of oak-cleaving thunderbolts,   5
Singe my white head! And thou, all-shaking thunder,
Strike flat the thick rotundity o' th' world![5]
Crack nature's molds; all germens spill[6] at once
That makes ingrateful man!

Fool

Oh, nuncle, court holy water[7] in a dry house is better   10
than this rainwater out o' door. Good nuncle, in. Ask
thy daughters blessing.[8] Here's a night pities neither
wise men nor fools.

Lear

Rumble thy bellyful! Spit, fire! Spout, rain!
Neither Nor° rain, wind, thunder, fire are my daughters.[9]   15
accuse/of I tax° not you, you elements, with° unkindness;[10]
I never gave you kingdom, called you children.
obedience You owe me no subscription.° Then let fall
Your horrible pleasure. Here I stand your slave,
A poor, infirm, weak, and despised old man,   20
agents (of the gods) But yet I call you servile ministers,°
That will with two pernicious daughters join
Your high-engendered battles[11] 'gainst a head
So old and white as this. Oh, ho! 'Tis foul.

Fool

He that has a house to put 's head in has a good   25
headpiece.[12]

1 *The codpiece that will house / Before the head has any, / The head and he shall louse; / So beggars marry many.*

   I.e., he that has sex before he has a home will find himself living in lice-infested destitution with a woman and many children (or many lice). A *codpiece* was a decorative append-age to a man's breeches worn over the genitals (here, the term implies the genitals themselves).

2 *The man that makes his toe / What he his heart should make / Shall of a corn cry woe / And turn his sleep to wake.*

   I.e., he who misplaces his affection will suffer pain and loss of sleep as a result.

3 *made mouths in a glass*

   Practiced facial expressions in a mirror (either for deceit or as a sign of vanity)

4 *Marry*

   Contraction of "by the Virgin Mary"; a mild oath

5 *grace and a codpiece*

   Royal grace (embodied in the King) and a fool (an exaggerated *codpiece* being a regular element of a fool's costume; see note 1 above)

6 *Gally the very wanderers of the dark*

   Frighten even nocturnal creatures

7 *sheets of fire*

   I.e., lightning

[*sings*] The codpiece that will house
  Before the head has any,
  The head and he shall louse;
  So beggars marry many. [1]   30
  The man that makes his toe
  What he his heart should make
  Shall of a corn cry woe
  And turn his sleep to wake. [2]
For there was never yet fair woman but she made   35
mouths in a glass. [3]

Lear

No, I will be the pattern of all patience;
I will say nothing.

          Enter **Kent**, [*in disguise*].

Kent

Who's there?

Fool

Marry, [4] here's grace and a codpiece: [5] that's a wise man   40
and a fool.

Kent

Alas, sir, are you here? Things that love night
Love not such nights as these. The wrathful skies
Gally the very wanderers of the dark [6]

stay inside And make them keep° their caves. Since I was man,   45
Such sheets of fire, [7] such bursts of horrid thunder,
Such groans of roaring wind and rain I never

endure Remember to have heard. Man's nature cannot carry°

physical suffering Th' affliction° nor the fear.

Lear

                    Let the great gods,

turmoil That keep this dreadful pother° o'er our heads,   50

1   *Find out*
     Reveal

2   *convenient seeming*
     Well-planned deception

3   *practiced on*
     Plotted against

4   *Close pent-up guilts, / Rive your conceal-
     ing continents and cry / These dreadful
     summoners grace!*
     **Secret and hidden sins, break out
     of the containers (i.e., the bodies
     of sinners) and yourselves beg for
     mercy. (*Summoners* were officials of
     the ecclesiastical courts, though
     here they are the wind and rain,
     which Lear imagines as God's
     agents.)**

5   *More sinned against than sinning*
     **Lear grudgingly admits some
     responsibility for what has
     happened, although he places the
     major blame upon Goneril and
     Regan. Even his incomplete
     awareness of his own sin, however,
     differentiates him from the hypo-
     critical sinners described in lines
     51–57.**

6   *demanding after you, / Denied me to
     come in*
     **When I asked for you, refused to
     let me in**

7   *The art of our necessities is strange / And
     can make vile things precious.*
     **Need has the remarkable power
     to turn what we once despised
     (the lowly *hovel*) into something
     precious (shelter from the raging
     storm).**

8   *He that has and a little tiny wit, / With
     heigh-ho, the wind and the rain, / Must
     make content with his fortunes fit, /
     Though the rain it raineth every day.*
     **A variation of the first stanza of the
     song sung by Feste at the end of
     Twelfth Night, which here suggests
     that one, like Lear, who acts fool-
     ishly must be prepared to be *content*
     with what results.**

Find out[1] their enemies now. Tremble, thou wretch,
That hast within thee undivulgèd crimes
by Unwhipped of° justice! Hide thee, thou bloody hand,
liar/counterfeiter Thou perjured,° and thou simular° of virtue
Villain That art incestuous! Caitiff,° to pieces shake, 55
That under covert and convenient seeming[2]
Secret Has practiced on[3] man's life! Close° pent-up guilts,
containers Rive your concealing continents° and cry
These dreadful summoners grace![4] I am a man
More sinned against than sinning.[5]

Kent

Alack, bareheaded? 60
near Gracious my lord, hard° by here is a hovel.
Some friendship will it lend you 'gainst the tempest.
cruel Repose you there, while I to this hard° house—
built More harder than the stones whereof 'tis raised,°
Which even but now, demanding after you, 65
Denied me to come in[6]—return and force
withheld Their scanted° courtesy.

Lear

My wits begin to turn.
[*to* **Fool**] Come on, my boy. How dost, my boy? Art
cold?
I am cold myself. [*to* **Kent**] Where is this straw, my fellow?
The art of our necessities is strange 70
And can make vile things precious.[7] Come, your hovel.
—Poor fool and knave, I have one part in my heart
That's sorry yet for thee.

Fool

[*sings*] He that has and a little tiny wit,
With heigh-ho, the wind and the rain, 75
Must make content with his fortunes fit,
Though the rain it raineth every day.[8]

1   *brave night to cool a courtesan*

    **Fine night to cool (the lustful heat
    of) a prostitute**

2   *I'll speak a prophecy ere I go*

    **There are actually two prophecies
    here. Lines 81–86 are a parody of
    one attributed to Chaucer, which is
    a familiar indictment of social ills.
    The second (lines 87–94) looks to
    a time of impossible virtue. (See
    LONGER NOTE, page 358.)**

3   *are more in word than matter*

    **Talk about virtue more than they
    practice it**

4   *nobles are their tailors' tutors*

    **I.e., when noblemen know more
    about fashion than their tailors**

5   *No heretics burned but wenches' suitors*

    **I.e., when lust is more important
    than faith. *Burned* plays on the fact
    that religious heresy was punished
    by burning at the stake, while the
    lecherous are punished by the
    burning of venereal disease.**

6   *When slanders do not live in tongues*

    When no one speaks slanders

7   *i' th' field*

    **I.e., openly (because they have
    nothing to hide)**

8   *That going shall be used with feet*

    **That walking will be done on foot
    (i.e., nothing will change)**

9   *Merlin shall make, for I live before his
    time*

    **Merlin was the legendary magician
    and prophet of King Arthur's court.
    Lear was thought to have ruled
    Britain in pre-Roman times (in the
    8th century B.C.), many centuries
    before Arthur's reign (supposedly
    in the 6th century A.D.).**

Lear

True, boy.—Come; bring us to this hovel.

[**Lear** *and* **Kent** *exit.*]

Fool

This is a brave night to cool a courtesan. ¹ I'll speak a
prophecy ere I go: ²   80

<table>
<tr><td></td><td>When priests are more in word than matter, ³</td></tr>
<tr><td>*ruin; dilute*</td><td>When brewers mar° their malt with water,</td></tr>
<tr><td></td><td>When nobles are their tailors' tutors, ⁴</td></tr>
<tr><td></td><td>No heretics burned but wenches' suitors, ⁵</td></tr>
<tr><td>*Britain*</td><td>Then shall the realm of Albion°</td></tr>
<tr><td></td><td>Come to great confusion.</td></tr>
<tr><td>*just*</td><td>When every case in law is right,°</td></tr>
<tr><td></td><td>No squire in debt nor no poor knight,</td></tr>
<tr><td></td><td>When slanders do not live in tongues, ⁶</td></tr>
<tr><td>*pickpockets*</td><td>Nor cutpurses° come not to throngs;</td></tr>
<tr><td>*count*</td><td>When usurers tell° their gold i' th' field, ⁷</td></tr>
<tr><td>*proprietors of brothels*</td><td>And bawds° and whores do churches build,</td></tr>
<tr><td>*whoever*</td><td>Then comes the time, who° lives to see 't,</td></tr>
<tr><td></td><td>That going shall be used with feet. ⁸</td></tr>
</table>

85

90

This prophecy Merlin shall make, for I live before   95
his time. ⁹   *He exits.*

1   *Go to*

     **I.e., enough; an expression of
     disapproval or impatience**

2   *power already footed*

     Army already landed

3   *incline to*

     Side with

4   *This courtesy forbid thee*

     **Your kindness toward Lear, which
     was forbidden**

5   *This seems a fair deserving, and must
     draw me / That which my father loses*

     **This (betrayal of my father) is what
     he deserves (or *deserving* of a nice
     reward), and will result in my
     receiving what will be taken from
     him.**

Act 3, Scene 3

Enter **Gloucester** *and* **Edmund**.

Gloucester

treatment Alack, alack, Edmund, I like not this unnatural dealing.°
permission / take pity on When I desire their leave° that I might pity° him, they
took from me the use of mine own house, charged me
on pain of perpetual displeasure neither to speak of
provide for him, entreat for him, or any way sustain° him. 5

Edmund

Most savage and unnatural!

Gloucester

Go to;[1] say you nothing. There is division between
the Dukes, and a worse matter than that. I have received
a letter this night. 'Tis dangerous to be spoken. I have
private chamber locked the letter in my closet.° These injuries the King 10
thoroughly now bears will be revenged home;° there is part of a
power already footed.[2] We must incline to[3] the King. I
seek / secretly will look° him and privily° relieve him. Go you and
so that maintain talk with the Duke, that° my charity be not of
him perceived. If he ask for me, I am ill and gone to 15
bed. If I die for it, as no less is threatened me, the King
helped my old master must be relieved.° There is strange things
about to happen toward,° Edmund. Pray you, be careful. *He exits.*

Edmund

This courtesy forbid thee[4] shall the Duke
Instantly know, and of that letter too. 20
This seems a fair deserving, and must draw me
That which my father loses[5]—no less than all.
The younger rises when the old doth fall. *He exits.*

1	*open night's*
	Night out in the open is

2	*i' th' mouth*
	I.e., head-on

Act 3, Scene 4

Enter **Lear**, **Kent** [*in disguise*], *and* **Fool**.

Kent
Here is the place, my lord. Good my lord, enter.
The tyranny of the open night's[1] too rough
human nature   For nature° to endure.   *Storm still.*

Lear
                  Let me alone.

Kent
Good my lord, enter here.

Lear
Will you   Wilt° break my heart?

Kent
I had rather break mine own. Good my lord, enter.   5

Lear
Thou think'st 'tis much that this contentious storm
Invades us to the skin. So 'tis to thee,
set   But where the greater malady is fixed°
The lesser is scarce felt. Thou'dst shun a bear,
But if thy flight lay toward the roaring sea   10
Thou'dst meet the bear i' th' mouth.[2] When the mind's
untroubled   free,°
sensitive (to pain)   The body's delicate.° This tempest in my mind
Doth from my senses take all feeling else
Except   Save° what beats there. Filial ingratitude!
as if   Is it not as° this mouth should tear this hand   15
thoroughly   For lifting food to 't? But I will punish home.°
No. I will weep no more. In such a night
To shut me out? Pour on; I will endure.
In such a night as this? O Regan, Goneril,
generous   Your old kind father, whose frank° heart gave all—   20

1   *unfed sides*

    Emaciated ribs

2   *looped and windowed*

    I.e., full of holes

3   *I have ta'en / Too little care of this*

    **Lear's descent into madness in
    the storm leads him to see certain
    things much more clearly than he
    had before, even though much of
    his moral and emotional blindness
    continues. In his first speech in this
    pivotal scene, he still blames his
    daughters for their *filial ingratitude*
    (line 14), but here starts to realize
    that he has not governed his king-
    dom as well as he might have and
    that he bears responsibility for the
    suffering of his people.**

4   *Take physic, pomp*

    **Heal yourself, you powerful and
    wealthy people**

5   *shake the superflux*

    **Give the surplus of your wealth and
    possessions**

6   *Fathom and half*

    **A sailor's cry when gauging the
    depth of water (literally "nine feet")**

Oh, that way madness lies; let me shun that!
No more of that.

Kent

　　　　　　Good my lord, enter here.

Lear

Prithee, go in thyself; seek thine own ease.
This tempest will not give me leave to ponder
that would On things would° hurt me more. But I'll go in.　　25
[*to* **Fool**] In, boy; go first. You houseless poverty—
Nay, get thee in. I'll pray, and then I'll sleep.

　　　　　　　　　　　[**Fool**]*exits* [*into the hovel*].

Poor naked wretches, wheresoe'er you are,
endure That bide° the pelting of this pitiless storm,
How shall your houseless heads and unfed sides, [1]　　30
Your looped and windowed [2] raggedness, defend you
From seasons such as these? Oh, I have ta'en
Too little care of this! [3] Take physic, pomp; [4]
Expose thyself to feel what wretches feel,
That thou mayst shake the superflux [5] to them　　35
And show the heavens more just.

Edgar

[*within*] Fathom and half, [6] fathom and half! Poor Tom!

　　　　　　Enter **Fool** [*from the hovel*].

Fool

demon Come not in here, nuncle; here's a spirit.° Help me;
help me!

Kent

Give me thy hand. Who's there?　　40

Fool

A spirit, a spirit! He says his name's Poor Tom.

1   *Humh!*

   Presumably Edgar shivers.

2   *that hath laid knives under his pillow and*
   halters in his pew, set ratsbane by his
   porridge

   The devil has tempted Tom to sin
   by providing him with the means to
   kill himself: a knife, a noose, and
   rat poison.

3   *five wits*

   Possibly the faculties of common
   wit, imagination, fantasy, estima-
   tion, and memory, but perhaps
   merely the five physical senses

4   *star-blasting*

   Destructive influence of the stars

5   *There could I have him now—and*
   there—and there again—and there.

   Edgar presumably fights off
   an (imaginary) devil, or perhaps
   attacks the lice and bugs on his
   body.

6   *reserved a blanket*

   Kept a blanket for himself (to cover
   his naked body)

Kent

mutter; mumble   What art thou that dost grumble° there i' th' straw?
Come forth.

Enter **Edgar** *[disguised as Poor Tom].*

Edgar

devil   Away!—The foul fiend° follows me! Through the
(a thorny shrub)   sharp hawthorn° blow the winds. Humh!¹ Go to thy   45
bed and warm thee.

Lear

Didst thou give all to thy daughters? And art thou
come to this?

Edgar

Who gives anything to Poor Tom, whom the foul
fiend hath led through fire and through flame, through   50
ford and whirlpool, o'er bog and quagmire; that hath
laid knives under his pillow and halters in his pew, set
ratsbane by his porridge,² made him proud of heart to
ride on a bay trotting horse over four-inched bridges
hunt; chase / as   to course° his own shadow for° a traitor? Bless thy five   55
Protect   wits!³ Tom's a-cold. Oh, do de, do de, do de. Bless°
infection   thee from whirlwinds, star-blasting,⁴ and taking!° Do
Poor Tom some charity, whom the foul fiend vexes.
There could I have him now—and there—and there
again—and there.⁵   *Storm still.*   60

Lear

predicament   Has his daughters brought him to this pass?°
—Couldst thou save nothing? Wouldst thou give 'em
all?

Fool

otherwise   Nay, he reserved a blanket,⁶ else° we had been all
shamed.

1   *Hang fated o'er men's faults*

Are ready to punish men's sins (like
star-blasting in line 57, this alludes to
the belief that disease results from
the influence of the stars)

2   *unkind*

(1) cruel; (2) unnatural

3   *pelican*

I.e., voracious. Baby pelicans were
proverbially believed to feed on
their parents' blood.

4   *Pillicock*

A term of affection (echoing
pelican), as well as slang for "penis"

5   *Obey thy parents; keep thy word's justice;*
swear not; commit not with man's sworn
spouse; set not thy sweet heart on proud
array.

Edgar alludes to five of the Ten
Commandments, the final phrase
here referring to the injunction
against covetousness (*proud*
array = rich apparel; see also
1 Timothy 2:9).

6   *gloves*

A love token from his mistress,
worn as a pledge (of his love). Edgar
provides a portrait of an affected
and foppish *servingman* not unlike
Oswald.

7   *slept in the contriving of lust*

Dreamed of sexual acts

8   *out-paramoured the Turk*

I.e., had more mistresses than a
sultan, with his harem

9   *light of ear*

Ready to believe malicious rumors

Lear

overhanging   Now all the plagues that in the pendulous° air   65

land   Hang fated o'er men's faults[1] light° on thy daughters!

Kent

He hath no daughters, sir.

Lear

reduced   Death, traitor! Nothing could have subdued° nature

To such a lowness but his unkind[2] daughters.

Is it the fashion that discarded fathers   70

bodies   Should have thus little mercy on their flesh?°

Judicious punishment! 'Twas this flesh begot

Those pelican[3] daughters.

Edgar

Pillicock[4] sat on Pillicock Hill. Alow, alow, loo, loo!

Fool

This cold night will turn us all to fools and madmen.   75

Edgar

Take heed o' th' foul fiend. Obey thy parents; keep

thy word's justice; swear not; commit not with man's

sworn spouse; set not thy sweet heart on proud array.[5]

Tom's a-cold.

Lear

What hast thou been?   80

Edgar

A servingman, proud in heart and mind, that curled

my hair, wore gloves[6] in my cap, served the lust of

my mistress' heart and did the act of darkness with

her; swore as many oaths as I spake words and broke

them in the sweet face of Heaven. One that slept in   85

the contriving of lust[7] and waked to do it. Wine loved I

dearly, dice dearly, and in woman out-paramoured the

Turk;[8] false of heart, light of ear,[9] bloody of hand; hog

in sloth, fox in stealth, wolf in greediness, dog in

1   *plackets*

Slits in petticoats or skirts

2   *suum, mun, nonny*

The first two of these nonsense
words may imitate the sound of
the wind, or, with the third, be a
fragment of a song refrain.

3   *Dolphin my boy*

Unexplained, perhaps another
song fragment. *Dolphin* is the
Anglicized spelling of *Dauphin*,
the title given to the crown prince
of France; *Dolphin* may also be a
euphemism for the devil.

4   *this extremity of the skies*

I.e., this extreme weather

5   *Thou ow'st the worm no silk, the beast
no hide, the sheep no wool, the cat no
perfume.*

Since Edgar is filthy and covered
only with a blanket, he owes nothing to those creatures that usually
contribute to human comfort.
Cat refers to the civet cat, which
produces a musky oil used to make
perfume.

6   *three on's are sophisticated; thou are the
thing itself*

I.e., three of us (Lear, Kent, and
the Fool) have been civilized by
society, but you are man in his essential aspect, [u]naccomodated by
the trappings of civilization.

7   *lendings*

Clothes (borrowed from *the worm,*

the beast, and *the sheep,* mentioned
in line 100)

8   *unbutton here*

Whether Lear actually takes off all
his clothes at this point is unclear.
(See LONGER NOTE, page 359).

9   *Flibbertigibbet*

Name of a devil in Samuel Harsnett's *Declaration of Egregious Popish
Impostures* (1603), a denunciation
of certain Catholic priests who
had been performing fraudulent
exorcisms as a way of attracting
converts. Other devils named in
the *Declaration* are mentioned in
lines 133, 136, 137, and 3.6.6.

10 *He begins at curfew and walks till the
first cock*

He roams from 9 pm (when the
curfew bell is rung) till dawn, when
the first cock crows

11 *web and the pin*

I.e., cataracts

12 *squints the eye*

Causes crossed eyes

13 *Swithold footed thrice the wold*

Saint Withold traveled over the
wold (or "countryside") three times

14 *her ninefold*

Either (1) her nine children; or (2)
the nine coils of her body (like that
of a snake)

hunting   madness, lion in prey.° Let not the creaking of shoes   90
nor the rustling of silks betray thy poor heart to
woman. Keep thy foot out of brothels,thy hand out of
moneylenders'   plackets, ¹ thy pen from lenders'° books, and defy the
foul fiend. Still through the hawthorn blows the cold
it says   wind; says,° suum, mun, nonny. ² Dolphin my boy, ³   95
cease; stop (French)   boy, *cessez!*° Let him trot by.

                                                    Storm still.

Lear

encounter   Thou wert better in a grave than to answer° with thy
uncovered body this extremity of the skies. ⁴ Is man
no more than this? Consider him well. Thou ow'st the
worm no silk, the beast no hide, the sheep no wool, the   100
cat no perfume. ⁵ Ha! Here's three on 's are sophisticated;
i.e., In his essence   thou art the thing itself. ⁶ Unaccommodated° man is no
more but such a poor, bare, forked animal as thou art.
Off, off, you lendings! ⁷ Come, unbutton here. ⁸

                                        [*Tearing at his clothes.*]

Fool

bad   Prithee, nuncle, be contented; 'tis a naughty° night to   105
uncultivated   swim in. Now a little fire in a wild° field were like an old
his   lecher's heart: a small spark; all the rest on 's° body cold.

                     Enter **Gloucester**, *with a torch.*

Look, here comes a walking fire.

Edgar

This is the foul Flibbertigibbet! ⁹ He begins at curfew
and walks till the first cock; ¹⁰ he gives the web and the   110
pin, ¹¹ squints the eye, ¹² and makes the harelip, mildews
ripening   the white° wheat, and hurts the poor creature of earth.
          Swithold footed thrice the wold; ¹³
a demon   He met the nightmare° and her ninefold; ¹⁴

1   *her troth plight*

    Pledge (to do no evil)

2   *ditch-dog*

    Dead dog tossed in a ditch

3   *the green mantle of the standing pool*

    **The green scum from the stagnant
    pond**

4   *three suits*

    **Kent earlier accused Oswald of be-
    ing *three-suited* (2.2.14), apparently
    a reference to the three suits of
    clothing allotted to a servant per
    year; Edgar, as Tom, represents
    himself as a servant; see line 81.**

5   *my follower*

    I.e., the devil that follows me

6   *Smulkin*

    **A minor devil who takes the form
    of a mouse, mentioned in Harsnett
    (see note 9 on page 208)**

7   *Prince of Darkness*

    I.e., the devil

8   *Modo he's called, and Mahu.*

    **Devils who commanded the military
    troops of Hell, according to
    Harsnett (see note 6 above)**

9   *Our flesh and blood, my lord, is grown so
    vile / That it doth hate what gets it.*

    **Our children have become so
    depraved that they loathe their
    parents (who *get* or *beget* them).**

Bid her alight   115
And her troth plight. [1]

begone   And aroint° thee, witch; aroint thee!

Kent

How fares your Grace?

Lear

[*pointing at* **Edgar**] What's he?

Kent

Who's there? What is 't you seek?   120

Gloucester

What are you there? Your names?

Edgar

Poor Tom, that eats the swimming frog, the toad, the
i.e., water newt   tadpole, the wall newt and the water;° that in the fury
of his heart, when the foul fiend rages, eats cow dung
for salads, swallows the old rat and the ditch-dog, [2]   125
drinks the green mantle of the standing pool; [3] who is
parish / put in the stocks   whipped from tithing° to tithing and stock-punished°
and imprisoned; who hath had three suits [4] to his
back, six shirts to his body,

Horse to ride, and weapon to wear;   130

animals   But mice and rats and such small deer°

Have been Tom's food for seven long year.

Beware my follower. [5] Peace, Smulkin! [6] Peace, thou
fiend!

Gloucester

What, hath your Grace no better company?   135

Edgar

The Prince of Darkness [7] is a gentleman. Modo he's
called, and Mahu. [8]

Gloucester

[*to* **Lear**] Our flesh and blood, my lord, is grown so vile
That it doth hate what gets it. [9]

1   *learnèd Theban*

I.e., Greek scholar. Perhaps this is
intended as a joke, since the inhab-
itants of Thebes were often held
to be particularly stupid, or, it has
been suggested, it could be a reference to a specific Cynic philosopher
known as the Theban Crates who
rejected wealth and pleasure in
favor of hard, impoverished living.

Edgar

Poor Tom's a-cold.   140

Gloucester

allow me   [*to* **Lear**] Go in with me. My duty cannot suffer°

every respect   T' obey in all° your daughters' hard commands.

Though their injunction be to bar my doors

And let this tyrannous night take hold upon you,

Yet have I ventured to come seek you out   145

And bring you where both fire and food is ready.

Lear

First let me talk with this philosopher.

[*to* **Edgar**] What is the cause of thunder?

Kent

Good my lord,

Take his offer. Go into th' house.

Lear

I'll talk a word with this same learnèd Theban.[1]   150

area of expertise   [*to* **Edgar**] What is your study?°

Edgar

avoid   How to prevent° the fiend, and to kill vermin.

Lear

Let me ask you one word in private.

[**Lear** *and* **Edgar** *move aside.*]

Kent

Urge   [*to* **Gloucester**] Importune° him once more to go, my
            lord.

His wits begin t' unsettle.

Gloucester

Canst thou blame him?   155

Storm still.

His daughters seek his death. Ah, that good Kent!

He said it would be thus, poor banished man.

1   *outlawed from my blood*

**Disinherited (and legally declared
an outlaw; see 2.1.79–84).**

2   *cry you mercy*

**Beg your pardon (for not paying
attention to Gloucester)**

3   *Take him you on.*

Bring him (Edgar) with you

4   *Athenian*

**This seems only to mean "philoso-
pher" here (Athens was renowned
for philosophical thought). Lear
either has forgotten he called Edgar
a *Theban* in line 150, or both words
merely mean "philosopher" to him
(and are applied to Edgar perhaps
because of his stoical acceptance of
his situation).**

Thou say'st the King grows mad; I'll tell thee, friend,
I am almost mad myself. I had a son,
Now outlawed from my blood;[1] he sought my life,   160
recently But lately,° very late. I loved him, friend,
No father his son dearer. True to tell thee,
The grief hath crazed my wits. What a night's this!
[*to* **Lear**] I do beseech your Grace—
Lear
                                Oh, cry you mercy,[2] sir.
[*to* **Edgar**] Noble philosopher, your company.   165
Edgar
Tom's a-cold.
Gloucester
[*to* **Edgar**] In, fellow, there, into th' hovel. Keep thee
    warm.
Lear
[*starting toward the hovel*] Come; let's in all.
Kent
                                This way, my lord.
Lear
                                        With him!
remain I will keep° still with my philosopher.
Kent
humor [*to* **Gloucester**] Good my lord, soothe° him. Let him
    take the fellow.   170
Gloucester
[*to* **Kent**] Take him you on.[3]
Kent
[*to* **Edgar**] Sirrah, come on. Go along with us.
Lear
Come, good Athenian.[4]

1 *Child Rowland*

An allusion to Roland (or Orlando),
the most famous of the knights
of the medieval Frankish king
Charlemagne; *child* is a title given to
a candidate for knighthood

2 *"Fie, foh, and fum, I smell the blood of a
British man"*

The giant's refrain in most versions of the folktale "Jack and the
Beanstalk"

Gloucester

No words, no words! Hush.

Edgar

Child Rowland[1] to the dark tower came;   175

motto/always   His word° was still° "Fie, foh, and fum,

I smell the blood of a British man."[2]   *They exit.*

1   *How, my lord, I may be censured, that*
     nature thus gives way to loyalty,
     something fears me to think of.

     How I might be judged, having
     placed natural affection (for my
     father) below my loyalty to you (as
     Duke), somewhat frightens me to
     consider.

2   *a provoking merit set awork by a reprov-*
     able badness in himself

     A sense of injured *merit* provoked
     by an obvious evil in his (i.e.,
     Gloucester's) own nature.

3   *approves him an intelligent party to the*
     advantages of France

     Proves Gloucester is providing
     France with secret information

4   *stuff his suspicion*

     Reinforce Cornwall's distrust (of
     Gloucester)

Act 3, Scene 5

Enter **Cornwall** *and* **Edmund**.

Cornwall
I will have my revenge ere I depart his house.

Edmund
judged How, my lord, I may be censured,° that nature thus
gives way to loyalty, something fears me to think of. [1]

Cornwall
I now perceive it was not altogether your brother's evil
i.e., Gloucester's disposition made him seek his° death, but a provoking   5
merit set awork by a reprovable badness in himself. [2]

Edmund
How malicious is my fortune that I must repent to
loyal be just!° [*showing a paper*] This is the letter he spoke of,
which approves him an intelligent party to the advan-
tages of France. [3] Oh, heavens, that this treason were   10
not, or not I the detector!

Cornwall
Go with me to the Duchess.

Edmund
If the matter of this paper be certain, you have mighty
business in hand.

Cornwall
True or false, it hath made thee Earl of Gloucester. Seek   15
out where thy father is, that he may be ready for our
arrest apprehension.°

Edmund
aiding [*aside*] If I find him comforting° the King, it will stuff his
continue suspicion [4] more fully.—I will persever° in my course

of loyalty, though the conflict be sore between that   20

family loyalty   and my blood.°

Cornwall

I will lay trust upon thee, and thou shalt find a dearer

father in my love.   *They exit.*

1   *piece out*

Increase; supplement

2   *his impatience*

His (Lear's) rage

3   *Frateretto*

Another devil from Harsnett's
*Declaration of Egregious Popish
Impostures* (see note to 3.4.109)

4   *Nero is an angler in the lake of darkness*

In Geoffrey Chaucer's "Monk's
Tale," the infamously cruel Roman
emperor Nero is depicted fishing
in Hell.

5   *yeoman*

A common landowner (below the
rank of gentleman)

6   *'em*

Most likely, Goneril and Regan.
Following this line, the Quarto has
37 additional lines of a mock trial,
which are reprinted in the Appendix page 343.

7   *five wits*

The mental faculties of common
wit, imagination, fantasy, estima-
tion, and memory. The phrase *bless
thy five wits* is also used by Edgar in
3.4.55–56.

Act 3, Scene 6

*Enter **Kent** [in disguise] and **Gloucester**.*

Gloucester
Here is better than the open air; take it thankfully. I
will piece out¹ the comfort with what addition I can. I
will not be long from you.

Kent
All the power of his wits have given way to his
impatience. ² The gods reward your kindness!   5
                                        [**Gloucester**] *exits.*

*Enter **Lear**, **Edgar** [as Poor Tom], and **Fool**.*

Edgar
Frateretto³ calls me, and tells me Nero is an angler in
the lake of darkness. ⁴ Pray, innocent, and beware the
foul fiend.

Fool
Prithee, nuncle, tell me whether a madman be a
gentleman or a yeoman?⁵   10

Lear
A king, a king!

Fool
No, he's a yeoman that has a gentleman to° his son;
for he's a mad yeoman that sees his son a° gentleman
before him.

Lear
To have a thousand with red burning spits   15
Come hissing in upon 'em⁶—

Edgar
Bless thy five wits!⁷

as
become a

1   *Tray, Blanch, and Sweetheart*

The three dogs named seem to
correlate to Lear's three daughters.
Tray could mean "pain" and *blanch*
may mean "flatter," thus suggesting Lear's treacherous elder daughters. The disowned Cordelia had
previously been Lear's *sweetheart*
and, given her sisters' behavior, has
presumably become so again.

2   *throw his head at them*

Threaten them (see also line 31)

3   *Bobtail tike or trundle-tail*

Short- or long-tailed dog

4   *leap the hatch*

Leap over the closed lower half of a
divided door

5   *horn*

An ox horn often carried by beggars, used for both drinking and
begging alms.

6   *entertain for one of my hundred*

Take into service as one of my
hundred retainers (the number
of attendants Lear had initially
demanded of Goneril and Regan)

Kent

Oh, pity! Sir, where is the patience now
That you so oft have boasted to retain?

Edgar

[aside] My tears begin to take his part so much   20
disguise   They mar my counterfeiting.°

Lear

The little dogs and all,
Tray, Blanch, and Sweetheart,¹ see, they bark at me.

Edgar

Get away   Tom will throw his head at them.²—Avaunt,° you curs!
either   Be thy mouth or° black or white,   25
Tooth that poisons if it bite,
Mastiff, greyhound, mongrel grim,
bitch/male dog   Hound or spaniel, brach° or him,°
Bobtail tike or trundle-tail,³
Tom will make them weep and wail;   30
shaking   For, with throwing° thus my head,
Dogs leap the hatch,⁴ and all are fled.
Cease/parish festivals   Do de, de, de. *Cessez!*° Come, march to wakes° and
fairs and market towns. Poor Tom, thy horn⁵ is dry.

Lear

dissect   Then let them anatomize° Regan; see what breeds   35
about her heart. Is there any cause in nature that makes
employ   these hard hearts? [to **Edgar**] You, sir, I entertain° for
one of my hundred,⁶ only I do not like the fashion of
exotic; luxurious   your garments. You will say they are Persian,° but let
them be changed.   40

Kent

Now, good my lord, lie here and rest awhile.

Lear

[lying down] Make no noise; make no noise. Draw

1   *go to bed at noon*   5   *away!*

The last words the Fool utters in the   In the 1608 Quarto Edgar has a
play. Some have argued that these   fourteen-line speech not in the
lines imply that the Fool is about to   Folio, which is reproduced in the
die or otherwise leave his master,   Appendix on page 347.
though they seem more likely to be
a jest generously acknowledging
Lear's *We'll go to supper i' th' morning.*
Lear has come to speak in the Fool's
idiom, perhaps indicating that he
has internalized the Fool's insights
into the condition of the world, and
the Fool confirms the insight with a
similarly topsy-turvy formulation.
The phrase itself also could mean
"play the fool," which might refer
back to the Fool's earlier comments
that it is Lear who is the real fool
in the play, and suggest that his
appointed Fool can now learn from
him.

2   *Dover*

Presumably, the current location of
Cordelia and the French army

3   *Stand in assurèd loss*

Will undoubtedly be lost

4   *that will to some provision / Give thee*
    quick conduct

Who will quickly lead you where
you can find supplies

(imaginary) bed curtains   the curtains.° So, so. We'll go to supper i' th' morning.

[*He sleeps.*]

Fool

And I'll go to bed at noon.¹

Enter **Gloucester**.

Gloucester

[*to* **Kent**] Come hither, friend. Where is the King my

master?   45

Kent

Here, sir, but trouble him not; his wits are gone.

Gloucester

Good friend, I prithee, take him in thy arms.

against   I have o'erheard a plot of death upon° him.

There is a litter ready; lay him in 't   ·

And drive towards Dover,² friend, where thou shalt meet   50

Both welcome and protection. Take up thy master.

If thou shouldst dally half an hour, his life,

With thine and all that offer to defend him,

Stand in assurèd loss.³ Take up, take up,

And follow me, that will to some provision   55

Give thee quick conduct.⁴ Come, come, away!⁵

They [pick up **Lear** *and] exit.*

1   *Advise the Duke, where you are going, to a*
    most festinate preparation
    Tell Albany, to whom you are going,
    to make immediate preparations
    (for battle)

2   *are bound to the like*
    Intend to do the same

3   *my Lord of Gloucester*
    I.e., Edmund (given the title "Earl"
    by Cornwall at 3.5.15), though
    Oswald refers to Gloucester by the
    title in line 14.

Act 3, Scene 7

Enter **Cornwall**, **Regan**, **Goneril**, *Bastard* [**Edmund**], *and servants.*

Cornwall

Ride　[*to* **Goneril**] Post° speedily to my lord your husband;
show him this letter. [*He gives a letter.*] The army of
France is landed.—Seek out the traitor Gloucester.

　　　　　　　　　　　　　　　　　　　　　　　　[Some servants exit.]

Regan

Hang him instantly.

Goneril

Pluck out his eyes.　　　　　　　　　　　　　　　　　　　　5

Cornwall

Leave him to my displeasure. Edmund, keep you our

sister-in-law / obligated　sister° company. The revenges we are bound° to take
upon your traitorous father are not fit for your behold-
ing. Advise the Duke, where you are going, to a most
festinate preparation;[1] we are bound to the like.[2] Our　　10

messengers　posts° shall be swift and intelligent betwixt us. Farewell, dear sister; farewell, my Lord of Gloucester.[3]

Enter steward [**Oswald**].

How now? Where's the King?

Oswald

Lear　My Lord of Gloucester hath conveyed him° hence.
Some five- or six-and-thirty of his knights,　　　　　　　15

seekers　Hot questrists° after him, met him at gate,

i.e., Gloucester's　Who, with some other of the Lord's° dependants,
Are gone with him toward Dover, where they boast
To have well-armèd friends.

1   *pass upon his life*

    Pass a death sentence upon him

2   *the form of justice*

    A formal trial

3   *our power / Shall do a court'sy to our*
    wrath

    I.e., my responsibility to dispense
    justice lawfully shall bow before
    my anger.

Cornwall

Get horses for your mistress.   20

[**Oswald** *exits.*]

Goneril

Farewell, sweet lord, and sister.

Cornwall

Edmund, farewell.   [**Goneril** *and* **Edmund** *exit.*]

—Go seek the traitor Gloucester.

Shackle   Pinion° him like a thief; bring him before us.

[*Servants exit.*]

Though well we may not pass upon his life [1]

Without the form of justice, [2] yet our power   25

Shall do a court'sy to our wrath, [3] which men

curb   May blame but not control.°

Enter **Gloucester**, *and servants* [*leading him*].

Who's there? The traitor?

Regan

Ingrateful fox! 'Tis he.

Cornwall

withered   Bind fast his corky° arms.

Gloucester

What means your Graces? Good my friends, consider   30

You are my guests. Do me no foul play, friends.

Cornwall

Bind him, I say.

Regan

Hard, hard. Oh, filthy traitor!

Gloucester

i.e., not a traitor   Unmerciful lady as you are, I'm none.°

1   *my hospitable favors / You should not*
    ruffle thus
    **My hospitality should not be so
    abused (*favors* may mean "appear-
    ance" rather than "actions," but the
    meaning of the phrase would not
    be substantially different).**

2   *Late footed*
    Recently landed

3   *guessingly set down*
    That merely guesses

Cornwall

To this chair bind him.—Villain, thou shalt find—

> [*Servants tie* **Gloucester** *to a chair and*
> **Regan** *pulls his beard.*]

Gloucester

By the kind gods, 'tis most ignobly done   35
To pluck me by the beard.

Regan

white-haired; venerable   So white° and such a traitor?

Gloucester

Wicked   Naughty° lady,
These hairs which thou dost ravish from my chin
come to life   Will quicken° and accuse thee. I am your host.
With robbers' hands my hospitable favors   40
You should not ruffle thus.¹ What will you do?

Cornwall

recently   Come, sir, what letters had you late° from France?

Regan

straightforward   Be simple-answered,° for we know the truth.

Cornwall

And what confederacy have you with the traitors
Late footed² in the kingdom?

Regan

                                To whose hands   45
You have sent the lunatic King. Speak.

Gloucester

I have a letter guessingly set down,³
Which came from one that's of a neutral heart,
And not from one opposed.

Cornwall

                                Cunning.

Regan

                                And false.

1   *charged at peril*

**Commanded at the risk of your
own life**

2   *I am tied to th' stake, and I must stand the
course.*

**Gloucester sees himself as a bear in
a bear-baiting contest; he is *tied to
'th stake* and must endure the attack
of the dogs (*stand the course*).**

3   *anointed*

**Sanctified; consecrated with holy
oils (referring to the sacred rite performed at the King's coronation)**

4   *quenched the stellèd fires*

Put out the fire of the stars

5   *he holp the heavens to rain*

**I.e., by augmenting the rain with his
own tears**

6   *turn the key*

I.e., let them in

7   *All cruels else subscribe.*

**I.e., all cruel beings at some point
show compassion except you.**

8   *wingèd vengeance*

Speedy revenge

Cornwall

Where hast thou sent the King?   50

Gloucester

To Dover.

Regan

Why   Wherefore° to Dover? Wast thou not charged at
         peril[1]—

Cornwall

Wherefore to Dover? Let him answer that.

Gloucester

I am tied to th' stake, and I must stand the course.[2]

Regan

Wherefore to Dover?   55

Gloucester

Because I would not see thy cruel nails
Pluck out his poor old eyes, nor thy fierce sister
In his anointed[3] flesh stick boarish fangs.
The sea, with such a storm as his bare head

risen; swelled   In hell-black night endured, would have buoyed° up   60
And quenched the stellèd fires;[4]

helped   Yet, poor old heart, he holp° the heavens to rain.[5]
If wolves had at thy gate howled that stern time,
Thou shouldst have said, "Good porter, turn the key."[6]
All cruels else subscribe.[7] But I shall see   65
The wingèd vengeance[8] overtake such children.

Cornwall

See 't shalt thou never.—Fellows, hold the chair.
Upon these eyes of thine I'll set my foot.

Gloucester

hope   He that will think° to live till he be old
Give me some help! Oh, cruel! O you gods!   70

                                   [**Cornwall** *puts out his eye.*]

1   *I'd shake it on this quarrel*

     I.e., for this cause, I'd pull it (i.e.,
     your beard) as a challenge to a
     fight.

2   *take the chance of anger*

     I.e., accept the risks of angry men
     fighting

Regan

One side will mock another. Th' other too.

Cornwall

[*to* **Gloucester**] If you see vengeance—

Servant

Stop   Hold° your hand, my lord!

I have served you ever since I was a child,

But better service have I never done you

Than now to bid you hold.

Regan

                                    How now, you dog?   75

Servant

[*to* **Regan**] If you did wear a beard upon your chin,

I'd shake it on this quarrel.¹ [**Cornwall** *draws his sword.*]

mean by this   —What do you mean?°

Cornwall

servant   My villain!°

Servant

[*drawing*] Nay, then, come on and take the chance of

anger.²   [*They fight.* **Cornwall** *is wounded.*]

Regan

[*to another servant*] Give me thy sword. —A peasant

stand up thus?   [*She takes a sword and stabs him.*]   80

Servant

Oh, I am slain! My lord, you have one eye left

injury   To see some mischief° on him. Oh!   [*He dies.*]

Cornwall

Lest it see more, prevent it. Out, vile jelly!

                        [*He plucks out* **Gloucester**'s *eye.*]

Where is thy luster now?

Gloucester

All dark and comfortless. Where's my son Edmund?   85

1   *How look you?*

     How are you?

2   *Give me your arm.*

     In the Quarto, after Regan and
     Cornwall exit the two remaining
     servants speak lines (printed here
     in the Appendix on page 349) that,
     in their horror at the act they have
     witnessed and gentle concern for
     Gloucester, somewhat ameliorate
     the monstrousness of the scene.
     Their absence from the Folio makes
     it a darker version of the tragedy.

filial love	Edmund, enkindle all the sparks of nature°
avenge	To quit° this horrid act.

Regan

                   Out, treacherous villain!

Thou call'st on him that hates thee. It was he

disclosure	That made the overture° of thy treasons to us,
	Who is too good to pity thee. 90

Gloucester

wronged	Oh, my follies! Then Edgar was abused.°
	Kind gods, forgive me that and prosper him!

Regan

Go thrust him out at gates and let him smell

His way to Dover. *[A servant starts to] exit with* **Gloucester**.

               How is 't, my lord? How look you?[1]

Cornwall

I have received a hurt. Follow me, lady.   95

—Turn out that eyeless villain. Throw this slave

i.e., extensively	Upon the dunghill.—Regan, I bleed apace.°
Inopportunely	Untimely° comes this hurt. Give me your arm.[2]

                                 They exit.

1   *Yet better thus, and known to be*
    condemned, / Than still condemned and
    flattered.

    But it is better to be like this (a
    beggar), when I know I am de-
    spised, than to be despised but
    flattered

2   *most dejected thing of fortune*
    Thing most cast down by fortune

3   *still in esperance*
    Always in hope

4   *The worst returns to laughter*
    I.e., when things are at their worst,
    any change must be for the good.

5   *Owes nothing*
    Has nothing left to expose

6   *poorly led*
    Led by a poor man (unworthy of
    Gloucester's rank)

7   *But that thy strange mutations make us*
    hate thee, / Life would not yield to age.
    I.e., we welcome the inevitability
    of aging and death because the
    terrible vicissitudes of fortune
    make us despise life.

Act 4, Scene 1

*Enter **Edgar** [as Poor Tom].*

Edgar

despised Yet better thus, and known to be condemned,°
Than still condemned and flattered. ¹ To be worst,
The lowest and most dejected thing of fortune, ²
Stands still in esperance, ³ lives not in fear.
The lamentable change is from the best;   5
The worst returns to laughter. ⁴ Welcome, then,
Thou unsubstantial air that I embrace.
The wretch that thou hast blown unto the worst
Owes nothing⁵ to thy blasts.

*Enter **Gloucester**, and an **Old Man** [leading him].*

But who comes here?
My father, poorly led? ⁶ World, world, O world!   10
But that thy strange mutations make us hate thee,
Life would not yield to age. ⁷

Old Man

Oh, my good lord, I have been your tenant
And your father's tenant these fourscore years.

Gloucester

Away, get thee away! Good friend, begone.   15
help Thy comforts° can do me no good at all;
Thee they may hurt.

Old Man

You cannot see your way.

Gloucester

need I have no way and therefore want° no eyes;
I stumbled when I saw. Full oft 'tis seen

1   *Our means secure us, and our mere*
    defects / Prove our commodities

    **Our possessions offer false secu-
    rity, while what we completely lack
    proves beneficial.**

2   *"This is the worst."*

    **Edgar uses the term *worse/worst*
    seven times within fourteen lines at
    the start of this scene, directing our
    attention to how extreme is his dis-
    tress. Although in his first speech
    he tried to convince himself that
    having reached *the worst* (line 6) he
    should be cheered since things can
    only improve, the awful sight of
    his blinded father makes him say *I
    am worse than e'er I was*. In this play,
    confidence that things must get
    better or at least can get no worse is
    usually a prelude to still more
    terrible events and experiences.**

3   *Bad is the trade that must play fool to*
    sorrow

    **It is a sad turn of events when one
    must play the fool in the face of
    such misery.**

Our means secure us, and our mere defects   20
Prove our commodities. [1] O dear son Edgar,

object / deceived The food° of thy abusèd° father's wrath!
with Might I but live to see thee in° my touch,
I'd say I had eyes again!

Old Man

How now? Who's there?

Edgar

[*aside*] O gods! Who is 't can say, "I am at the worst"?   25
I am worse than e'er I was.

Old Man

'Tis poor mad Tom.

Edgar

[*aside*] And worse I may be yet. The worst is not
So long as we can say, "This is the worst." [2]

Old Man

[*to* **Edgar**] Fellow, where goest?

Gloucester

Is it a beggar-man?

Old Man

Madman and beggar too.   30

Gloucester

sanity He has some reason,° else he could not beg.
I' th' last night's storm I such a fellow saw,
Who Which° made me think a man a worm. My son
Came then into my mind, and yet my mind
Was then scarce friends with him. I have heard more
     since.   35
irresponsible As flies to wanton° boys are we to th' gods:
amusement They kill us for their sport.°

Edgar

[*aside*] How should this be?
Bad is the trade that must play fool to sorrow, [3]

1   *Ang'ring itself*

Vexing himself

5   *I cannot daub it further.*

I can no longer play this role.

2   *ancient love*

Old attachments; long-standing affection

3   *'Tis the time's plague*

It is an appropriate image of the horror of the present time. Gloucester's words wryly express his awareness of the inversion of order in the Britain of the play, but they also invoke all-too familiar aspects of Shakespeare's London, like the *madmen* who were kept in Bethlehem (Bedlam) Hospital, on the north bank of the Thames. It was easy to visit the hospital in order to see them, and many Jacobean plays represented madmen on the stage, such as John Webster's *The Duchess of Malfi* (c.1614) and Thomas Middleton and William Rowley's *The Changeling* (c.1622–1623); begging was only permitted by those with a disability, and there were many *blind* or crippled beggars in London; and the theaters were regularly closed during outbreaks of *plague* for fear of its spread where large crowds were allowed to gather.

4   *Above the rest*

Above all else; whatever you do

Ang'ring itself[1] and others.—Bless thee, master!

Gloucester

Is that the naked fellow?

Old Man

                    Ay, my lord.   40

Gloucester

Get thee away. If for my sake

two   Thou wilt o'ertake us hence a mile or twain°

i.e., On I'° th' way toward Dover, do it for ancient love,[2]

And bring some covering for this naked soul,

Whom Which° I'll entreat to lead me.

Old Man

                  Alack, sir, he is mad.   45

Gloucester

'Tis the time's plague,[3] when madmen lead the blind.

Do as I bid thee, or rather do thy pleasure;

Above the rest,[4] begone.

Old Man

apparel I'll bring him the best 'parel° that I have,

of   Come on° 't what will.   *He exits.*

Gloucester

               Sirrah, naked fellow—   50

Edgar

Poor Tom's a-cold. [*aside*] I cannot daub it further.[5]

Gloucester

Come hither, fellow.

Edgar

[*aside*] And yet I must.—Bless thy sweet eyes, they
     bleed.

Gloucester

Know'st thou the way to Dover?

1   *stile*

   An arrangement of rungs or posts
   permitting access to a *footpath*

2   *goodman's son*

   Son of a man of some substance,
   but not of noble birth (though
   Gloucester is, of course, a nobleman)

3   *humbled to all strokes*

   Brought to accept all misfortune

4   *superfluous and lust-dieted man*

   Man who has more than he needs
   and indulges his desires

5   *slaves your ordinance*

   I.e., subjugates your divine law to
   his own will

6   *confinèd deep*

   I.e., the waters of the straits of
   Dover (the channel between
   England and France)

7   *rich about me*

   Of value that I have with me

Edgar

Both stile[1] and gate, horseway and footpath. Poor Tom   55
hath been scared out of his good wits. Bless thee, goodman's son,[2] from the foul fiend!

Gloucester

[*giving a purse*] Here, take this purse, thou whom the
    heavens' plagues
Have humbled to all strokes.[3] That I am wretched

always   Makes thee the happier. Heavens deal so still!°   60
Let the superfluous and lust-dieted man[4]
That slaves your ordinance,[5] that will not see

feel sympathy   Because he does not feel,° feel your power quickly!

eliminate   So distribution should undo° excess
And each man have enough. Dost thou know Dover?   65

Edgar

Ay, master.

Gloucester

overhanging   There is a cliff, whose high and bending° head

into   Looks fearfully in° the confinèd deep.[6]
Bring me but to the very brim of it,
And I'll repair the misery thou dost bear   70
With something rich about me.[7] From that place
I shall no leading need.

Edgar

                    Give me thy arm.
Poor Tom shall lead thee.   *They exit.*

1   *turned the wrong side out*

    I.e., misunderstood everything

2   *He'll not feel wrongs / Which tie him to an*
    answer.

    He disregards insults that should
    provoke a response.

3   *Our wishes on the way / May prove effects.*

    The hopes you and I discussed on
    our journey may come to pass.

4   *musters*

    Assembling of troops

5   *change names*

    Exchange roles (i.e., husband and
    wife) with Albany

6   *distaff*

    Spinning staff (a spindle on which
    wool is wound and a symbol of
    femininity)

7   *mistress's*

    Both "ruler's" and "lover's"

8   *Conceive*

    Think about what I have just said
    (but with a sexual innuendo that
    runs through the last five lines of
    this speech; see 1.1.11 and note)

Act 4, Scene 2

Enter **Goneril,** *Bastard* [**Edmund**], *and steward* [**Oswald**].

Goneril

Welcome, my lord. I marvel our mild husband

Has not Not° met us on the way. [*to* **Oswald**]

Now, where's your master?

Oswald

Madam, within, but never man so changed.

i.e., French army I told him of the army° that was landed;

He smiled at it. I told him you were coming;   5

His answer was "The worse." Of Gloucester's treachery

And of the loyal service of his son

fool When I informed him, then he called me sot°

And told me I had turned the wrong side out. [1]

What most he should dislike seems pleasant to him;   10

he should like What like,° offensive.

Goneril

[*to* **Edmund**] Then shall you go no further.

cowardly It is the cowish° terror of his spirit,

take responsibility That dares not undertake.° He'll not feel wrongs

Which tie him to an answer. [2] Our wishes on the way

brother-in-law May prove effects. [3] Back, Edmund, to my brother;°   15

escort / armies Hasten his musters [4] and conduct° his powers.°

I must change names [5] at home and give the distaff [6]

Into my husband's hands. This trusty servant

likely Shall pass between us. Ere long you are like° to hear,

If you dare venture in your own behalf,   20

A mistress's [7] command. Wear this; spare speech.

Bend down Decline° your head. [*places a scarf around his neck and kisses him*] This kiss, if it durst speak,

Would stretch thy spirits up into the air.

Conceive [8] and fare thee well.

1   *My fool usurps my body*

     **My foolish husband claims pos-
     session of me (some copies of the
     Quarto have "bed" for *body*).**

2   *worth the whistle*

     **I.e., worthy of your concern. From
     the proverbial expression, "It is
     a poor dog that is not worth the
     whistle."**

3   *Who hast not in thy brows an eye
     discerning / Thine honor from thy
     suffering*

     **Who cannot differentiate between
     what your *honor* insists must
     be confronted and what can be
     endured**

4   *Proper deformity shows not in the fiend /
     So horrid as in woman.*

     **I.e., the ugliness that is proper for
     the devil is even more horrible
     when it appears in a woman.**

Edmund

Yours in the ranks of death.

Goneril

i.e., Edmund   My most dear Gloucester!° 25

[**Edmund**] *exits.*

Oh, the difference of man and man!

To thee a woman's services are due;

My fool usurps my body. ¹

Oswald

Madam, here comes my lord.   *He exits.*

Enter **Albany.**

Goneril

I have been worth the whistle. ²

Albany

Oh, Goneril,   30

You are not worth the dust which the rude wind

Blows in your face.

Goneril

Cowardly   Milk-livered° man,

That bear'st a cheek for blows, a head for wrongs,

Who hast not in thy brows an eye discerning

Thine honor from thy suffering. ³

Albany

See thyself, devil! 35

Proper deformity shows not in the fiend

So horrid as in woman. ⁴

Goneril

useless   Oh, vain° fool!

Enter a **Messenger.**

1　*A servant that he bred, thrilled with*
　remorse

**I.e., a servant that Cornwall
himself raised, moved by pity (for
Gloucester)**

2　*Flew on him and amongst them felled him*
　dead

**Turned upon (the servant), and
amongst them (either "surrounded by
everyone" or "between them," i.e.,
with the help of Regan) killed him.**

3　*But not without that harmful stroke*
　which since / Hath plucked him after

**But not before he received the
injurious blow, which has since
killed him**

4　*our nether crimes / So speedily can venge*

**Our earthly crimes you can punish
so quickly**

5　*One way I like this well*

**On one hand, this news (of Corn-
wall's death) is welcome (since his
death will lessen Regan's power)**

6　*But being widow, and my Gloucester with*
　her, / May all the building in my fancy
　pluck / Upon my hateful life

**But now that Regan is a widow
and free to be with Edmund, she
may prevent the happiness I have
imagined and leave me trapped in
my hateful life (with Albany).**

Messenger

Oh, my good lord, the Duke of Cornwall's dead,
Slain by his servant, going to put out
The other eye of Gloucester.

Albany

                        Gloucester's eyes!   40

Messenger

A servant that he bred, thrilled with remorse,[1]

In opposition / aiming   Opposed° against the act, bending° his sword

by that   To his great master, who, thereat° enraged,
Flew on him and amongst them felled him dead,[2]
But not without that harmful stroke which since   45
Hath plucked him after.[3]

Albany

                    This shows you are above,

divine judges   You justicers, ° that these our nether crimes
So speedily can venge![4] But, oh, poor Gloucester!
Lost he his other eye?

Messenger

                Both, both, my lord.
—This letter, madam, craves a speedy answer;   50
'Tis from your sister.   [*handing her a letter*]

Goneril

              [*aside*] One way I like this well;[5]

i.e., Edgar   But being widow, and my Gloucester° with her,
May all the building in my fancy pluck

That other   Upon my hateful life.[6] Another° way

bitter   The news is not so tart.°—I'll read and answer. [*She exits.*] 55

Albany

i.e., Gloucester's   Where was his son when they did take his° eyes?

Messenger

Come with my lady hither.

1   *their punishment*

     **I.e., the punishsment meted out
by Regan and Cornwall (upon
Gloucester)**

2   They exit.

     **Following this, the Quarto has an
entire scene absent from the Folio,
which here is printed in the Appendix on page 351.**

Albany

>   He is not here.

Messenger

returning No, my good lord. I met him back° again.

Albany

Knows he the wickedness?

Messenger

i.e., Gloucester Ay, my good lord. 'Twas he informed against him°   60
And quit the house on purpose that their punishment[1]
Might have the freer course.

Albany

>   Gloucester, I live

To thank thee for the love thou show'dst the King
And to revenge thine eyes.—Come hither, friend.
Tell me what more thou know'st.   *They exit.*[2]   65

1   colors

    Military banners

2   *rank fumitor and furrow weeds, / With*
    hardocks, hemlock, nettles, cuckooflowers, /
    Darnel, and all the idle weeds that grow

    Cordelia lists all the *idle weeds* with
    which Lear has adorned himself.
    The image of *idle* (i.e., useless)
    ***weeds*, which spread like Lear's**
    madness, is presented in op-
    position to the *sustaining corn* (i.e.,
    grain), on which we depend.

3   *What can man's wisdom / In the restoring*
    his bereavèd sense?

    What can human knowledge do to
    restore his sanity, which grief has
    taken from him?

4   *outward worth*

    Material wealth

5   *That to provoke in him/ Are many simples*
    operative

    There are many effective herbs to
    help him (to sleep).

6   *unpublished virtues*

    Hidden healing herbs

Act 4, Scene 3

Enter, with drum and colors,[1] **Cordelia, Gentlemen,** *and soldiers.*

Cordelia

Alack, 'tis he! Why, he was met even now

turbulent   As mad as the vexed° sea, singing aloud,

bad-smelling   Crowned with rank° fumitor and furrow weeds,

With hardocks, hemlock, nettles, cuckooflowers,

Darnel, and all the idle weeds that grow[2]   5

hundred soldiers   In our sustaining corn. A century° send forth!

Search every acre in the high-grown field

And bring him to our eye.   *[Some soldiers exit.]*

                  What can man's wisdom

In the restoring his bereavèd sense?[3]

He that helps him take all my outward worth.[4]   10

Gentleman

There is means, madam.

sleep   Our foster nurse of nature is repose,°

The which he lacks. That to provoke in him

Are many simples operative,[5] whose power

Will close the eye of anguish.

Cordelia

                All blest secrets,   15

All you unpublished virtues[6] of the earth,

Grow/helpful/remedying   Spring° with my tears! Be aidant° and remediate°

In the good man's distress. Seek, seek for him,

madness   Lest his ungoverned rage° dissolve the life

lacks/sense   That wants° the means° to lead it.

Enter **Messenger.**

1   *No blown ambition doth our arms incite, /*
    But love, dear love, and our aged father's
    right.

    **It is not a grasping ambition that
    prompts this battle, but rather
    precious love and the desire to
    restore our elderly father's rights.**

Messenger

News, madam. 20

armies The British powers° are marching hitherward.

Cordelia

already 'Tis known before.° Our preparation stands

In expectation of them. O dear father,

It is thy business that I go about;

the King of France Therefore great France° 25

beseeching My mourning and importuned° tears hath pitied.

proud No blown° ambition doth our arms incite,

But love, dear love, and our aged father's right. [1]

Soon may I hear and see him! *They exit.*

1   *What might import my sister's letter to*
    him?

    (1) what is the subject of my sister's
    letters to Edmund?; (2) what does
    it signify that my sister is writing
    to him?

2   *Faith*

    In faith (a common oath or
    interjection)

3   *is posted hence*

    Has ridden quickly away

4   *dispatch / His nighted life*

    End his *nighted* (i.e., both ignorant
    and literally blinded) life

Act 4, Scene 4

*Enter **Regan** and steward [**Oswald**].*

Regan

i.e., Albany's But are my brother's° powers set forth?

Oswald

Ay, madam.

Regan

Himself in person there?

Oswald

fussing Madam, with much ado.°

Your sister is the better soldier.

Regan

Lord Edmund spake not with your lord at home?

Oswald

No, madam.   5

Regan

What might import my sister's letter to him?[1]

Oswald

I know not, lady.

Regan

Faith,[2] he is posted hence[3] on serious matter.

stupidity It was great ignorance,° Gloucester's eyes being out,

Gloucester To let him° live. Where he arrives he moves   10

All hearts against us. Edmund, I think, is gone,

Gloucester's In pity of his° misery, to dispatch

discover His nighted life;[4] moreover, to descry°

The strength o' th' enemy.

Oswald

I must needs after him, madam, with my letter.   15

261

1   *charged my duty*
    Gave me my orders

2   *most speaking*
    Very expressive

3   *of her bosom*
    In her confidence

4   *take this note*
    Take note of this

5   *more convenient is he for my hand / Than*
    for your lady's
    It is more appropriate that Edmund
    marry me than Goneril

6   *this*
    Probably a letter; when Oswald is
    killed in 4.5, Edgar does not men-
    tion this letter but reads one from
    Goneril (4.5.259–266).

7   *thus much*
    What I have said

8   *desire her call her wisdom to her*
    Entreat her to come to her senses

9   *cuts him off*
    I.e., kills him (as at line 4.5.260)

Regan

Our troops set forth tomorrow. Stay with us;

roads The ways° are dangerous.

Oswald

                       I may not, madam.

My lady charged my duty[1] in this business.

Regan

Why should she write to Edmund? Might not you

Perhaps Transport her purposes by word? Belike°   20

Some things—I know not what. I'll love thee much;

Let me unseal the letter.

Oswald

                  Madam, I had rather—

Regan

I know your lady does not love her husband.

recent I am sure of that; and at her late° being here

amorous glances She gave strange oeillades° and most speaking[2] looks 25

To noble Edmund. I know you are of her bosom.[3]

Oswald

I, madam?

Regan

you I speak in understanding; y'° are, I know 't.

Therefore I do advise you, take this note:[4]

My lord is dead. Edmund and I have talked,   30

And more convenient is he for my hand

infer Than for your lady's.[5] You may gather° more.

If you do find him, pray you give him this;[6]

And when your mistress hears thus much[7] from you,

I pray, desire her call her wisdom to her.[8]   35

So, fare you well.

If you do chance to hear of that blind traitor,

Advancement Preferment° falls on him that cuts him off.[9]

Oswald

I wish Would° I could meet him, madam! I should show
What party I do follow.

Regan

Fare thee well.   40

They exit [separately].

1   *that same hill*

    I.e., one of the cliffs of Dover (which
    Gloucester previously described at
    4.1.67–68)

2   *low*

    Far down (over the edge of the cliff)

3   *choughs*

    Small birds of the crow family (pro-
    nounced "chuffs")

4   *wing the midway air*

    Fly halfway down to the sea (from
    the top of the cliff)

5   *samphire*

    An aromatic plant often used in
    pickling. As it grows mainly on the
    sides of cliffs, the collection of it
    could be dangerous, hence *dreadful
    trade.*

Act 4, Scene 5

Enter **Gloucester** *and* **Edgar** *[still disguised].*

Gloucester

When shall I come to th' top of that same hill?[1]

Edgar

You do climb up it now. Look how we labor.

Gloucester

flat   Methinks the ground is even.°

Edgar

                                                   Horrible steep.

Hark, do you hear the sea?

Gloucester

                                          No, truly.

Edgar

Why, then, your other senses grow imperfect   5

Because of   By° your eyes' anguish.

Gloucester

                                  So may it be, indeed.

Methinks thy voice is altered, and thou speak'st

language / content   In better phrase° and matter° than thou didst.

Edgar

Y' are much deceived. In nothing am I changed

But in my garments.

Gloucester

                                  Methinks y' are better spoken.   10

Edgar

Come on, sir; here's the place. Stand still. How fearful

And dizzy 'tis to cast one's eyes so low![2]

The crows and choughs[3] that wing the midway air[4]

large   Show scarce so gross° as beetles. Halfway down

terrifying   Hangs one that gathers samphire[5]—dreadful° trade!   15

267

1   *anchoring bark / Diminished to her cock;*
     her cock, a buoy
     **That ship over there looks like a
     rowboat, and her rowboat looks
     like a buoy.**

2   *Lest my brain turn, and the deficient*
     sight / Topple down headlong
     **Lest I become dizzy, and my result-
     ing blurry sight cause me to fall
     over the edge**

3   *all beneath the moon*
     I.e., all the world

4   *leap upright*
     **Jump straight up (for fear of losing
     his balance)**

5   *Fairies and gods / Prosper it with thee!*
     **May fairies and gods multiply its
     contents for you.**

6   *Why I do trifle thus with his despair / Is*
     done to cure it.
     **I.e., I toy with his despair in order
     to cure it.**

Methinks he seems no bigger than his head.
The fishermen that walk upon the beach
Appear like mice, and yond tall anchoring bark
Diminished to her cock; her cock, a buoy¹

waves   Almost too small for sight. The murmuring surge,°   20

innumerable/breaks   That on th' unnumbered° idle pebble chafes,°
Cannot be heard so high. I'll look no more,
Lest my brain turn, and the deficient sight
Topple down headlong.²

Gloucester

                 Set me where you stand.

Edgar

Give me your hand. You are now within a foot   25

edge   Of th' extreme verge.° For all beneath the moon³
Would I not leap upright.⁴

Gloucester

                 Let go my hand.

is   Here, friend, 's° another purse; in it a jewel
Well worth a poor man's taking. [*He gives a purse.*] Fairies
    and gods

Prosper it with thee!⁵ Go thou further off.   30
Bid me farewell, and let me hear thee going.

Edgar

[*moving away*] Now fare ye well, good sir.

Gloucester

                 With all my heart.

Edgar

[*aside*] Why I do trifle thus with his despair
Is done to cure it.⁶

Gloucester

                 [*kneeling*] O you mighty gods!
This world I do renounce and, in your sights,   35
Shake patiently my great affliction off.

1   *To quarrel with*

     Into challenging

2   *My snuff and loathèd part of nature*

     The last hateful remains of my life (a
     snuff **being a partially extinguished**
     candle)

3   *I know not how conceit may rob / The*
     treasury of life, when life itself / Yields to
     the theft

     I wonder if imagination alone might
     not cause his death, since he is so
     ready to die.

4   *where he thought*

     Where he thought he was (i.e., on
     the cliff)

5   *Alive or dead? / Ho, you, sir! Friend! Hear*
     you, sir? Speak!

     As he addresses his father here,
     Edgar adopts yet another persona.
     No longer playing the role of Poor
     Tom, Edgar pretends to be a
     concerned passerby. He has yet to
     reveal himself as Gloucester's son.

6   *Thou'dst shivered*

     You would have shattered

7   *Ten masts at each*

     Ten ship masts, laid end to end

8   *chalky bourn*

     Chalky boundary. The Dover cliffs
     (with the heavy chalk deposits that
     earn them the name "the white
     cliffs of Dover") mark the edge of
     England's south-eastern border.

If I could bear it longer and not fall

irresistible   To quarrel with [1] your great opposeless° wills,

My snuff and loathèd part of nature [2] should

Burn itself out. If Edgar live, oh, bless him!   40

Now, fellow, fare thee well.   [*He falls*.]

Edgar

                                        Gone, sir. Farewell.

—And yet I know not how conceit may rob

The treasury of life, when life itself

Yields to the theft. [3] Had he been where he thought, [4]

this act (of falling)   By this° had thought been past.—Alive or dead?   45

Ho, you, sir! Friend! Hear you, sir? Speak! [5]

die   [*aside*] Thus might he pass° indeed; yet he revives.

Who   —What° are you, sir?

Gloucester

                                        Away and let me die.

Edgar

anything   Hadst thou been aught° but gossamer, feathers, air,

i.e., feet / plunging   So many fathom° down precipitating,°   50

Thou'dst shivered [6] like an egg; but thou dost breathe,

whole; healthy   Hast heavy substance, bleed'st not, speak'st, art sound.°

Ten masts at each [7] make not the altitude

Which thou hast perpendicularly fell.

Thy life's a miracle. Speak yet again.   55

Gloucester

But have I fall'n or no?

Edgar

From the dread summit of this chalky bourn. [8]

on high / shrill-voiced   Look up aheight;° the shrill-gorged° lark so far

Cannot be seen or heard. Do but look up.

Gloucester

Alack, I have no eyes.   60

1 *beguile the tyrant's rage / And frustrate*
   his proud will

   I.e., by committing suicide, thereby
   thwarting the intentions of the
   tyrant

2 *happy father*

   Fortunate old man (though
   expressing Edgar's actual relationship without Edgar intending it be
   understood)

3 *clearest gods, who make them honors / Of*
   men's impossibilities

   Most righteous gods, who earn our
   reverence by performing miracles

Is wretchedness deprived that benefit
To end itself by death? 'Twas yet some comfort
cheat When misery could beguile° the tyrant's rage
And frustrate his proud will. [1]

Edgar

Give me your arm.

[*He lifts* **Gloucester** *up.*]

Up—so. How is 't? Feel you your legs? You stand.   65

Gloucester

Too well, too well.

Edgar

This is above all strangeness.
Upon the crown o' th' cliff, what thing was that
Which parted from you?

Gloucester

A poor unfortunate beggar.

Edgar

As I stood here below, methought his eyes
Were two full moons; he had a thousand noses,   70
twisted Horns whelked° and waved like the enragèd sea.
It was some fiend. Therefore, thou happy father, [2]
Think that the clearest gods, who make them honors
Of men's impossibilities, [3] have preserved thee.

Gloucester

endure I do remember now. Henceforth I'll bear°   75
Affliction till it do cry out itself
"Enough, enough," and die. That thing you speak of,
I took it for a man; often 'twould say
"The fiend, the fiend." He led me to that place.

Edgar

carefree Bear free° and patient thoughts.

Enter **Lear**.

1   *The safer sense will ne'er accommodate /*
    His master thus.

    **A sane mind would never permit its
    owner to dress like that.**

2   *they cannot touch me for crying.*

    **They cannot criticize me for crying.
    (The 1608 Quarto has "coining," a
    reference to the minting of coins as
    a royal prerogative.)**

3   *Nature's above art in that respect.*

    (See LONGER NOTE, page 359)

4   *press money*

    **Sum paid to a military recruit at
    the time of his conscription or
    enlistment.**

5   *crowkeeper*

    **Either a scarecrow or a live person
    hired to drive crows away from
    crops**

6   *Draw me a clothier's yard.*

    **I.e., draw your bow the full length
    of the arrow. A *clothier's yard* was
    a unit of length set at thirty-six
    inches long.**

7   *gauntlet*

    **A challenge was declared by the
    throwing down of an armored glove
    (*gauntlet*); possibly, Lear throws
    down the cheese as his challenge
    against the mouse—both of
    which, cheese and mouse, may**

be figments of Lear's tortured
imagination.

8   *I'll prove it on*

    I'll maintain my claim even against

9   *brown bills*

    **I.e., pike-carrying soldiers (*brown
    bills* were spear-like weapons that
    were painted *brown* to prevent them
    from rusting, though the term
    could be used for those who carried
    them)**

10 *hewgh*

    (Sound of an arrow in flight)

11 *Sweet marjoram*

    **An herb thought to cure some
    diseases of the brain**

12 *like a dog*

    I.e., fawningly

13 *told me I had the white hairs in my beard
    ere the black ones were there*

    **I.e., told me I was wise before I was
    old enough to have grown a beard**

14 *To say "ay" and "no" to everything that
    I said "ay" and "no" to was no good
    divinity.*

    **To agree with me about everything
    was not true obedience (since it
    taught me falsely to believe I was
    god-like and infallible).**

But who comes here? 80
The safer sense will ne'er accommodate
Its His° master thus. [1]

Lear

No, they cannot touch me for crying.[2] I am the King
himself.

Edgar

heart-rending Oh, thou side-piercing° sight! 85

Lear

Nature's above art in that respect.[3] There's your press
money.[4] That fellow handles his bow like a crowkeeper.[5]
Draw me a clothier's yard.[6] Look, look, a mouse!
Peace, peace; this piece of toasted cheese will
i.e., trap do° 't. There's my gauntlet;[7] I'll prove it on[8] a giant. 90
i.e., arrow Bring up the brown bills.[9] Oh, well flown, bird!° I' th'
bull's-eye / password clout,° i' th' clout—hewgh![10] Give the word.°

Edgar

Sweet marjoram.[11]

Lear

Pass.

Gloucester

I know that voice. 95

Lear

Ha! Goneril with a white beard? They flattered me like
a dog[12] and told me I had the white hairs in my beard
ere the black ones were there.[13] To say "ay" and "no"
to everything that I said "ay" and "no" to was no good
divinity.[14] When the rain came to wet me once and the 100
shiver wind to make me chatter,° when the thunder would not
understood; discovered peace at my bidding, there I found° 'em; there I smelt 'em
out. Go to; they are not men o' their words. They told
immune to fever me I was everything. 'Tis a lie. I am not ague-proof.°

1   *goes to 't*

     Has sex (see also lines 116 and 121)

2   *Whose face between her forks presages*
     snow

     Who pretends by her facial expres-
     sions that she is chaste (*forks*
     are clips used to hold elaborate
     hairdos). It is possible, however,
     that *forks* means "legs," and the
     word order of a bawdier image has
     been transposed from the more ex-
     pected form: "Whose face presages
     snow between her legs." Either way,
     the meaning is the same: that she
     tries to appear chaste.

3   *minces virtue*

     Acts as if she's virtuous (with her
     coy fastidiousness)

4   *of pleasure's name*

     Any mention of sex

5   *fitchew*

     Polecat (ferret), an animal thought
     to breed enthusiastically (and
     hence slang for "prostitute")

6   *centaurs*

     Mythological creatures that were
     half human (head, upper torso),
     half horse (lower torso, legs), and
     notoriously lustful

Gloucester

distinct sound | The trick° of that voice I do well remember.   105
Is 't not the King?

Lear

              Ay, every inch a king.
When I do stare, see how the subject quakes.

crime; offense | I pardon that man's life. What was thy cause?°
Adultery?
Thou shalt not die. Die for adultery? No.   110
The wren goes to 't,¹ and the small gilded fly

copulate | Does lecher° in my sight.
Let copulation thrive, for Gloucester's bastard son
Was kinder to his father than my daughters

Begot | Got° 'tween the lawful sheets.   115

lechery / in a hurry | To 't, luxury,° pell-mell,° for I lack soldiers.
Behold yond simpering dame,
Whose face between her forks presages snow,²
That minces virtue³ and does shake the head
To hear of pleasure's name.⁴   120

Neither the / well-fed | The° fitchew⁵ nor the soilèd° horse goes to 't
With a more riotous appetite.
Down from the waist they are centaurs,⁶
Though women all above.

Only / waist / rule | But° to the girdle° do the gods inherit;°   125
Beneath is all the fiend's.
There's Hell, there's darkness, there is the sulfurous pit,
burning, scalding, stench, consumption. Fie, fie, fie!

perfume / druggist | Pah, pah! Give me an ounce of civet,° good apothecary,°
sweeten my imagination. There's money for thee.   130

Gloucester

Oh, let me kiss that hand!

Lear

Let me wipe it first; it smells of mortality.

1   *piece*

Probably "masterpiece" in light of
Lear's royalty, but may merely have
its familiar meaning "portion," in
comparison to the *great world* that
will itself eventually be destroyed.

2   *so wear out to naught*

Be reduced to nothing in the same
manner (as Lear)

3   *are you there with me*

Do you follow my meaning?

4   *heavy case*

sad state (punning on *case* as "eye-
socket")

5   *feelingly*

(1) only by touch; (2) intensely

6   *handy-dandy*

I.e., whatever you please; literally,
choose a hand; a children's game
where the child must guess which
hand has something hidden in it

Gloucester

Oh, ruined piece ¹ of nature! This great world

Shall so wear out to naught.² Dost thou know me?

Lear

squint I remember thine eyes well enough. Dost thou squinny° 135

at me? No, do thy worst, blind Cupid; I'll not love. Read

handwriting thou this challenge. Mark but the penning° of it.

Gloucester

Were all thy letters suns, I could not see.

Edgar

believe / is happening [*aside*] I would not take° this from report. It is,°

And my heart breaks at it. 140

Lear

Read.

Gloucester

sockets What, with the case° of eyes?

Lear

Oh, ho, are you there with me?³ No eyes in your head,

nor no money in your purse? Your eyes are in a heavy

empty case,⁴ your purse in a light,° yet you see how this world 145

goes.

Gloucester

I see it feelingly. ⁵

Lear

What, art mad? A man may see how this world goes with

no eyes. Look with thine ears. See how yond justice rails

lowly upon yond simple° thief. Hark in thine ear: change places 150

and, handy-dandy,⁶ which is the justice, which is the

thief? Thou hast seen a farmer's dog bark at a ˈ

Gloucester

Ay, sir.

Lear

i.e., the beggar And the creature° run from the cur? There th

1   *beadle*

Parish officer, one of whose duties
was the whipping of petty offenders

2   *The usurer hangs the cozener.*

The moneylender punishes the
cheat (i.e., one criminal judges
another).

3   *great vices*

The vices of great men

4   *Plate sin with gold*

I.e., dress sin in golden armor. The
image demonstrates that Lear has
grasped the unfair nature of hierar-
chical society, recognizing that it is
easier to escape the consequences
of your actions if you are powerful
and wealthy.

5   *matter and impertinency*

Sense and nonsense

6   *block*

Probably here a mold to shape a
hat; perhaps Lear is referring to the
garland of weeds he has been wear-
ing as a crown.

7   *felt*

Fabric; Lear desires a surprise attack (on Albany and Corwall) and
suggests the horses have padding
added to their shoes in order to
mute the sound of their approach.

8   *in proof*

To the test

likeness / even a   behold the great image° of authority: a° dog's obeyed   155
in office.
Thou rascal beadle, ¹ hold thy bloody hand!
Why dost thou lash that whore? Strip thy own back;
way   Thou hotly lusts to use her in that kind°
For which thou whipp'st her. The usurer hangs the
cozener. ²   160
Through tattered clothes great vices ³ do appear;
Robes and furred gowns hide all. Plate sin with gold, ⁴
harmlessly   And the strong lance of justice hurtless° breaks;
Arm it in rags, a pygmy's straw does pierce it.
vouch for   None does offend, none, I say, none. I'll able° 'em.   165
i.e., protection   Take that° of me, my friend, who have the power
spectacles   To seal th' accuser's lips. Get thee glass eyes°
contemptible   And, like a scurvy° politician, seem
To see the things thou dost not. Now, now, now, now!
Pull off my boots. Harder, harder! So.   170

Edgar
[*aside*] Oh, matter and impertinency ⁵ mixed:
Reason in madness!

Lear
If thou wilt weep my fortunes, take my eyes.
I know thee well enough; thy name is Gloucester.
Thou must be patient. We came crying hither.   175
Thou know'st the first time that we smell the air
howl / Pay attention   We wawl° and cry. I will preach to thee. Mark.°

Gloucester
Alack, alack the day!

Lear
When we are born, we cry that we are come
This is   To this great stage of fools.—This'° a good block. ⁶   180
ingenious   It were a delicate° stratagem to shoe
A troop of horse with felt. ⁷ I'll put 't in proof, ⁸

1 *natural fool of fortune*

   Born to be fortune's plaything

2 *bravely*

   **Courageously (but also can mean
   "well dressed," hence *smug* later in
   the line)**

3 *jovial*

   **Both "majestic" (i.e., Jove-like) and
   "jolly"**

4 *Sa, sa, sa, sa.*

   **A hunting cry (from the French
   ça, ça!)**

And when I have stol'n upon these son-in-laws,
Then, kill, kill, kill, kill, kill, kill!

Enter a **Gentleman** *[with attendants].*

Gentleman

Oh, here he is. Lay hand upon him.—Sir,   185
Your most dear daughter—

Lear

No rescue? What, a prisoner? I am even
The natural fool of fortune.[1] Use me well;
You shall have ransom. Let me have surgeons;

wounded I am cut° to th' brains.

Gentleman

                              You shall have anything.   190

Lear

supporters No seconds?° All myself?

i.e., tears Why, this would make a man a man of salt°
To use his eyes for garden waterpots.

neat; dapper I will die bravely,[2] like a smug° bridegroom. What?
I will be jovial.[3] Come, come, I am a king.   195
Masters, know you that?

Gentleman

You are a royal one, and we obey you.

Lear

if Then there's life in't. Come; an° you get it, you shall
get it by running. Sa, sa, sa, sa.[4]

                         He exits [followed by attendants].

Gentleman

lowest A sight most pitiful in the meanest° wretch,   200
Past speaking of in a king! Thou hast a daughter

1   *twain*

     (1) Goneril and Regan; (2) Adam and
     Eve (i.e., original sin)

2   *her to*

     (1) upon Britain; (2) upon human
     nature

3   *Everyone hears that / Which can distin-*
     guish sound.

     Anyone who can hear knows of it.

4   *The main descry / Stands on the hourly*
     thought.

     I.e., the appearance (of the army) is
     expected at any time.

5   *on special cause*

     For a special reason (i.e., to aid
     Lear)

6   *worser spirit*

     Evil angel (or perhaps merely "my
     melancholy thoughts")

7   *father*

     Respectful address for an old man
     (see line 72 and note)

universal Who redeems nature from the general° curse
Which twain ¹ have brought her to. ²

Edgar

noble Hail, gentle° sir.

Gentleman

God reward   Sir, speed° you. What's your will?

Edgar

anything / impending Do you hear aught,° sir, of a battle toward?°   205

Gentleman

widely known Most sure and vulgar.° Everyone hears that
Which can distinguish sound. ³

Edgar

                          But, by your favor,
How near's the other army?

Gentleman

Near and on speedy foot. The main descry
Stands on the hourly thought. ⁴   210

Edgar

I thank you, sir; that's all.

Gentleman

Though that the Queen on special cause ⁵ is here,
Her army is moved on.

Edgar

                          I thank you, sir.

                          [**Gentleman**] *exits.*

Gloucester

You ever-gentle gods, take my breath from me;
Let not my worser spirit ⁶ tempt me again   215
To die before you please!

Edgar

                          Well pray you, father. ⁷

Gloucester

who Now, good sir, what° are you?

1   *the art of known and feeling sorrows*

    The instruction of misfortune both
    seen in others and experienced
    myself

2   *pregnant to good pity*

    Inclined to compassion

3   *The bounty and the benison of Heaven /*
    To boot, and boot!

    In addition (to my thanks) I wish
    for you the riches and blessings of
    Heaven (*to boot* = (1) in addition; (2)
    to profit)

4   *A proclaimed prize*

    A person with a bounty on his head

5   *framed flesh*

    I.e., conceived and born

6   *thyself remember*

    Pray for forgiveness

7   *friendly*

    I.e., because Gloucester is eager
    to die

8   *'Chill*

    I will; Edgar speaks in a dialect that
    suggests he is an unsophisticated
    country dweller.

Edgar

resigned A most poor man, made tame° to fortune's blows,
Who, by the art of known and feeling sorrows,[1]
Am pregnant to good pity.[2] Give me your hand.   220
dwelling I'll lead you to some biding.°

Gloucester
                                        Hearty thanks.
The bounty and the benison of Heaven
To boot, and boot![3]

                    *Enter steward [**Oswald**].*

Oswald

fortunate   A proclaimed prize![4] Most happy!°
                                [He draws his sword.]
That eyeless head of thine was first framed flesh[5]
To raise my fortunes. Thou old unhappy traitor,   225
Quickly Briefly° thyself remember.[6] The sword is out
That must destroy thee.

Gloucester
                            Now let thy friendly[7] hand
welcome Put strength enough to 't.

                                *[**Edgar** stops **Oswald**.]*

Oswald

Why   Wherefore,° bold peasant,
publicly proclaimed Dar'st thou support a published° traitor? Hence,
Lest that th' infection of his fortune take   230
A similar Like° hold on thee. Let go his arm.

Edgar

i.e., further / occasion 'Chill[8] not let go, zir, without vurther° 'casion.°

Oswald

Let go, slave, or thou diest!

Edgar

way / i.e., folk Good gentleman, go your gait° and let poor volk° pass.

1   *An 'chud ha' bin zwaggered out of my life*

If I could have been killed by swag-
gering (i.e., bragging)

2   *'twould not ha' bin zo long as 'tis by a*
vortnight

It would not have been so long
as it is by a fortnight (i.e., my life
wouldn't have lasted two weeks)

3   *'che vor ye*

I warn you

4   *wax*

I.e., the wax seal on the letter

An 'chud ha' bin zwaggered out of my life,[1] 'twould not   235
ha' bin zo long as 'tis by a vortnight.[2] Nay, come not
near th' old man; keep out, 'che vor ye,[3] or

i.e., shall / head / club   I' se° try whether your costard° or my ballow° be the
I will   harder. 'Chill° be plain with you.

Oswald

Out, dunghill!   240

Edgar

i.e., sir / i.e., for   'Chill pick your teeth, zir.° Come; no matter vor° your
sword thrusts   foins.°

[*They fight.* **Edgar** *hits him in the head.*]

Oswald

Peasant   Slave, thou hast slain me. Villain,° take my purse.
If ever thou wilt thrive, bury my body

on   And give the letters which thou find'st about° me   245
To Edmund, Earl of Gloucester. Seek him out

On / side   Upon° the English party.° Oh, untimely
Death! Death!   [*He dies.*]

Edgar

conscientious   I know thee well: a serviceable° villain,
As duteous to the vices of thy mistress   250
As badness would desire.

Gloucester

                         What, is he dead?

Edgar

Sit you down, father. Rest you.   [**Gloucester** *sits.*]
Let's see these pockets; the letters that he speaks of
May be my friends. He's dead; I am only sorry

executioner   He had no other deathsman.° Let us see.   255

[*He finds a letter and opens it.*]

With your permission   Leave,° gentle wax,[4] and, manners, blame us not.
To know our enemies' minds we rip their hearts;

i.e., To rip open their   Their° papers is more lawful.   *Reads the letter.*

1   *if your will want not*
    If you do not lack the desire

2   *supply the place for your labor*
    **Fill Albany's place as reward for
    your efforts**

3   *indistinguished space of woman's will*
    **Unimaginable scope of woman's
    lust**

4   *post unsanctified*
    Wicked messenger

5   *in the mature time*
    When the time is ripe

6   *the death-practiced Duke*
    Albany, whose murder is planned

7   *How stiff is my vile sense, / That I stand
    up and have ingenious feeling / Of my
    huge sorrows!*
    **How stubborn are my senses,
    which keep me conscious and make
    me feel this terrible grief intensely.**

8   *wrong imaginations*
    Delusions

"Let our reciprocal vows be remembered. You have
i.e., Albany   many opportunities to cut him° off; if your will want   260
not, [1] time and place will be fruitfully offered. There
accomplished is nothing done° if he return the conqueror. Then am
I the prisoner, and his bed my jail, from the loathed
warmth whereof deliver me and supply the place for
your labor. [2] Your—wife, so I would say—affectionate   265
servant, Goneril."
Oh, indistinguished space of woman's will! [3]
A plot upon her virtuous husband's life,
And the exchange my brother! Here in the sands
cover   Thee I'll rake° up, the post unsanctified [4]   270
Of murderous lechers; and in the mature time [5]
wicked   With this ungracious° paper strike the sight
Of the death-practiced Duke. [6] For him 'tis well
That of thy death and business I can tell.
                                      [He exits with the body.]

Gloucester
The King is mad. How stiff is my vile sense,   275
That I stand up and have ingenious feeling
mad   Of my huge sorrows! [7] Better I were distract; °
So should my thoughts be severed from my griefs,
And woes by wrong imaginations [8] lose
The knowledge of themselves.
                                              Drum afar off.

                   [Enter **Edgar**.*]*

Edgar
                              Give me your hand.   280
Far off, methinks, I hear the beaten drum.
lodge   Come, father, I'll bestow° you with a friend.   *They exit.*

1   *every measure fail me*

   **All attempts will be inadequate
   (when compared to your goodness)**

2   *All my reports go with the modest truth, /
   Nor mine nor clipped, but so.*

   **May everything that is said about
   me be straightforward, neither
   exaggerated nor diminished, but
   just as it happened.**

3   *Yet to be known shortens my made intent*

   **To reveal myself now would precipi-
   tously alter my own plan**

4   *My boon I make it*

   The favor I request is

5   *wind up*

   **Put in tune; tighten (as strings on
   a lute)**

6   *child-changèd*

   **(1) changed by the actions of his
   children; or (2) changed into a child**

Act 4, Scene 6

Enter **Cordelia**, **Kent** [*in disguise*], *and* **Gentleman**.

Cordelia

O thou good Kent, how shall I live and work
To match thy goodness? My life will be too short,
And every measure fail me.[1]

Kent

more than is deserved   To be acknowledged, madam, is o'erpaid.°
All my reports go with the modest truth,   5
Nor more nor clipped, but so.[2]

Cordelia

dressed   Be better suited.°
clothes / reminders   These weeds° are memories° of those worser hours;
I prithee, put them off.

Kent

                        Pardon, dear madam;
Yet to be known shortens my made intent.[3]
acknowledge   My boon I make it[4] that you know° me not   10
fit   Till time and I think meet.°

Cordelia

Then be 't so, my good lord. [*to the* **Gentleman**] How
    does the King?

Gentleman

he sleeps   Madam, sleeps° still.

Cordelia

O you kind gods,
Cure this great breach in his abusèd nature!   15
Th 'untuned and jarring senses, oh, wind up[5]
Of this child-changèd[6] father!

Gentleman

So please your Majesty

1   *I' th' sway of your own will*
    As you see fit

2   *To hovel thee with swine and rogues*
    forlorn
    To be housed with pigs and
    wretched vagrants

3   *concluded all*
    Ended altogether

That we may wake the King? He hath slept long.

Cordelia

Be governed by your knowledge and proceed 20

clothed I' th' sway of your own will.[1]—Is he arrayed?°

Enter **Lear** *in a chair carried by servants.*

Gentleman

Ay, madam. In the heaviness of sleep

We put fresh garments on him.

Be by, good madam, when we do awake him.

self-control I doubt not of his temperance.° 25

Cordelia

[*kissing him*] O my dear father! Restoration hang

Thy medicine on my lips, and let this kiss

Repair those violent harms that my two sisters

venerable condition Have in thy reverence° made!

Kent

       Kind and dear princess!

Cordelia

Even had / locks of hair Had° you not been their father, these white flakes° 30

demand Did challenge° pity of them. Was this a face

To be opposed against the jarring winds?

Mine enemy's dog,

Though he had bit me, should have stood that night

In front of / glad Against° my fire; and wast thou fain,° poor father, 35

To hovel thee with swine and rogues forlorn[2]

broken In short° and musty straw? Alack, alack!

'Tis wonder that thy life and wits at once

Had not concluded all.[3]—He wakes! Speak to him.

Gentleman

Madam, do you; 'tis fittest. 40

1   *wheel of fire*

**Damnable torment. Lear imagines
himself in Hell.** His vision of its tor-
ments could be pagan or Christian,
with the wheel referring either to
the punishment of Ixion, who was
condemned to turn forever on a
wheel for trying to seduce Zeus's
wife, Hera, or to the all too familiar
method of torture in early modern
Europe in which people were tied
and broken on the rack.

2   *pinprick*

Presumably, Lear takes something
(perhaps some piece of jewelry or a
piece of broken straw still caught in
his hair) to prick himself.

Cordelia

How does my royal lord? How fares your Majesty?

Lear

You do me wrong to take me out o' th' grave.

Heaven   Thou art a soul in bliss,° but I am bound

so that   Upon a wheel of fire, ¹ that° mine own tears

Do scald like molten lead.

Cordelia

                 Sir, do you know me?   45

Lear

You are a spirit, I know. Where did you die?

Cordelia

wide of the mark   Still, still far wide!°

Gentleman

He's scarce awake. Let him alone awhile.

Lear

Where have I been? Where am I? Fair daylight?

wronged; deceived   I am mightily abused.° I should ev'n die with pity   50

as I am   To see another thus.° I know not what to say.

I will not swear these are my hands. Let's see;

I feel this pinprick.² Would I were assured

Of my condition!

Cordelia

           [*kneeling*] Oh, look upon me, sir,

And hold your hands in benediction o'er me.   55

                [**Lear** *begins to kneel.*]

You must not kneel.

Lear

              Pray, do not mock me.

silly   I am a very foolish fond° old man,

more   Fourscore and upward,° not an hour more nor less;

And, to deal plainly,

I fear I am not in my perfect mind.   60

1   *till further settling*

Until his mind becomes more calm

i.e., Kent   Methinks I should know you and know this man,°

entirely   Yet I am doubtful; for I am mainly° ignorant

What place this is, and all the skill I have

Remembers not these garments, nor I know not

Where I did lodge last night. Do not laugh at me,   65

For, as I am a man, I think this lady

To be my child Cordelia.

Cordelia

[*weeping*] And so I am, I am.

Lear

i.e., real   Be your tears wet?° Yes, faith. I pray, weep not.

If you have poison for me I will drink it.   70

I know you do not love me, for your sisters

Have, as I do remember, done me wrong.

You have some cause; they have not.

Cordelia

No cause, no cause.

Lear

Am I in France?

Kent

             In your own kingdom, sir.   75

Lear

deceive   Do not abuse° me.

Gentleman

madness   Be comforted, good madam. The great rage,°

Ask   You see, is killed in him. Desire° him to go in.

Trouble him no more till further settling. [1]

Cordelia

Will 't please your Highness walk?   80

Lear

You must bear with me.

Pray you now, forget and forgive.

I am old and foolish.   *They exit.*

1   *Know of the Duke if his last purpose hold*

**Ask Albany if he is still committed
(to fight).**

2   *since he is advised by aught*

**Since then he has been led by
anything**

3   *He's full of alteration / And self-reproving.*

**He continually changes his mind
and finds fault with himself**

4   *constant pleasure*

Firm decision

5   *is certainly miscarried*

Has surely come to harm

6   *found my brother's way / To the forfended
place*

**Taken my brother-in-law's (i.e.,
Albany's) place in his marital bed
(*forfended* = forbidden)**

7   *I never shall endure her.*

I.e., I can't stand her anymore.

Act 5, Scene 1

Enter, with drum and colors, **Edmund**, **Regan**, *gentlemen, and soldiers.*

Edmund

Inquire [*to a gentleman*] Know° of the Duke if his last purpose
    hold,[1]
Or whether since he is advised by aught[2]
To change the course. He's full of alteration
And self-reproving.[3] Bring his constant pleasure.[4]

                          [*Gentleman exits.*]

Regan

i.e., Oswald Our sister's man° is certainly miscarried.[5]   5

Edmund

feared 'Tis to be doubted,° madam.

Regan

                       Now, sweet lord,

i.e., intend to bestow You know the goodness I intend° upon you.
Tell me, but truly—but then speak the truth—
Do you not love my sister?

Edmund

honorable   In honored° love.

Regan

But have you never found my brother's way   10
To the forfended place?[6]

Edmund

                 No, by mine honor, madam.

Regan

I never shall endure her.[7] Dear my lord,
intimate Be not familiar° with her.

Edmund

Doubt   Fear° me not.
—She and the Duke her husband!

301

1   *rigor of our state*

   Harshness of our rule

2   *cry out*

   Protest

3   *Why is this reasoned?*

   Why are we discussing this?

4   *domestic and particular broils*

   **Internal and personal problems (as
   opposed to the international crisis
   with the invasion by France)**

5   *th' ancient of war*

   Our most experienced soldiers

6   *I know the riddle*

   **I understand your meaning (i.e.,
   you want to keep me close because
   you do not trust me around
   Edmund)**

Enter, with drum and colors, **Albany,**
Goneril, *[and]* **soldiers.**

Albany

met   Our very loving sister, well bemet.°   15

[*to* **Edmund**] Sir, this I heard: the King is come to his
     daughter,

With others whom the rigor of our state[1]

Forced to cry out.[2]

Regan

                          Why is this reasoned?[3]

Goneril

i.e., We must combine   Combine° together 'gainst the enemy,

For these domestic and particular broils[4]   20

Are not the question here.

Albany

decide   Let's then determine°

With th' ancient of war[5] on our proceeding.

Regan

Sister, you'll go with us?

Goneril

No.

Regan

desirable   'Tis most convenient.° Pray, go with us.   25

Goneril

[*aside*] Oh, ho, I know the riddle.[6]—I will go.

Enter **Edgar** [*still disguised*].

Edgar

[*to* **Albany**] If e'er your Grace had speech with man so
     poor,

Hear me one word.

1   *this letter*

    **The letter found on Oswald's body,
which Edgar reads at 4.5.259–266**

2   *greet the time*

    Be prepared when the time comes

Albany

                  [*to the others*] I'll overtake you.

                            Both the armies exit.

                                  Speak.

Edgar

[*giving a letter*] Before you fight the battle, ope this letter. [1]

If you have victory, let the trumpet sound   30

For him that brought it. Wretched though I seem,

i.e., prove in combat I can produce a champion that will prove°

asserted / lose; die What is avouchèd° there. If you miscarry,°

Your business of the world hath so an end,

plotting And machination° ceases. Fortune love you.   35

Albany

Stay till I have read the letter.

Edgar

I was forbid it.

When time shall serve, let but the herald cry,

And I'll appear again.   **[Edgar]** *exits.*

Albany

read Why, fare thee well. I will o'erlook° thy paper.   40

Enter **Edmund**.

Edmund

troops The enemy's in view. Draw up your powers.°

                  [*He shows* **Albany** *a paper.*]

estimate Here is the guess° of their true strength and forces

reconnaissance By diligent discovery,° but your haste

Is now urged on you.

Albany

                We will greet the time. [2]   *He exits.*

Edmund

To both these sisters have I sworn my love,   45

1   *hardly shall I carry out my side*

    It will be difficult to fulfill my vows (to Goneril)

2   *taking off*

    Murder

3   *my state / Stands on me to defend, not to debate*

    My welfare rests on my actions not my words.

suspicious	Each jealous° of the other as the stung	
serpent	Are of the adder.° Which of them shall I take?	
	Both? One? Or neither? Neither can be enjoyed	
i.e., Regan	If both remain alive. To take the widow°	
	Exasperates, makes mad her sister Goneril,	50
	And hardly shall I carry out my side,¹	
Goneril's	Her° husband being alive. Now then, we'll use	
authority; backing	His countenance° for the battle, which being done,	
	Let her who would be rid of him devise	
	His speedy taking off.² As for the mercy	55
	Which he intends to Lear and to Cordelia,	
	The battle done and they within our power,	
They shall	Shall° never see his pardon, for my state	
	Stands on me to defend, not to debate.³ *He exits.*	

1   Alarum

     Call to battle

2   *father*

     **Edgar continues to use this word
     as a term of respect; he has not yet
     revealed himself to his father.**

3   retreat

     Trumpet call for withdrawal

4   *Ripeness is all*

     **Timing is everything (see Ecclesi-
     astes 3:1: "To all things there is an
     appointed time"). The line here is
     ambiguous, however, indicating
     either that human lives ripen (as
     opposed to *rot*, line 8) or that
     the gods control our destinies,
     determining when the time is *ripe*
     (not necessarily when we are). The
     phrase has a compelling aphoris-
     tic ring but, like much of Edgar's
     moralizing, its meaning is not clear
     enough to be taken as words of
     genuine wisdom.**

Act 5, Scene 2

*Alarum [1] within. Enter, with drum and colors, **Lear**, **Cordelia**,*
*and soldiers over the stage; and they exit. Enter **Edgar** [still*
*disguised] and **Gloucester**.*

Edgar

Here, father, [2] take the shadow of this tree

i.e., shelter For your good host. ° Pray that the right may thrive.

If ever I return to you again,

I'll bring you comfort.

Gloucester

Grace go with you, sir!

[**Edgar**] *exits.*

*Alarum and retreat [3] within. Enter **Edgar**.*

Edgar

Away, old man! Give me thy hand. Away!   5

(have been) taken King Lear hath lost, he and his daughter ta'en. °

Give me thy hand. Come on.

Gloucester

No further, sir. A man may rot even here.

Edgar

What? In ill thoughts again? Men must endure

Their going hence even as their coming hither;   10

Ripeness is all. [4] Come on.

Gloucester

And that's true too.

They exit.

1   *Good guard / Until their greater pleasures*
     first be known / That are to censure them.

     **Guard them well until we know the
     desires of those powerful persons
     (Albany, Goneril, and Regan) who
     are to pass judgment on them.**

2   *cast down*

     Defeated

3   *these daughters and these sisters*

     I.e., Goneril and Regan

4   *gilded butterflies*

     I.e., fashionable courtiers

5   *take upon 's*

     Profess to understand

6   *wear out*

     Outlive

7   *packs and sects of great ones, / That ebb*
     and flow by th' moon

     **Parties and factions at court, whose
     status constantly changes**

8   *such sacrifices*

     **I.e., their renunciation of worldly
     power (though the language antici-
     pates Cordelia's death)**

9   *throw incense*

     I.e., celebrate (the sacrifice)

Act 5, Scene 3

Enter, in conquest, with drum and colors, **Edmund**; **Lear** *and*
Cordelia, *as prisoners; soldiers,* **Captain**, *[and trumpeters].*

Edmund

Some officers take them away. Good guard
Until their greater pleasures first be known
That are to censure them. [1]

Cordelia

                       [*to* **Lear**] We are not the first

intentions   Who with best meaning° have incurred the worst.
For thee, oppressèd King, I am cast down;[2]   5
otherwise   Myself could else° outfrown false Fortune's frown.
Shall we not see these daughters and these sisters?[3]

Lear

No, no, no, no! Come; let's away to prison.
We two alone will sing like birds i' th' cage.
When thou dost ask me blessing, I'll kneel down   10
And ask of thee forgiveness. So we'll live,
And pray, and sing, and tell old tales, and laugh
At gilded butterflies,[4] and hear poor rogues
Talk of court news; and we'll talk with them too—
Who loses and who wins; who's in, who's out—   15
And take upon 's[5] the mystery of things,
As if we were God's spies; and we'll wear out,[6]
In a walled prison, packs and sects of great ones,
That ebb and flow by th' moon.[7]

Edmund

                         Take them away.

Lear

Upon such sacrifices,[8] my Cordelia,   20
The gods themselves throw incense.[9] Have I caught
    thee?   [*embracing* **Cordelia**]

1 *He that parts us shall bring a brand from*
Heaven / And fire us hence like foxes.

**I.e., only an act of the gods could
separate us now (the reference is
to firebrands being used to smoke
foxes out of their holes).**

2 *The good years shall devour them, flesh
and fell*

**Time will destroy them completely
(*fell* = skin)**

3 *Are as the time is*

I.e., change with the circumstances

4 *Does not become a sword*

Is not suitable for a soldier

5 *bear question*

Permit discussion

6 *write "happy"*

I.e., consider yourself lucky.

7 *carry it so*

Carry it out exactly

8 **Captain** exits.

**In the 1608 Quarto, the Captain
exits only after saying: "I cannot
draw a cart, nor eat dried oats; / If it
be man's work I'll do it."**

He that parts us shall bring a brand from Heaven
And fire us hence like foxes. [1] Wipe thine eyes;
The good years shall devour them, flesh and fell, [2]

Before   Ere° they shall make us weep. We'll see 'em starved first.   25

Come.   *He exits [with* **Cordelia**, *guarded*].

Edmund

Come hither, Captain. Hark.

Take thou this note. [*He gives a paper.*] Go follow them to
   prison.

promoted   One step I have advanced° thee; if thou dost

As this instructs thee, thou dost make thy way   30

To noble fortunes. Know thou this: that men

Are as the time is. [3] To be tender-minded

Does not become a sword. [4] Thy great employment

Will not bear question; [5] either say thou'lt do't

Or thrive by other means.

Captain

                I'll do 't, my lord.   35

Edmund

thou   About it, and write "happy" [6] when th'° hast done.

Attend (to this)   Mark,° I say, instantly, and carry it so [7]

As I have set it down.   **Captain** *exits.* [8]

Flourish. Enter **Albany**, **Goneril**, **Regan**, [*another*
Captain, *and*] *soldiers.*

Albany

quality; lineage   Sir, you have showed today your valiant strain,°

And fortune led you well. You have the captives   40

opponents   Who were the opposites° of this day's strife.

I do require them of you, so to use them

As we shall find their merits and our safety

May equally determine.

1   *Whose age has charms in it, whose title*
     more, / To pluck the common bosom on
     his side / And turn our impressed lances in
     our eyes / Which do command them

     **The reverence for Lear's age and
     even more for his title (as king) will
     elicit sympathy from the people
     and turn our own conscripted
     (*impressed*) soldiers against us**

2   *by your patience*

     With your permission

3   *subject of*

     Subordinate in

4   *we list to grace him*

     **I choose to think of him (i.e., as an
     equal). Regan uses the royal plural.**

5   *in your addition*

     By the titles you have granted him

6   *In my rights, / By me invested*

     **Endowed with my power and
     authority**

7   *That were the most*

     That would only be achieved

Edmund

                             Sir, I thought it fit

To send the old and miserable King   45

confinement   To some retention° and appointed guard,

i.e., Lear's   Whose° age had charms in it, whose title more,

on to   To pluck the common bosom on° his side

And turn our impressed lances in our eyes

i.e., Cordelia   Which do command them.[1] With him I sent the Queen,°   50

My reason all the same. And they are ready

time   Tomorrow or at further space° t' appear

judicial hearing   Where you shall hold your session.°

Albany

                         Sir, by your patience,[2]

consider   I hold° you but a subject of[3] this war,

equal   Not as a brother.°

Regan

                    That's as we list to grace him.[4]   55

wishes / sought after   Methinks our pleasure° might have been demanded°

troops   Ere you had spoke so far. He led our powers,°

rank   Bore the commission of my place° and person,

relation to me   The which immediacy° may well stand up

And call itself your brother.

Goneril

fast   Not so hot!°   60

merit   In his own grace° he doth exalt himself

More than in your addition.[5]

Regan

                          In my rights,

equals   By me invested,[6] he compeers° the best.

Albany

That were the most[7] if he should husband you.

1   *The eye that told you so looked but*
    asquint.

    I.e., your judgment is flawed (*as-
    quint* = awry). "Love, being jealous,
    makes a good eye look asquint"
    was proverbial.

2   *full-flowing stomach*

    I.e., heart filled with anger

3   *the walls is thine*

    I.e., I am yours; Regan gives herself
    to Edmund in terms of a castle sur-
    rendering to an attack or seige.

4   *strike*

    Either to issue a challenge to Albany
    or to announce the betrothal. In
    Q the line is spoken by Edmund,
    which clearly makes it a challenge.

5   *and, in thy arrest / This gilded serpent*

    And, in the charge against you, I
    also arrest Goneril

Regan

prove to be Jesters do oft prove ° prophets.

Goneril

i.e., Stop   Holla, ° holla!   65

That eye that told you so looked but asquint.[1]

Regan

Lady, I am not well, else I should answer

From a full-flowing stomach.[2] [*to* **Edmund**] General,

inheritance Take thou my soldiers, prisoners, patrimony; °

Dispose of them, of me; the walls is thine.[3]   70

Let witness Witness ° the world that I create thee here

My lord and master.

Goneril

                    Mean you to enjoy him?

Albany

power to stop it The let-alone ° lies not in your good will.

Edmund

Nor in thine, lord.

Albany

Bastard   Half-blooded ° fellow, yes.

Regan

[*to* **Edmund**] Let the drum strike [4] and prove my title

        thine.   75

Albany

Stay yet; hear reason. Edmund, I arrest thee

On capital treason, and, in thy arrest,

(on Edmund) This gilded serpent.[5] [*pointing to* **Goneril**] For your claim, °

sister-in-law   fair sister, °

I bar it in the interest of my wife;

betrothed 'Tis she is subcontracted ° to this lord,   80

1   *banns*

Proclamation of intent to marry

2   *make your loves to me*

If Goneril and Edmund are
betrothed then only Albany is available to marry.

3   *prove upon thy person*

I.e., confirm by a trial of combat

4   *in nothing less*

In no regard less guilty

5   *exchange*

I.e., my glove for yours as a sign of a
willingness to meet in combat

6   *single virtue*

Unassisted strength

oppose   And I, her husband, contradict° your banns.[1]

           If you will marry, make your loves to me;[2]

spoken for   My lady is bespoke.°

Goneril

farce   An interlude!°

Albany

           Thou art armed, Gloucester. Let the trumpet sound.

           If none appear to prove upon thy person[3]   85

           Thy heinous, manifest, and many treasons,

prove   There is my pledge. [*He throws down a glove.*] I'll make° it

                on thy heart,

           Ere I taste bread, thou art in nothing less[4]

           Than I have here proclaimed thee.

Regan

                                        Sick, oh, sick!

Goneril

i.e., poison   [*aside*] If not, I'll ne'er trust med'cine.°   90

Edmund

Whoever   [*throwing down a glove*] There's my exchange.[5] What° in

                the world he is

           That names me traitor, villain-like he lies.

Summon   Call° by the trumpet. He that dares approach,

           On him, on you—who not?—I will maintain

           My truth and honor firmly.

Albany

                              A herald, ho!   95

                    Enter a **Herald**.

Albany

           [*to* **Edmund**] Trust to thy single virtue,[6] for thy soldiers,

           All levied in my name, have in my name

           Took their discharge.

1   *manifold*

    Many times over (or "in various ways")

2   armed

    In full armor

Regan

My sickness grows upon me.

Albany

[*to soldiers*] She is not well. Convey her to my tent.

[**Regan** *exits, with soldiers.*]

Come hither, herald. Let the trumpet sound, 100

And read out this. [*He gives a paper.*] *A trumpet sounds.*

Herald

birth / rank (*reads*) "If any man of quality° or degree° within the

roster lists° of the army will maintain upon Edmund, sup-

posèd Earl of Gloucester, that he is a manifold¹ traitor,

i.e., Edmund let him appear by the third sound of the trumpet. He° 105

is bold in his defense." *First trumpet.*

Again! *Second trumpet.*

Again! *Third trumpet.*

Trumpet answers within.

Enter **Edgar**, *armed.*²

Albany

Ask him his purposes, why he appears

Upon this call o' th' trumpet.

Herald

Who What° are you? 110

Your name, your quality, and why you answer

This present summons?

Edgar

Know my name is lost,

worm-eaten By treason's tooth bare-gnawn and canker-bit.°

Yet am I noble as the adversary

fight with I come to cope.°

1 *mine honors, / My oath, and my*
   profession

   My reputation, the oath I took
   when I became a knight, and my
   knighthood itself

2 *victor sword and fire-new fortune*

   Victorious sword and brand-new
   position

3 *that thy tongue some 'say of breeding*
   breathes

   Since your speech gives some
   signs of noble birth ('*say* = assay,
   or proof)

4 *What safe and nicely I might well delay /*
   By rule of knighthood, I disdain and spurn

   I reject the rules of knighthood, by
   which I could legitimately refuse
   to fight one of lower rank (or one
   whose name I do not know)

5 *Back do I toss these treasons to thy head*

   Your accusations of treason I turn
   against you.

6 *the hell-hated lie*

   The lie that I hate as much as I hate
   Hell

Albany

                              Which is that adversary?   115

Edgar

What's he that speaks for Edmund, Earl of Gloucester?

Edmund

Himself. What say'st thou to him?

Edgar

                                          Draw thy sword,

That, if my speech offend a noble heart,

Thy arm may do thee justice. Here is mine.

                              [*He draws his sword.*]

i.e., my challenge Behold, it° is the privilege of mine honors,   120

My oath, and my profession.[1] I protest,

In spite of Maugre° thy strength, place, youth, and eminence,

Despite thy victor sword and fire-new fortune,[2]

courage Thy valor, and thy heart,° thou art a traitor—

False to thy gods, thy brother, and thy father,   125

Conspirator Conspirant° 'gainst this high-illustrious Prince,

top And, from th' extremest upward° of thy head

lowest part (i.e., the sole) To the descent° and dust below thy foot,

venomous A most toad-spotted° traitor. Say thou "no,"

set; determined This sword, this arm, and my best spirits are bent°   130

To prove upon thy heart, whereto I speak,

Thou liest.

Edmund

prudence In wisdom° I should ask thy name.

But since thy outside looks so fair and warlike,

And that thy tongue some 'say of breeding breathes,[3]

What safe and nicely I might well delay   135

By rule of knighthood, I disdain and spurn.[4]

Back do I toss these treasons to thy head,[5]

With the hell-hated lie[6] o'erwhelm thy heart,

i.e., those treasons Which°—for they yet glance by and scarcely bruise—

1   *for they yet glance by and scarcely*
    bruise— / This sword of mine shall give
    them instant way, / Where they shall rest
    forever

    Since the mere accusations of trea-
    son do not harm you, I will use my
    sword to give them direct access (to
    your heart) where they shall stick;
    i.e., Edmund claims he will win the
    trial by combat and prove that the
    charges of treason against Edgar
    are valid.

2   *Hold*

    The word could be addressed to Ed-
    gar, asking him to stop his attack,
    or, more likely, the fallen Edmund
    is asked to take the incriminating
    letter.

This sword of mine shall give them instant way, 140
Where they shall rest forever. [1]—Trumpets, speak!
[*He draws.*] *Alarums. Fights* [*and* **Edmund** *falls*].

Albany

Spare   [*to* **Edgar**] Save° him; save him!

Goneril

trickery / i.e., Edmund   This is practice,° Gloucester.°
By th' law of war thou wast not bound to answer
opponent   An unknown opposite.° Thou art not vanquished
cheated / deceived   But cozened° and beguiled.°

Albany

                                                   Shut your mouth, dame, 145
close   Or with this paper shall I stop° it.—Hold, [2] sir.
Thou worse than any name, read thine own evil.
                                                   [*He shows the letter.*]
[*to* **Goneril**] No tearing, lady; I perceive you know it.

Goneril

Say if I do, the laws are mine, not thine.
Who can arraign me for 't?   *She exits.*

Albany

                                                   Most monstrous! Oh! 150
Know'st thou this paper?

Edmund

                                   Ask me not what I know.

Albany

restrain   Go after her. She's desperate; govern° her.
                                                   [*A soldier exits.*]

Edmund

What you have charged me with, that have I done,
And more, much more. The time will bring it out.
'Tis past, and so am I. But what art thou 155
victory   That hast this fortune° on me? If thou 'rt noble,
I do forgive thee.

1   *The wheel is come full circle*

    (1) I have been appropriately pun-
    ished for my crimes; (2) fortune's
    wheel has turned a full circle (see
    2.2.166–167 and note).

2   *I am here*

    I am back where I started.

3   *That followed me so near*

    I.e., that almost resulted in my
    capture

4   *That we the pain of death would hourly
    die / Rather than die at once*

    That we would rather be alive
    and continue to suffer, than die
    instantly (and end the suffering)

Edgar

forgiveness   Let's exchange charity.°

nobility   I am no less in blood° than thou art, Edmund;

thou   If more, the more th'° hast wronged me.

             My name is Edgar, and thy father's son.   160

pleasurable   The gods are just, and of our pleasant° vices

             Make instruments to plague us.

begot   The dark and vicious place where thee he got°

             Cost him his eyes.

Edmund

                                   Th' hast spoken right. 'Tis true.

             The wheel is come full circle;¹ I am here.²   165

Albany

bearing   [*to* **Edgar**] Methought thy very gait° did prophesy

regal   A royal° nobleness. I must embrace thee.

             Let sorrow split my heart if ever I

             Did hate thee or thy father!   [*They embrace.*]

Edgar

                                          Worthy prince,

             I know 't.   170

Albany

             Where have you hid yourself?

             How have you known the miseries of your father?

Edgar

Listen to   By nursing them, my lord. List° a brief tale,

             And when 'tis told, oh, that my heart would burst!

deadly; fatal The bloody° proclamation to escape   175

             That followed me so near³—oh, our lives' sweetness,

             That we the pain of death would hourly die

             Rather than die at once!⁴—taught me to shift

             Into a madman's rags, t' assume a semblance

clothing   That very dogs disdained; and in this habit°   180

eye sockets   Met I my father with his bleeding rings,°
i.e., eyes   Their precious stones° new lost; became his guide,
                 Led him, begged for him, saved him from despair;
                 Never—oh, fault!—revealed myself unto him
ago   Until some half hour past,° when I was armed.   185
outcome   Not sure, though hoping, of this good success,°
                 I asked his blessing, and from first to last
damaged   Told him our pilgrimage. But his flawed° heart—
                 Alack, too weak the conflict to support—
                 Twixt two extremes of passion, joy and grief,   190
                 Burst smilingly.

Edmund

                                        This speech of yours hath moved me
                 And shall perchance do good. But speak you on;
                 You look as you had something more to say.

Albany

                 If there be more, more woeful, hold it in,
melt (in tears) For I am almost ready to dissolve,°   195
                 Hearing of this.

Enter a **Gentleman** [*with a knife*].

Gentleman
Help, help, oh, help!
Edgar

                                        What kind of help?

Albany

                                                    Speak, man.

Edgar
What means this bloody knife?
Gentleman

steams   'Tis hot; it smokes.°
It came even from the heart of—Oh, she's dead!

1 *very manners urges*

Common decency demands

Albany

Who dead? Speak, man.   *200*

Gentleman

Your lady, sir, your lady! And her sister

By her is poisoned; she confesses it.

Edmund

I was contracted to them both. All three

Now marry in an instant.

Edgar

                              Here comes Kent.

Enter **Kent**.

Albany

Produce the bodies, be they alive or dead.   *205*

                              [**Gentleman** *exits*.]

This judgment of the heavens, that makes us tremble,

Touches us not with pity.—Oh, is this he?

politeness [*to* **Kent**] The time will not allow the compliment°

Which very manners urges.[1]

Kent

                              I am come

forever To bid my King and master aye° good night.   *210*

Is he not here?

Albany

                  Great thing of us forgot!

Speak, Edmund, where's the King? And where's

    Cordelia?

                        Goneril *and* **Regan**'s *bodies* [*are*] *brought out*.

i.e., spectacle See'st thou this object,° Kent?

Kent

                              Alack, why thus?

1   *my writ*

My written orders of execution

2   *thy token of reprieve*

Some indication that the reprieve
comes with your authority

Edmund

Yet Edmund was beloved.

The one the other poisoned for my sake   215

And after slew herself.

Albany

                              Even so.—Cover their faces.

Edmund

I pant for life. Some good I mean to do,

Despite of mine own nature. Quickly send—

Be brief in it—to th' castle, for my writ[1]

Is on the life of Lear and on Cordelia.   220

Nay, send in time!

Albany

                              Run, run, oh, run!

Edgar

commission   To who, my lord? Who has the office?°

[*to* **Edmund**] Send thy token of reprieve.[2]

Edmund

Well thought on. Take my sword.

Give it the Captain.

Albany

                              Haste thee, for thy life.   225

                    [*Gentleman exits with* **Edmund**'s *sword.*]

Edmund

He hath commission from thy wife and me

To hang Cordelia in the prison and

To lay the blame upon her own despair,

killed   That she fordid° herself.

Albany

The gods defend her! Bear him hence awhile.   230

                              [**Edmund** *is carried out.*]

1   *men of stones*

I.e., statues (and thus unfeeling)

2   *dead as earth*

Lear had hoped that he and Cordelia could be permitted to live together as *birds in a cage* (5.3.9), insignificant creatures beneath notice, but even this hope is frustrated. Cordelia is now united with nature in its most basic form, as she is as *dead as earth*, though Lear continues to hope she might be alive, as he asks for *a looking glass* to see if she breathes and momentarily persuades himself *She lives* (line 239), before the crushing recognition at lines 280–283.

3   *stone*

Mirror; polished or semitransparent stone used as a mirror

4   *promised end*

I.e., Doomsday

5   *Fall and cease.*

Possibly Albany asks for all things to come to an end, but more likely he calls for the gods to allow Lear to *fall and cease* being (to put him out of his misery).

Enter **Lear**, *with* **Cordelia** *in his arms* [*followed
by a* **Gentleman**].

Lear

Howl, howl, howl! Oh, you are men of stones! [1]
Had I your tongues and eyes, I'd use them so
That Heaven's vault should crack. She's gone forever.
I know when one is dead and when one lives;
She's dead as earth. [2] Lend me a looking glass;   235
If that her breath will mist or stain the stone, [3]
Why, then she lives.   [*He lays her down.*]

Kent

                              Is this the promised end? [4]

Edgar

mere likeness Or image° of that horror?

Albany

                              Fall and cease. [5]

Lear

This feather stirs; she lives! If it be so,
It is a chance which does redeem all sorrows   240
That ever I have felt.

Kent

                              [*kneeling*] O my good master!

Lear

Prithee, away.

Edgar

                              'Tis noble Kent, your friend.

Lear

A plague upon you murderers, traitors all!
I might have saved her; now she's gone forever!
Cordelia, Cordelia! Stay a little. Ha?   245
What is 't thou say'st? Her voice was ever soft,

1   *crosses spoil me*

     **Troubles (of old age) weaken me (as
     a swordsman)**

2   *tell you straight*

     Recognize you in a moment

3   *If Fortune brag of two she loved and
     hated, / One of them we behold.*

     **If Fortune had one person she most
     loved and another she most hated,
     then Lear is the hated one.**

4   *This' a dull sight.*

     **Either (1) this is a dismal scene; or (2)
     my sight is failing**

5   *Caius*

     **Apparently Kent's name when
     disguised; the only time the name
     is mentioned in the play, as Kent
     hopes Lear will recognize his
     loyalty.**

6   *That from your first of difference and
     decay*

     **Who from the beginning of your
     transformation and the decline of
     your fortune**

7   *Nor no man else.*

     **(1) I am he (Caius) and no one else;
     or (2) no one more deserves your
     welcome than I do.**

Gentle, and low, an excellent thing in woman.
I killed the slave that was a-hanging thee.

Gentleman

'Tis true, my lords, he did.

Lear

                      Did I not, fellow?

sword   I have seen the day, with my good biting falchion°   *250*
I would have made him skip. I am old now,
And these same crosses spoil me. [1]—Who are you?
Mine eyes are not o' th' best; I'll tell you straight. [2]

Kent

If Fortune brag of two she loved and hated,
One of them we behold. [3]   *255*

Lear

This' a dull sight. [4] Are you not Kent?

Kent

                          The same,
Your servant Kent. Where is your servant Caius? [5]

Lear

He's a good fellow, I can tell you that;
He'll strike, and quickly too. He's dead and rotten.

Kent

No, my good lord. I am the very man—   *260*

Lear

attend to / straightaway   I'll see° that straight.°

Kent

That from your first of difference and decay [6]
Have followed your sad steps.—

Lear

                        You are welcome hither.

Kent

Nor no man else. [7] All's cheerless, dark, and deadly.

1   *What comfort to this great decay may*
    come / Shall be applied

    Whatever opportunity we have to
    comfort Lear we will take

2   *boot and such addition*

    Additional honors and whatever
    titles

3   *poor fool*

    I.e., Cordelia (*fool* is intended here
    as a term of endearment, but it
    inevitably recalls the Fool who had
    accompanied Lear through 3.6, and
    has been taken by some to suggest
    that Cordelia and the Fool were
    played by one actor, but see note 6
    on p. 96.

killed   Your eldest daughters have fordone° themselves,   265
in despair   And desperately° are dead.

Lear

                  Ay, so I think.

Albany

He knows not what he says, and vain is it

ourselves   That we present us° to him.

Edgar

useless   Very bootless.°

Enter a **Messenger***.*

Messenger

Edmund is dead, my lord.

Albany

That's but a trifle here.   270

You lords and noble friends, know our intent:

What comfort to this great decay may come

As for   Shall be applied.[1] For° us, we will resign,

During the life of this old Majesty,

To him our absolute power; [*to* **Edgar** *and* **Kent**] you, to

        your rights,   275

honorable deeds   With boot and such addition[2] as your honors°

Have more than merited. All friends shall taste

The wages of their virtue, and all foes

The cup of their deservings.—Oh, see, see!

Lear

And my poor fool[3] is hanged! No, no, no life?   280

Why should a dog, a horse, a rat have life,

And thou no breath at all? Thou'lt come no more,

Never, never, never, never, never!

Pray you, undo this button. Thank you, sir.

1   **Kent**

In the Quarto this line is assigned
to Lear.

2   *rack*

Instrument of torture (where one's
limbs are stretched and broken)

3   *He but usurped his life.*

I.e., he clung to life, but the life he
led in recent months was hardly the
one for which he was born.

4   **Edgar**

In the Quarto, this final speech is
spoken by Albany. Even the differences in speech prefixes for this
speech and line 287 suggest how
significantly the Folio text of *King
Lear* differs from that of the 1608
Quarto.

Do you see this? Look on her; look, her lips.   285
Look there; look there!   *He dies.*

Edgar

He faints.—My lord, my lord!

Kent [1]

Break, heart. I prithee, break!

Edgar

Look up, my lord.

Kent

soul; spirit   Vex not his ghost.° Oh, let him pass! He hates him
That would upon the rack[2] of this tough world
Stretch him out longer.

Edgar

He is gone indeed.   290

Kent

The wonder is he hath endured so long.
He but usurped his life.[3]

Albany

Bear them from hence. Our present business
Is general woe. [*to* **Kent** *and* **Edgar**] Friends of my
    soul, you twain

wounded   Rule in this realm and the gored° state sustain.   295

Kent

(to death)   I have a journey,° sir, shortly to go.
My master calls me; I must not say no.

Edgar [4]

accept   The weight of this sad time we must obey;°
Speak what we feel, not what we ought to say.

i.e., Lear   The oldest° hath borne most; we that are young   300
Shall never see so much nor live so long.

They exit, with a dead march.

1   *the tameness of a wolf, a horse's*
health, a boy's love, or a whore's oath
**All four things were commonly
said not to be trustworthy.**

2   *I will arraign them straight*
**Lear imagines a trial for Goneril
and Regan. (*Straight* = "straightaway")**

3   *he*
**Probably referring to one of
Edgar's imagined fiends, or pos-
sibly Lear himself**

4   *Want'st thou eyes*
**Directed at the imagined Goneril
and Regan; either (1) do you lack
onlookers; or (2) can't you see
who's looking at you**

5   *"Come o'er the burn, Bessy, to me—"*
**Fragment from a popular ballad.
(A *burn* is a brook.)**

6   *Her boat hath a leak, / And she must
not speak / Why she dares not come
over to thee.*
**The Fool's extension of the song
has no known source.**

7   *nightingale*
**Edgar pretends to mistake the
Fool's singing for the singing of
the devil.**

8   *Hoppedance*
**A version of *Hobberdidance*,
another devil from Harsnett (see
3.4.109 and note)**

9   *their evidence*
The evidence against them

10   *robèd man*
**Probably an ironic reference to
the blanket that Edgar wears as
part of his disguise (see 2.3. 10)**

11   *yokefellow of equity*
Judicial partner

Appendix:
King Lear Quarto-only Readings

In the Quarto (1608), the following appears after 3.6.16:

Edgar

The foul fiend bites my back.

Fool

He's mad that trusts in the tameness of a wolf, a
horse's health, a boy's love, or a whore's oath.[1]

Lear

It shall be done; I will arraign them straight.[2]   20

judge   [*to* **Edgar**] Come, sit thou here, most learnèd justicer.°

wise   [*to* **Fool**] Thou, sapient° sir, sit here. —No, you she-
       foxes!

Edgar

Look where he[3] stands and glares!—Want'st thou
eyes[4] at trial, madam?

     [*sings*] "Come o'er the burn, Bessy, to me—"[5]   25

Fool

     [*sings*] Her boat hath a leak,
     And she must not speak
     Why she dares not come over to thee.[6]

Edgar

The foul fiend haunts Poor Tom in the voice of a night-

i.e., unsmoked   ingale.[7] Hoppedance[8] cries in Tom's belly for two white°   30

rumble (with hunger)   herring. Croak° not, black angel; I have no food for thee.

Kent

bewildered   [*to* **Lear**] How do you, sir? Stand you not so amazed.°
Will you lie down and rest upon the cushions?

Lear

I'll see their trial first. Bring in their evidence.[9]

     [*to* **Edgar**] Thou robèd man[10] of justice, take thy place;   35
     [*to* **Fool**] And thou, his yokefellow of equity,[11]

1   *o' th' commission*

     I.e., one of the judges

2   *I took you for a joint stool*

     **I.e., I'm sorry I didn't notice you (a
     proverbial insult). Apparently the
     Fool in line 48 directs his remarks
     to a stool that is on stage, and
     Lear in his madness follows
     along. (A *joint stool* is a well-made
     stool with fitted legs and struts.)**

Sit	Bench° by his side. [*to* **Kent**] You are o' th' commission;¹
	Sit you too. [*They sit.*]

Edgar

Let us deal justly.

	[*sings*] Sleepest or wakest thou, jolly shepherd?	40
grain	Thy sheep be in the corn,°	
dainty	And for one blast of thy minikin° mouth	
	Thy sheep shall take no harm.	

Purr the cat is gray.

Lear

	Arraign her first; 'tis Goneril—I here take my oath	45
who kicked	before this honorable assembly—kicked° the poor	
	King her father.	

Fool

Come hither, mistress. Is your name Goneril?

Lear

She cannot deny it.

Fool

Cry you mercy, I took you for a joint stool.²	50

Lear

i.e., Regan / perverse	And here's another,° whose warped° looks proclaim
material / of	What store° her heart is made on.° Stop her there!
	Arms, arms! Sword, fire! Corruption in the place!
	False justicer, why hast thou let her scape?

1   *our woes*

     Our same affliction

2   *We scarcely think our misery our foes*

     **We find our own suffering easier
     to bear.**

3   *Who alone suffers*

     He who suffers in solitude

4   *He childed as I fathered*

     **I.e., his children cause him as
     much pain as my father does me.**

5   *Mark the high noises, and thyself
     bewray / When false opinion, whose
     wrong thoughts defile thee, / In thy just
     proof repeals and reconciles thee.*

     **Listen to the rumors about
     powerful people, and don't
     reveal yourself until evidence
     has cleared your name and
     reconciled you with your father.**

6   *safe 'scape the King!*

     May the King safely escape!

In the Quarto, the following appears after 3.6.56:

Edgar

When we our betters see bearing our woes,[1]

We scarcely think our miseries our foes.[2]

Who alone suffers[3] suffers most i' th' mind,

Leaving free things and happy shows behind;   60

But then the mind much sufferance doth o'erskip

When grief hath mates, and bearing fellowship.

bearable How light and portable° my pain seems now,

When that which makes me bend makes the King

    bow—

He childed as I fathered.[4] Tom, away!   65

Mark the high noises, and thyself bewray

When false opinion, whose wrong thoughts defile

    thee,

In thy just proof repeals and reconciles thee.[5]

Whatever What° will hap more tonight, safe 'scape the King![6]

Hide Lurk,° lurk.   [*He exits.*]   70

1   *Allows itself to anything*

     **Will let him get away with
     anything**

2   *flax and whites of eggs*

     **A common treatment for eye
     injuries**

In the Quarto, the following appears after 3.7.98:

Second Servant
I'll never care what wickedness I do
If this man come to good.
Third Servant
                                        If she live long,   100
natural   And in the end meet the old° course of death,
Women will all turn monsters.
Second Servant
i.e., Edgar in disguise   Let's follow the old Earl, and get the Bedlam°
To lead him where he would. His roguish madness
Allows itself to anything. [1]   105
Third Servant
Go thou. I'll fetch some flax and whites of eggs [2]
To apply to his bleeding face. Now, Heaven help him!
                        They exit [with the body].

1   *imports*

   Carries as a consequence

2   *Who should express her goodliest*

   **To see which would make her the
   more beautiful**

*In the Quarto, the following scene, completely absent from the
Folio, appears following 4.2.*

Kent

Why the King of France is so suddenly gone back know
you no reason?

Gentleman

unfinished   Something he left imperfect° in the state, which since
his coming forth is thought of, which imports¹ to the
kingdom so much fear and danger that his personal   5
return was most required and necessary.

Kent

as his general   Who hath he left behind him general?°

Gentleman

The Marshal of France, Monsieur la Far.

Kent

move   Did your letters pierce° the Queen to any demonstra-
tion of grief?   10

Gentleman

Ay, sir. She took them, read them in my presence,
trickled   And now and then an ample tear trilled° down
Her delicate cheek. It seemed she was a queen
which   Over her passion, who,° most rebel-like,
Sought to be king o'er her.

Kent

                                     Oh, then it moved her?   15

Gentleman

Not to a rage. Patience and sorrow strove
Who should express her goodliest.² You have seen
Sunshine and rain at once. Her smiles and tears

1   *like a better way*

I.e., better than *sunshine and rain*

2   *those happy smilets / That played on*
her ripe lip seemed not to know / What
guests were in her eyes

Those happy little smiles that
played on her red lips seemed
ignorant of the tears in her eyes.

3   *a rarity most beloved*

A most precious emotion

4   *If all could so become it*

If everyone could bear it so
gracefully

5   *Let pity not be believed*

Do not trust in pity (since Goneril
and Regan seem to have none)

6   *clamor-moistened*

Her state of grief thus dampened
with tears (the 1608 Quarto prints
"clamour moystened her")

7   *Else one self mate and make could not*
beget / Such different issues

Otherwise the same parents
could not produce such different
children.

8   *before the King returned*

Before the King of France
returned home

Were like a better way; [1] those happy smilets
That played on her ripe lip seemed not to know   20
(i.e., the tears) What guests were in her eyes, [2] which° parted thence
As pearls from diamonds dropped. In brief,
Sorrow would be a rarity most beloved [3]
If all could so become it. [4]

Kent

Made she no verbal question?   25

Gentleman

sighed Faith, once or twice she heaved° the name of "father"
Pantingly forth, as if it pressed her heart;
Cried, "Sisters, sisters! Shame of ladies, sisters!
Kent! Father! Sisters! What, i' th' storm, i' th' night?
Let pity not be believed!" [5] There she shook   30
The holy water from her heavenly eyes,
went And, clamor-moistened, [6] then away she started,°
To deal with grief alone.

Kent

It is the stars,
dispositions The stars above us, govern our conditions,°
Else one self mate and make could not beget   35
Such different issues. [7] You spoke not with her since?

Gentleman

No.

Kent

Was this before the King returned? [8]

Gentleman

No, since.

Kent

Well, sir, the poor distressèd Lear's i' th' town,
state of mind Who sometime in his better tune° remembers   40
What we are come about, and by no means
consent Will yield° to see his daughter.

1   *elbows him*

I.e., jogs his memory

2   *turned her / To foreign casualties*

**Drove her to take her chances
living abroad**

3   *Detains him from*

Keeps him from seeing

Gentleman

Why, good sir?

Kent

overwhelming A sovereign° shame so elbows him.[1] His own unkindness

blessing That stripped her from his benediction,° turned her

To foreign casualties,[2] gave her dear rights 45

To his dog-hearted daughters—these things sting

His mind so venomously that burning shame

Detains him from[3] Cordelia.

Gentleman

Alack, poor gentleman!

Kent

armies Of Albany's and Cornwall's powers° you heard not? 50

Gentleman

on the march 'Tis so. They are afoot.°

Kent

Well, sir, I'll bring you to our master Lear

important And leave you to attend him. Some dear° cause

Will in concealment wrap me up awhile.

by my true identity / regret When I am known aright,° you shall not grieve° 55

Lending me this acquaintance. I pray you, go

Along with me. *They exit.*

Longer Notes

PAGE 45

1.1.2 *Albany than Cornwall*

Brutus, the legendary first king of Britain, gave all land north of the Humber to his son, Albanact, and thus the northern lands of Britain were known as Albany. Cornwall was often used as a term for the west of Britain, which would include Wales. Cordelia's proposed *third more opulent* (1.1.85) is therefore the main part of England. Lear's division of the kingdoms is in effect a division of Britain into England, Scotland, and Wales, exactly the opposite plan of King James, who made every effort to unite the kingdoms under his rule, once he became King of England in 1603. The topical nature of the play is even clearer if we bear in mind that James's two sons, Henry and Charles, were the Dukes of Cornwall and Albany when the play was first performed.

PAGE 45

1.1.8 *breeding*

The word has two distinct and nearly opposite meanings: (1) upbringing; (2) parentage. One points to nurture, the other to nature. The play wonders about what makes people as they are. "Is there any cause in nature that makes these hard hearts," Lear asks (3.6.36–37), thinking about the cruelty of Regan. But the play offers no certain answer to the mystery of evil, although it seeks its source more in terms of human psychology than abstract morality (or astrological determinism).

PAGE 49

1.1.51—52   *That we our largest bounty may extend / Where nature doth with merit challenge*

In England, normally the monarch's eldest son or daughter would succeed to the throne on the death of the ruling parent. According to this system, Goneril should be made sole queen, but here, Lear wants to award the largest share of his kingdom to his youngest daughter because she *deserves* it most, though the terms of this deserving, "Which of you shall we say doth love us most" (1.1.50) are hardly politically responsible. Nonetheless, the difference in practice would have drawn the attention of Shakespeare's audience to the strangeness of the pre-Christian Britain in which the play is set. It would also have called to mind the arguments made in the late 1590s, when it was unclear who would succeed Elizabeth, who had no obvious heir. James had the strongest claim to the throne through his birth, but many wanted to exclude him because he was the son of an executed traitor, Mary Stuart, Queen of Scots (1542–1587), as well as a foreigner. This situation led to arguments about whether a monarch had to be a suitable ruler or whether the bloodline was the only issue.

PAGE 197

3.2.79—80   *I'll speak a prophecy ere I go*

This prophecy (lines 81-94) exists only in the Folio text and does not appear in the 1608 Quarto. Some commentators think that the speech is not authentically Shakespearean; others defend its place in the play as an important revision. The first half of the speech describes the sort of moral degeneracy and social confusion that is evident in Britain in the play: priests urging behavior they do not themselves demonstrate; brewers diluting their beer to make higher profits; nobles paying too much attention to fashion; and lovers burned by venereal disease. The second part depicts an ideal state that will never happen: legal cases being resolved fairly; no one in debt; sexually immoral people unable to excuse their sins by giving money to the church. When this happy state comes about, says the Fool in his characteristic idiom, everyone will be so confused that they will actually act appropriately, i.e., walk on their feet. The Fool's prophecy reminds the audience of how much the world of the play has perverted social and moral norms even as it acts as a parody of prophecies of Britain's future that circulated in Shakespeare's lifetime.

PAGE 209

3.4.104   *unbutton here*

There is no stage direction in the Folio or Quarto, but a long tradition has Lear being restrained by Gloucester and the Fool from exposing himself to the elements. Lear had started off trying to retain the trappings of power and status with his demand for a hundred knights, but now he is prepared to become a *poor, bare, forked animal* (line 103). Whatever his action, the lines raise the question of what man is in a state of nature; that is, what human nature essentially is, away from the restraints of civilization. In seeking to take off his clothing, Lear may be lowering himself to the status of a beast, or he may

be getting rid of what is superfluous and at last discovering what it truly means to be human.

PAGE 275

4.5.86   *Nature's above art in that respect.*

If Lear is responding to Edgar, the line means that life provides more heart-rending examples of suffering than ever art did. If he is continuing his own thought that he is *the King himself*, it means that the King cannot lose his natural rights and be subject to censure. This was a contentious political issue. For some political commentators, notably King James himself, the monarch was always above the law. For others, the monarch was subject to the law just as everyone else was. What was at stake was the very nature of monarchy. If, however, it is the first meaning that is intended, the line encourages the audience to think about the relationship between the play as art and the world beyond it. Is the real world actually more pleasant than this exceptionally bleak play, or does it tell us the truth that others are too afraid to face?

THE TRAGEDIE OF KING LEAR.

Actus Primus. Scœna Prima.

Enter Kent, Gloucester, and Edmond.

Kent.

I Thought the King had more affected the Duke of *Albany*, then *Cornwall*.

Glou. It did alwayes seeme so to vs : But now in the diuision of the Kingdome, it appeares not which of the Dukes hee valewes most, for qualities are so weigh'd, that curiosity in neither, can make choise of eithers moity.

Kent. Is not this your Son, my Lord?

Glou. His breeding Sir, hath bin at my charge. I haue so often blush'd to acknowledge him, that now I am braz'd too't.

Kent. I cannot conceiue you.

Glou. Sir, this yong Fellowes mother could; whereupon she grew round womb'd, and had indeede (Sir) a Sonne for her Cradle, ere she had a husband for her bed. Do you smell a fault?

Kent. I cannot wish the fault vndone, the issue of it, being so proper.

Glou. But I haue a Sonne, Sir, by order of Law, some yeere elder then this ; who, yet is no deerer in my account, though this Knaue came somthing sawcily to the world before he was sent for : yet was his Mother fayre, there was good sport at his making, and the horson must be acknowledged. Doe you know this Noble Gentleman, *Edmond*?

Edm. No, my Lord.

Glou. My Lord of Kent :

Remember him heereafter, as my Honourable Friend.

Edm. My seruices to your Lordship.

Kent. I must loue you, and sue to know you better.

Edm. Sir, I shall study deseruing.

Glou. He hath bin out nine yeares, and away he shall againe. The King is comming.

Sennet. Enter King Lear, Cornwall, Albany, Generill, Regan, Cordelia, and attendants.

Lear. Attend the Lords of France & Burgundy, Gloster.

Glou. I shall, my Lord. *Exit.*

Lear. Meane time we shal expresse our darker purpose. Giue me the Map there. Know, that we haue diuided In three our Kingdome : and 'tis our fast intent, To shake all Cares and Businesse from our Age, Conferring them on yonger strengths, while we Vnburthen'd crawle toward death. Our son of *Cornwal*, And you our no lesse louing Sonne of *Albany*,

We haue this houre a constant will to publish Our daughters seuerall Dowers, that future strife May be preuented now. The Princes, *France* & *Burgundy*, Great Riuals in our yongest daughters loue, Long in our Court, haue made their amorous soiourne, And heere are to be answer'd. Tell me my daughters (Since now we will diuest vs both of Rule, Interest of Territory, Cares of State) Which of you shall we say doth loue vs most, That we, our largest bountie may extend Where Nature doth with merit challenge. *Generill*, Our eldest borne, speake first.

Gon. Sir, I loue you more then word can weild y matter, Deerer then eye-sight, space, and libertie, Beyond what can be valewed, rich or rare, No lesse then life, with grace, health, beauty, honor : As much as Childe ere lou'd, or Father found. A loue that makes breath poore, and speech vnable, Beyond all manner of so much I loue you.

Cor. What shall *Cordelia* speake ? Loue, and be silent.

Lear. Of all these bounds euen from this Line, to this, With shadowie Forrests, and with Champains rich'd With plenteous Riuers, and wide-skirted Meades We make thee Lady. To thine and *Albanies* issues Be this perpetuall. What sayes our second Daughter? Our deerest *Regan*, wife of *Cornwall*?

Reg. I am made of that selfe-mettle as my Sister, And prize me at her worth. In my true heart, I finde she names my very deede of loue : Onely she comes too short, that I professe My selfe an enemy to all other ioyes, Which the most precious square of sense professes, And finde I am alone felicitate In your deere Highnesse loue.

Cor. Then poore *Cordelia*, And yet not so, since I am sure my loue's More ponderous then my tongue.

Lear. To thee, and thine hereditarie euer, Remaine this ample third of our faire Kingdome, No lesse in space, validitie, and pleasure Then that confer'd on *Generill*. Now our Ioy, Although our last and least ; to whose yong loue, The Vines of France, and Milke of Burgundie, Striue to be interest. What can you say, to draw A third, more opilent then your Sisters? speake.

Cor. Nothing my Lord.

Lear. Nothing?

qq 2 *Cor.*

Editing *King Lear*

by David Scott Kastan

K*ing Lear* was first published in 1608 in a quarto edition that proudly announces itself as *Mr. William Shakespeare: HIS True Chronicle Historie of the Life and Death of King LEAR and His Three Daughters*. It seems likely that the unique emphasis upon this as Shakespeare's play was to differentiate it in the bookstalls from another play on the same subject, *The True Chronicle History of King Leir, and His Three Daughters*, which had been published anonymously in 1605. A significantly different version of Shakespeare's play was published in the Folio of 1623. It appeared as the ninth play in the section of tragedies, located between *Hamlet* and *Othello*. Whatever the intended generic difference from the quarto *Chronicle Historie*, the Folio tragedy has about 110 lines not in the Quarto *Lear* and lacks about 290 lines that do appear in it. Numerous speeches vary to small and great degree, even on the fact of their speaker. Traditionally editors have conflated the two versions, taking some of each, to produce an idealized text imagined as the one Shakespeare wrote, but which each of the two printed versions somehow corrupted and misrepresented. However, in recent years, scholars have come to think of these two versions as independent and discrete, each representing a different stage of Shakespeare's imagination of the play.

This Barnes & Noble edition is based on the Folio text, as it seems to be Shakespeare's most fully considered version of the play, a thorough revision that sharpens (and shortens) the dramatic action of the play, subtly modifies some of the Quarto's characterizations (especially Kent, Albany, and Edgar), and rewrites the ending, giving Edgar rather than Albany the last word. It is impossible to know exactly what motivated the changes, even to know who was responsible for them (although stylistic tests seem to prove it was Shakespeare himself). It seems likely that Shakespeare began his revisions by marking up a copy of the 1608 Quarto, and, as his changes became too numerous and substantial to be easily followed, a manuscript copy of the now revised play was prepared for the use of the acting company. This copy (or a transcript of it) was probably what the printers of the Folio worked from, though, on the evidence of spelling and punctuation, they also consulted a copy of the second edition of the Quarto (Q2), which had been published in 1619 with a title page falsely dated 1608.

The editorial work of this present edition of *King Lear* is conservative, for the most part accepting the evidence of the printed Folio text. Most of the changes from the original merely involve the normalizing of spelling, capitalization, and punctuation, the removal of superfluous italics, the regularization of the names of characters, minor repositioning of stage directions, and the rationalizing of entrances and exits. Emendations are made only when the reading of the Folio seems manifestly wrong. A comparison of the edited text of 1.1.1–88 with the facsimile page of the Folio (on p. 360) reveals some of the issues in this process. The speech prefixes are expanded and normalized for clarity, so that *Glou.* and *Edm.* become **Gloucester** and **Edmund**. Spelling, capitalization, and italicization in this edition follow modern practices rather than the habits of the Folio's printers. As neither spelling nor punctuation in Shakespeare's time had yet been standardized, words were spelled in various ways that indicated their proximate pronunciation, and punctuation, which then was largely a rhythmical pointer rather than predominantly designed, as it is now, to clarify logical relations, was necessarily far more idiosyncratic than today. In any case, compositors were under no obligation to follow either the spelling or punctuation of their copy. For most readers, then, there is little advantage in an edition that reproduces the spelling and punctuation of the early printed text. It does not accurately represent Shakespeare's writing habits, and it makes reading difficult, in a way Shakespeare could never have anticipated or desired.

Therefore the Folio's "alwayes" in line 3 becomes the familiar "always" in this edition, while the next word "seeme" becomes "seem," both words here omitting the intrusive "e." In the same line of this edition, the Folio's "vs" becomes "us," while "diuision" becomes "division," though it is interesting to note that "u" was then often used where we use a "v," and sometimes vice versa, just as "i" could be used where we use a "j," as with the Folio's "ioyes" (for "joys")" in line 72. Other modernizations are similarly straightforward: the Folio's "valewes" becomes "value", and in line 8 "bin" becomes the modern "been." In line 73, however, something more than modernization is required: the Folio's "professes" seems clearly wrong (probably a result of the printer being misled by the similarity of "f" and the long "s" and possibly affected by "professe" two lines earlier) and here is emended to "possesses."

Punctuation is modernized throughout. The colon after the Folio's "vs" in line 3 marks a heavy pause rather than defines a precise grammatical relation as it would in modern usage, and in this text it is replaced with a semi-colon that accords with modern practice. Commas that modern usage would not introduce are omitted (as that in line 2 of the Folio, and the Folio's "then" is modernized to the intended "than"), and added when the syntax demands them. The superfluous, "literary" capitalizations of nouns in the Folio are removed, as the Folio's "Son" in line 7 becomes "son," just as "Cradle" in line 14 becomes "cradle." In all these cases, editing is intended to clarify rather than alter Shakespeare's intentions. Thus, Gloucester's speech at 1.1.18–24 reads in the Folio:

> But I haue a Sonne, Sir, by order of Law, some yeere elder then this;
> who, yet is no deerer in my account, though this Knaue came somth-
> ing sawcily to the world before he was sent for : yet was his Mother
> fayre, there was good sport at his making, and the horson must be
> acknowledged. Doe you know this Noble Gentleman, *Edmond?*

Modernized this reads:

> But I have a son, sir, by order of law, some year elder than this, who
> yet is no dearer in my account. Though this knave came something
> saucily to the world before he was sent for, yet was his mother fair,
> there was good sport at his making, and the whoreson must be
> acknowledged.——Do you know this noble gentleman, Edmund?

Though modernization clarifies the logic of the speech, admittedly the process involves some loss. Clarity and consistency is gained at the expense of expressive detail, but normalizing spelling, capitalization, and punctuation allows the text to be read with far greater ease than the original, and essentially as it was intended to be understood. We lose the archaic feel of the text in exchange for clarity of meaning. Old spellings are consistently modernized in this edition, but old *forms* of words are retained (e.g., "Vnburthened" is modernized to Unburdened" in line 40, although "brazed" [braz'd] in line 10 is retained). If, inevitably, in such modernization we lose some of the historical feel of the text Shakespeare's contemporaries read, it is important to remember that Shakespeare's contemporaries would not have thought the book they read in any sense archaic or quaint, as these details inevitably make it for a reader today. The text would have seemed to them as modern as this one does to us.

Modern readers, however, cannot help but be distracted by the different conventions they encounter on the Folio page. While it is indeed of interest to see how orthography and typography have changed over time, these changes are not primary concerns for most readers of this edition. What little, then, is lost in a careful modernization of the text is more than made up for by the removal of the artificial obstacle of unfamiliar spelling forms and punctuation habits, which Shakespeare or his publishers never could have intended as interpretive difficulties for his readers.

Textual Notes

The list below records all substantive departures in this edition from the Folio text of 1623. It does not usually record modernizations of spelling, normalization in the use of capitals, corrections of obvious typographical errors, adjustments of lineation, minor repositioning or rewording of stage directions (SD), or rationalizations of speech prefixes (SP). The adopted reading in this edition is given first in boldface and followed by the original, rejected reading of the Folio or noted as being absent from the Folio text. If the adopted reading appears in the 1608 Quarto or a later Folio, this is indicated in brackets (and **corr** or **uncorr** refers there respectively to the corrected or uncorrected state of the edition where that is relevant). Editorial stage directions are not collated but are enclosed within brackets in the text. Latin stage directions are translated (e.g., *They all exit* for *Exeunt omnes*).

1.1.5 equalities [Q] qualities; **1.1.73 possesses** [Q] professes; **1.1.84 interessed** interest; **1.1.108 mysteries** [F2] miseries; **1.1.154 a** [Q] [Not in F]; **1.1.155 nor** [Q] nere; **1.1.189SP Gloucester** [Q] Cor.; **1.1.215 best** [Q] [Not in F]; **1.1.290 not** [Q] [Not in F]; **1.2.1SP Edmund** Bastard (and generally throughout); **1.2.21 top** to; **1.2.122 Fut** [Q] [Not in F]; **1.2.124 Edgar** [Q] [Not in F]; **1.2.125 and** [Q] [Not in F]; **1.3.3SP Oswald** Ste. (Steward, and throughout; **1.4.1 well** [Q] will; **1.4.134 crown** [Q] Crownes; **1.4.150 fools** [Q] Foole; **1.4.169 nor crumb** not crumb; **1.5.32 more** mo

2.1.2 you [Q] your; **2.1.69 I should** [Q] should I; **2.1.78 why** [Q] wher; **2.1.86 strange news** [Q] strangenesse; **2.1.120 price** prize; **2.1.123 thought** [Q] though; **2.2.15 worsted-stocking** [Q corr] woosted-stocking; **2.2.21 clamorous** [Q] clamours; **2.2.71 too intrinse** t'intrince; **2.2.74 Renege** [Q] Reuenge; **2.2.75 gale** [Q] gall; **2.2.104 flickering** flicking; **2.2.119 dread** [Q] dead; **2.2.143 For . . . legs.** [Q] [Not in F]; **2.2.145 Duke's** [Q] Duke; **2.3.18 sheepcotes** [Q] Sheeps-Coates; **2.4.2 messenger** [Q] Messengers; **2.4.28 panting** [Q] painting; **2.4.31 those** [Q] whose; **2.4.53 Hysterica** Historica; **2.4.59 the** [Q] the the; **2.4.71 have** [Q] hause; **2.4.125 you** [Q] your; **2.4.127 mother's** [Q] Mother; **2.4.184 fickle** [Q] fickly

3.2.3 drowned [Q] drown; **3.2.13 wise men** Wisemen; **3.2.40 wise man** Wiseman; **3.4.10 thy** [Q] they; **3.4.12 This** [Q corr] the; **3.4.31 looped** [Q loopt] lop'd; **3.4.50 through fire** [Q] though Fire; **3.4.51 ford and whirlpool** [Q foord, and whirli-poole] Sword, and Whirle-poole; **3.4.55 Bless** [Q] Blisse; **3.4.56 Bless** [Q] blisse; **3.4.110 till the** [Q] at; **3.4.112 wold** old; **3.4.128 had** [Q] [Not in F]; **3.5.8 letter** [Q] letter which; **3.5.22 dearer** [Q] deere; **3.6.29 Bobtail tike** [Q] Or Bob-taile tight; **3.6.29 trundle-tail** [Q] Troudle taile; **3.6.32 leap** [Q] leapt; **3.6.36 makes** [Q] make; **3.7.10 festinate** fetiuate

4.1.49 'parel Parrell; **4.1.56 scared** scarr'd; **4.2.36 shows** [Q corr] seemes; **4.2.43 thereat enraged** [Q] threat-enrag'd; **4.2.47 justicers** [Q corr] Iustices; **4.3.3 fumitor** Fenitar; **4.3.18 distress** [Q] desires; **4.4.39 him** [Q] [Not in F]; **4.5.17 walk** [Q] walk'd; **4.5.162 Plate sin** Place sinnes; **4.6.25 not** [Q] [Not in F]; **4.6.45 scald** [Q] scal'd

5.1.13 me [Q] [Not in F]; **5.1.35 love** [Q] loues; **5.3.13 hear poor rogues** [Q] heere (poore Rogues); **5.3.78 sister** [Q] Sisters; **5.3.91 he is** [Q] hes; **5.3.120 Behold . . . honors** Behold it is my priuiledge, / The priuiledge of mine Honours; **5.3.123 Despite** [Q] Despise; **5.3.231 you** [Q] your; **5.3.263 You are** [Q Y'are] Your are

King Lear on the Early Stage
by Andrew Hadfield

King Lear was probably written at some point in 1605, within two years of James I becoming King of England. A play on the same subject, *The True Chronicle History of King Leir*, was published in 1605, having been entered in the Stationers' Register on May 8. Evidence suggests that the anonymous play was first performed by the Earl of Sussex's Men in April 1594, but the fact that it was republished might also mean that it had recently been revived. The title of the First Quarto of Shakespeare's play, the *True Chronicle Historie of the Life and Death of King LEAR and His Three Daughters* (1608) suggests that this play was designed to supersede its rival. The fact that two plays on the same subject were published at the same time indicates how topical the story of the British king had become, undoubtedly because England had just become part of a multiple kingdom of Britain, ruled by the Scottish monarch, James VI of Scotland and I of England. The title page to the Quarto mentions three things that distinguish it from its rival: first, the addition of a new subplot with Edgar disguised as Poor Tom; second, the first performance in front of the King at Whitehall; and third, the author's name prominently displayed. None of the play quartos published in the 1590s made much of Shakespeare's authorship, and usually he was not even mentioned. But it was clear that after

Fig 1. In the large London playhouses, the balcony above the stage could be used for staging, seating, or to house musicians.

Fig 2. English Renaissance drama made minimal use of sets or backdrops. In the absence of a set, the stage pillars could be incorporated into the action, standing in for trees and other architectural elements.

Fig 3. *The discovery space, located in the middle of the backstage wall, could be used as a third entrance as well as a location for scenes requiring special staging, such as in a tomb or bedchamber.*

Fig 4. *A trapdoor led to the area below the stage, known as "Hell" (as contrasted with the painted ceiling, known as "Heaven" or the "heavens"). Ghosts or other supernatural figures could descend through the trap, and it could also serve as a grave.*

1600 Shakespeare had become a literary celebrity who was worth advertising.

Such information suggests that *King Lear* was an important play for Shakespeare's company, who had become the King's official players soon after the King's accession in 1603. James was interested in spectacle and often enjoyed seeing masques at court. He was also aware of the power of patronage and the need for a monarch to act in a regal manner, dispensing favors to his subjects. But we should not assume from this that he actually paid much attention to drama itself. What evidence we have indicates that he was frequently bored by complex and worthy plays and was invariably keen to see his favorite courtiers dancing athletically (he was supposed to have fallen for his favorite, George Villiers, Duke of Buckingham, when he saw him dancing). Although *King Lear* was chosen as a play to be performed at court, after it had first appeared on the public stage at the Globe, we need not assume that the King was especially interested in the play. It might have been chosen because of its topical appeal to prominent courtiers and success with the public.

King Lear is indeed a play of topical interest, showing a monarch giving away the kingdom of "Britain" (not England) just at the time that the incumbent monarch had tried to unite it but failed. James had attempted to unite England and Scotland formally in the parliament of 1604, but the proposal had been rejected, much to his chagrin. Forever afterward, James styled himself "King of Britain" (see "Introduction to *King Lear*," p. 11). Whether or not we read Shakespeare's play as critical of James, the suggestion is there that the events of ancient Britain were produced on stage in order to encourage the audience to think about their relationship to current events.

So, although no records survive of the play's early stage history, we can safely assume that *King Lear* excited interest because of its relevance, even if the connection the audience made was to recognize the alien nature of ancient British history rather than its similarity to recent times. Significantly, a later post-Reformation tradition had the King dressed in magnificent robes of scarlet with ermine trim, and it was probably the case that Shakespeare's Lear dressed in similar finery, making the connection to the current monarch—and his predecessor—for the audience. We might also bear in mind Lear's disparaging comment to Goneril: "Thou art a lady; / If only to go warm were gorgeous, / Why, nature needs not what thou gorgeous wear'st, / Which scarcely keeps thee warm" (2.4.265–268). These lines suggest that Goneril was also dressed in a beautiful, elaborate, and skimpy dress, appropriate for a lady at the Jacobean court (perhaps like the one worn by Frances Howard, Countess of Somerset, in a portrait of 1615).

The play would have made use of the costumes available in order to highlight its themes. Emphasis is placed on the splendor of the royal clothing in the first half of the play in order to draw a pointed contrast to the rags worn by Poor Tom in Acts Three and Four, clothes that have such an impact on Lear, impressing him with the poignant reality of poverty. The elaborate sumptuary laws established in the late Middle Ages and codified by the Tudors are spectacularly flouted by the King himself, who has the indignity of appearing naked in Act Three. Lear's exclamation, "Off, off, you lendings! Come, unbutton here" (3.4.104), after his long conversation with Edgar disguised as Poor Tom, functions as an appropriate philosophical conclusion to his thoughts on the inauthentic nature of clothes as a means of covering up real existence. Such an action would have been extraordinarily shocking for audiences in 1605–1606, given the elaborate, carefully codified laws about appropriate clothing, which were designed to match appropriate clothing to the right occasion, limit extravagance, and preserve ideas of social rank. Oswald, Goneril's steward, is evidently more elaborately dressed than he needs to be when Kent confronts him in Act Two. Kent declares with considerable contempt, "A tailor made thee," a line echoed by the Duke of Cornwall ("A tailor make a man?"), which enables Kent to insult Oswald further: "A tailor, sir. A stonecutter or a painter

could not have made him so ill, though they had been but two years /
o' th' trade" (2.2.51–56). Oswald's fancy clothes cannot hide his
essentially inadequate and superficial nature, a pointed contrast to
the loyal and authentic characters in the play—Kent, the Fool, Cordelia, Edgar—who are not deceived by surfaces. Oswald looks as if he
had been designed by a bad craftsman, an image that suggests that
he is not a real person. It is little wonder that the mad Lear strives for
authenticity by getting rid of his clothes.

There is also the Fool, who would probably have been
dressed in a jester's costume, an outfit that would have emphasized
the theatrical nature of the performance, then as now. The King's
Men were famous for their fools. When they had been the Chamberlain's Men before the advent of James, one of their key performers
had been Will Kemp, who had left the company in 1599 just as they
were about to establish themselves at the Globe Theatre, perhaps
because of a rift with Shakespeare. The role of Falstaff in the two Henry IV plays (1597–1598) had been written for Kemp. The Fool in *King Lear*
clearly followed in the same tradition, and was probably played by the
resident actor who succeeded Kemp, Robert Armin (1568–1616).

Armin was noted as a skilled improviser who could also
dance and had a gift for clowning. He wrote his own play, *The Two Maids
of More-clack* (1608), which served as a showcase for his various skills
and in which he acted two roles, that of a foolish clown and a rather
more sophisticated steward. But it is also possible that the Fool was
played by the same actor who played Cordelia, as neither is on stage
together. Cordelia disappears after the first scene and then reappears
in Act Four, while the Fool is on stage from the end of Act One and
until Act Three. If the parts are doubled, then the Fool's disappear-
ance in Act Three, after the enigmatic line, "And I'll go to bed at noon"
(3.6.44), is so he can change into his other costume. If this is the case,
then the Fool must have been a slender and delicate boy actor, who
did not appear robust enough to survive long and whose relationship

with Lear was more of a favored and precocious child correcting the excesses of an overbearing parent than of an equal in wit but not status.

The wealth of references to clothing suggests that costumes
played a vital role in the early performances of *King Lear*. This was in
stark contrast to the stage setting, which was undoubtedly fairly
simple and straightforward. There are no stage directions or lines
that indicate that elaborate props were required, as they were in plays
such as Christopher Marlowe's *Dr. Faustus* (c. 1589, published in Quarto
1604), or Shakespeare's *Henry VIII* (1613), which led to the destruction
of the Globe Theatre when stray discharge from a cannon set the
thatched roof alight. The props that are required are all relatively
ordinary objects that any theater company would have possessed:
letters, torches, weapons, and so on. The play does require a map
in the opening scene; stocks for Kent; and some means of imitat-
ing the noise of the storm, which was probably made by rolling can-
nonballs over a metal sheet, or drumrolls—nothing that would have
challenged the ingenuity of the King's Men.

Stage directions indicate that virtually all of the action
would have taken place on the stage in front of the audience, and little use would have been made of the wider spaces within the theater
(as would have happened in plays such as John Webster's *The Duchess of Malfi* (c. 1614), or Thomas Middleton and William Rowley's *The
Changeling* (1622–1623), both of which contained extensive scenes
involving madmen who would have been separate from the main
actors and perhaps even stationed around the theater). Edmund asks
Edgar to descend at 2.1.19, so Edgar must have been standing on the
balcony of the playhouse above the main stage, but this is the only
indication that this part of the acting space was used. What about
the "hovel" on the heath (3.2.61)? Or the tree or bush under which
Edgar tells Gloucester to shelter in Act Five, scene two? These would
have been simple to construct, or they may have been suggested by
the columns on the stage, or may merely have been things that the
audience had to imagine.

Although the staging is simple, the play is punctuated by spectacle and scenes of physical action. There is the blinding of Gloucester (3.7) and then his supposed fall from a cliff (4.5), both of which would have required imaginative collusion between actors and audience. The early performances of *Lear* relied upon the play being dramatic enough to establish a bond between those on the stage and those watching. *Lear* is a very verbal play, even though the speeches within it are not as extensive or dense as they are in plays such as *Hamlet* or *Troilus and Cressida*. Still, it does contain some of the most demanding lines in the Shakespeare canon, most notoriously Lear's repetitions and exclamations in the final scene, culminating in "Never, never, never, never, never!" (5.3.283). But there is a regular supply of dramatic action that engages the audience: the tearing of the map (1.1); the fight between Edgar and Edmund (5.3); Kent being put in the stocks (2.2); the expulsion of Lear into the storm (2.4); the scenes on the heath (3.2, 3.4, 3.6, et al.); the blinding of Gloucester and the death of Cornwall (3.7); the pretense that Gloucester is thrown from Dover cliff (4.5); Lear's madness crowned with flowers (4.6); and the battle scenes and the deaths that conclude the play (5.2–3). The audience is never left without an action-packed scene for long.

However, the real heart of *King Lear* is its language. The costumes and moments of action would have been vital for the success of the early performances, but they are present to prevent the play from becoming excessively labored and cerebral. Perhaps the revisions (see Editing *King Lear*, page 361) undertaken after 1605 were made to speed up and make the play more theatrical. In any case, such revisions indicate that *Lear* was a play that received special attention from its author and his company. If some of the changes may have been demanded by changing political conditions or by the desire to darken the tragedy, all seem to function to make the play work better on stage. Its greatness is not only a result of its profound if dispiriting vision of life but also of its mastery of the resources of the theater.

Significant Performances
by Andrew Hadfield

1605 *King Lear* is first performed at the Globe at some point in 1605. Richard Burbage, the leading actor of the company, played Lear.

December 26, 1606 The first recorded performance occurs at court on this date, as advertised on the title page of the Quarto (1608). *King Lear* was the first play performed at court in the post-Christmas season and the first play performed by the newly renamed King's Men after an outbreak of the plague in July 1606.

1609 *King Lear* is performed during the Christmas season at Gowthwaite Hall, Yorkshire, for Sir John Yorke, a prominent Catholic nobleman, along with *Pericles, Saint Christopher,* and *The travails of the Three English Brothers* by a traveling troupe, the Simpsons.

No further records of performances exist until after the Restoration in 1660. This absence might indicate that *King Lear* was not a particularly popular play, especially if we consider that it did not enjoy great public acclaim even after the theaters, which had been closed in 1642, reopened in 1660.

January 1664 *King Lear* is performed at Lincoln Inn Fields by the Duke's Men (one of two companies established after the Restoration, the other being the King's Men). Lear would have been played by the company's chief actor, Thomas Betterton.

June 25, 1675   *King Lear* is performed at Dorset Garden Theatre, which was built in 1671 by Christopher Wren.

1681   Nahum Tate rewrites *King Lear*, carefully consulting both Quarto and Folio texts. Tate changed the style and language of the play, making it less offensive and abrasive; he introduced some new characters, such as Arante, a confidante for Cordelia; and he eliminated others, most notably, the Fool. The play was given a happy ending, as Cordelia marries Edgar, and Lear retires with Gloucester and Kent to live the last parts of their lives in contemplation and reasoned debate. Tate's adaptation became the version of *Lear* that most audiences would see until well into the nineteenth century, even though some eighteenth-century editors criticized his version.

1747–1776   The play's popularity increases because Lear is often performed by David Garrick, the most important actor of his generation. Garrick restored some of Shakespeare's text, but left the Fool out, placing great emphasis on his own performance as the King and establishing Lear as one of the key roles for any great actor to attempt. There are a number of records of Garrick's virtuoso performances that reveal him straining every sinew and limb in anger at key moments, such as his speech in the climax to Act One, after which he bursts into tears. Garrick was also notable for dressing royally, in scarlet trimmed with ermine, a tradition that was to continue into the twentieth century. Garrick's chief rivals, Spranger Barry and William Powell, also performed the role of Lear.

1752   Lewis Hallam tours America, including *King Lear* in his repertoire.

1768   George Coleman performs a more authentic version of *King Lear* at Covent Garden, but he does not attract audiences.

1788   John Philip Kemble plays Lear with his sister, Sarah Siddons, as Cordelia. Kemble used Garrick's modified version of the play but later returned to Tate's play. Kemble no longer produced a spare and spartan work, but employed a large cast, particularly in the 1795 production at Drury Lane. Kemble's performance was notable for its brilliant spectacle, and he played the part of an old, afflicted king to perfection. His voice, however, was thought by many observers to be weak, inadequate to represent the majesty of a monarch.

1810–1820   There are few performances of any plays because of George III's mental disorders.

April 13, 1820   Performing in London at Covent Garden, Junius Brutus Booth is the first to revive *King Lear* after King George's death, though still in Tate's version.

April 24, 1820   Edmund Kean plays Lear at London's Drury Lane, the first great Romantic version of the play, setting the agenda for the next few decades. Kean was not a physically imposing actor, but he had an impressively clear voice, and his performances were notable for their passion. Kean was lavishly praised by his contemporaries for his version of the curse of Goneril, the storm scenes, and Lear's reconciliation with Cordelia (Act Four). Kean apparently wanted to restore the ending of the play and eventually got his way in 1823. However, his attempt to carry Cordelia onstage proved beyond his physical capacity, reducing the audience to laughter, and Tate's conclusion was reinstated.

August 1833   William Charles Macready performed the role of Lear for the first time. Macready became the great Lear of the middle years of the nineteenth century, making it one of his most significant roles. He restored more of Shakespeare's text, especially the style and language, and a version of the original ending (although he still omitted the Fool). The play gradually became more spectacular and lavish in its production values. In addition to larger casts, nineteenth-century directors created spectacular stage designs with castles, druid circles based on Stonehenge, and violent storms.

1881   Edwin Booth performs Lear in London and on tour in America.

1892   Jacob Gordin performs *The Jewish King Lear* in New York, one of many adaptations/appropriations of the play by non-English-speaking directors.

From 1900–1999, especially after the Second World War, *King Lear* is performed more often than in any previous century.

1931   John Gielgud plays Lear at London's Old Vic when only twenty-six. He was praised for the sensitivity and intelligibility of his portrayal. He also played Lear in 1940, under the direction of Harley Granville-Barker at the same theater; in 1950 at Stratford-upon-Avon, with Peggy Ashcroft as Cordelia; and in 1955 at London's Palace Theatre. The 1950 production made Lear into a weak and doddering old man and was much criticized, while in 1955 he was a more vigorous, angry man competing in his rage with the fury of the elements.

1941   Gregori Kozintsev produces *King Lear* in Moscow in a version that stresses Lear's suffering humanity.

1943 Donald Wolfit plays Lear, to critical acclaim, as a powerful and grand king aware of his own impending destruction.

1946 Laurence Olivier plays Lear for the first time at the Old Vic. Olivier's performance got mixed reviews, and his attempt to inject some humor into the role was not considered an unqualified success.

1962 Peter Brook produces *King Lear* for the Royal Shakespeare Company, probably the most influential version of the play in the twentieth century. Brook saw *Lear* as a brutal existential fable, and he cut lines that softened his stark interpretation. Paul Scofield played Lear as an austere, flawed figure, an Oedipus for modern times. The set was flat and spartan, more like productions of the play in the seventeenth century than those of more recent years. Brook himself said that his intention was to provoke questions and not provide answers.

1969 Peter Brook's film of *King Lear*, based on his stage version, opens. It stressed the helplessness of mankind in the face of angry and indifferent gods. Various cuts and changes were made so that Cordelia's role almost disappeared, as well as other moments that might offer significant hope. Lear's reunion with Gloucester at Dover, however, has been praised by some as a moving image of human resilience. Both appear as "tough old losers" (Robert Hapgood) in a desperate landscape.

1971 Gregori Kozintsev's Russian film of *King Lear* opens. Kozintsev emphasized the suffering and oppression of the poor. Lear's fate cannot be separated from that of the oppressed that he governs, a lesson the King, accompanied by his loyal Fool to the bitter end, eventually learns.

1971   Edward Bond's *Lear* is first performed (see pp. 9 and 383–384 for comment). It is revived in 1982 by the Royal Shakespeare Company.

1982   Adrian Noble's Royal Shakespeare Company version was notable for its tender and affecting representation of the relationship between Lear (Michael Gambon) and the Fool (Antony Sher). Together they enacted vaudeville routines, and homage was played to Samuel Beckett in the mock trial scene, when Lear plunged a dagger into the Fool, who stands in an oil drum like characters in *Endgame*.

1982   Michael Horden plays Lear in Jonathan Miller's BBC television version, as an old man more forlorn than furious.

1983   Olivier's last performance as Lear comes in a Granada television version directed by Michael Elliott. Olivier's performance was a tour de force, as he dominated the play to the virtual exclusion of all other actors, apart from John Hurt's Fool, who remains loyal to his master though clearly seeing the disasters that are coming. Olivier's Lear was an egotistical old man, whose physical frailty belied the intensity of his emotions. The set was largely based on the megaliths of Stonehenge.

1985   *Ran*, directed by Akira Kurosawa, based on *King Lear* (see pp. 10–11, 387 for comment).

January 1989   Aribert Reimann's opera of *King Lear* is staged in London.

1991   J. A. Seazer produces *King Lear* in Japanese at the Tokyo Globe Theatre. The production included additional scenes, many of them in mime, including a "Festival of Fools" at the start, and "Roses of the Sterile Woman," a dance performed by Goneril and Oswald.

1997 Sir Richard Eyre directs *King Lear* at the Royal National Theatre with Ian Holm in the title role. The production concentrated on the destruction of the family from within, using the intimate set to help make the play a domestic tragedy, but one no less poignant or painful than more majestic versions.

2002 At the Stratford Festival of Canada, the play is directed by Jonathan Miller, starring Christopher Plummer as Lear. This production emphasized the social disorder at the heart of the play, though Plummer's Lear movingly explored the psychological tragedy, as the old King's pitifully vulnerable self emerges from behind his regal trappings.

Inspired by *King Lear*

Stage

As is well known, Restoration audiences disliked *King Lear*'s conclusion, specifically the tragic demise of both Lear and Cordelia, and found Shakespeare's verse too rough and archaic for their tastes. In 1681, the Irish poet Nahum Tate revised the play as *The History of King Lear.* Tate's version, which was immensely popular for many years, makes three key changes to the play: it invents a romantic subplot for Edgar and Cordelia, introduces the idea that Lear is beloved by his own people, and provides a happy ending, transforming the play from a tragedy into a tragicomedy. In the final scene of Tate's *Lear*, the King, restored to rule by a popular uprising of British citizens, cedes the throne to the now-betrothed Edgar and Cordelia and resolves to live out his days in religious retirement with his faithful servant Kent and the blinded Duke of Gloucester.

Edward Bond's violent 1971 play *Lear* (also discussed in the Introduction) charts the fall and rise, respectively, of a king named Lear (based on Shakespeare's Lear, but ruling over an unnamed country in an unspecified time period) and of a young woman named Cordelia, who comes to power even as the King's authority crumbles and disappears. At the start of the play, the paranoid Lear is supervising the construction of a protective wall around his kingdom. Lear is soon deposed by his daughters, Bodice and Fontanelle, who throw their

father in prison and embark on a cruel reign that provokes a popular rebellion headed by a young woman named Cordelia, whose husband was
killed for trying to help the old King. In prison, Lear begins to repent
his ways. As the King's insight grows, so, too, does the rebel campaign
under Cordelia, which succeeds in capturing Bodice and Fontanelle. But
the subsequent government under Cordelia is no less corrupt. A com-
mittee condemns Lear's older daughters to death without a trial, and
the two women are executed in front of their father. In an attempt to
gain favor with his captors, a fellow prisoner uses a gruesome machine
to remove Lear's eyeballs. Lear staggers out into his former kingdom
and comes upon the wall, where construction is beginning again to
ensure the safety of Cordelia's regime. Lear, having turned prophet
and dissident, loses his life in an attempt to tear down the barrier that
he himself conceived and built. Bond's vicious, dispassionate play has
drawn controversy and mixed reviews since its premiere—as have
most of Bond's pieces—but it is still considered a major work by one of
Britain's foremost contemporary playwrights.

   Lear's Daughters, a 1987 play by Elaine Feinstein and the Women's
Theatre Group, writes the prehistory of Goneril, Regan, and Cordelia.
The play argues that the tragedy of Shakespeare's *King Lear* derives from
Lear's patriarchal parenting style, which has a warping effect on the
nascent personalities of his three young daughters. The play also depicts
how the attitudes and experiences of the adult women in Lear's court
shape the young girls' future conduct. Goneril, Regan, and Cordelia learn
from their Nurse a personal mythology that describes each child as a
miraculous, individual event. At the same time, the submissive behavior
of their mother, the Queen, teaches them that women should be naturally subservient to the wishes of husbands and fathers. By the end of
the play, the eldest sisters have been considerably embittered by the in-
herent conflict between these lessons. Future divisions between Lear's
daughters are foreshadowed by Cordelia's status as Lear's favorite child
and Goneril's harsh domination of the easily led but increasingly angry

Regan. The drama concludes with the image of the three sisters catching and holding, together, a single crown—a symbol of trouble to come.

The title of Howard Barker's *Seven Lears* (1989) is a reference to the early modern convention of dividing the human lifespan into seven ages distinguished by seven different roles: infant, schoolchild, lover, soldier, justice, pantaloon (a foolish old man), and finally the second infancy of extreme old age. Barker's psychological drama follows Lear's progression through these seven ages. The King begins his life as a thoughtful child whose rejection of the injustices of his own father's reign seems to bode well for the future. At the start of the play, Lear discovers the gaol, or jail, within which prisoners are kept and vows to stop the practice. But as he grows older, Lear becomes absorbed with his own thoughts, leading him first to neglect and then enjoy the cries of the jailed prisoners. Barker gives Lear a wife whose clear-sightedness and firm morality place her in opposition to her vacillating husband. Her name, appropriately enough, is Clarissa—"clear"—and when she discovers the jail, which has become her husband's most precious secret, Lear chooses to destroy her, an act which, Barker argues, explains the suppression of any mention of Lear's wife in the text of Shakespeare's play. *Seven Lears* is the tragedy of a man who might have been a decent man had he remained a private citizen, but whom authority and public responsibility turn into a tyrant and a murderer.

In Julia Pascal's *The Yiddish Queen Lear* (1999), King Lear becomes Madame Esther Laranovska, the matriarch of a Yiddish theater clan. The play is set in WWII-era New York City, where Esther has settled with her daughters Rachele, Gitelle, and Channelle. The two eldest daughters, who take issue with Esther's diva-like personality, feel that their mother's traditional theater practice is outdated. When Esther decides to retire, the two women open a nightclub together. Esther moves in with Gitelle and her husband, but she soon discovers that Gitelle is having an affair with Rachele's husband, Irving. Seeking to protect herself, Gitelle accuses Esther of insanity and throws her out.

In the spirit of creative improvisation, the now-homeless Esther joins the destitute members of her former acting company—out of work since Esther's retirement—and together they form a kind of begging theater: the "Yiddish Theater of the Streets." Channelle eventually finds her mother and, vowing to restore Esther's money, travels back to Europe with her and the company. But in Europe, the rise of Hitler has begun. Meanwhile, in America, Rachele discovers Irving and Gitelle's affair and stabs her sister to death in a jealous rage. Channelle tries and fails to buy passage to France for her mother and the rest of the company, but it is too late: France is now occupied by the Nazis. Deprivation and the news of Gitelle's murder send Esther over the brink of sanity. In the final scene of the play, Channelle is struck and mortally wounded by a car as she dashes away from the painful sight of her mother's madness. The ragged remnants of the Yiddish Theater of the Streets attend Esther's last moments as she grieves for her daughters before perishing herself, the last of her kind.

Film

The phrase "Hobson's choice" refers to a choice in which only one option is truly viable. In David Lean's 1954 film *Hobson's Choice* (based on a 1915 stage comedy by Harold Brighouse), a widowed bootmaker named Henry Hobson lives at ease while his three daughters run the house and look after the successful family business. Hobson, wishing for things to continue as they are, forbids his daughters to marry. But Maggie, his eldest daughter, has other ideas: she falls in love with Hobson's head bootmaker, Will Mossop, and secretly arranges to marry him. The new couple starts a competing bootmaking business, and the two younger daughters follow their sister's example by similarly deserting their father for new husbands. As Hobson watches his trade dwindle and his house decay, he begins drinking heavily. When his health begins to fail, Maggie and Will return to offer him a take-it-or-leave-it Hobson's choice: he can take them on as business partners and have them return to the household, or he can continue along a certain path to ruin. Backed into a corner, Hobson agrees. In its own way, the movie ends happily, with the promise of good care for Hobson himself and of successful marriage and business settlements for Maggie and her sisters.

The most famous film adaptation of _Lear_ is most likely Akira Kurosawa's _Ran_ (c. 1985). Kurosawa sets the action in feudal Japan and gives his Lear, the Great Lord Hidetora Ichimonji, three sons rather than three daughters. In _Ran_, it is evident that only the Great Lord's sustained ruthlessness has allowed him to create a united territory out of a patchwork of warring, petty lordships. This ruthlessness, however, has also been his children's only model of conduct. Therefore, when Hidetora announces his intention to retire and live as his sons' honored guest, his actions strike his sons as unexpectedly sentimental. Ichimonji presumes that his heirs, Taro, Jiro, and Saburo, have learned filial loyalty as well as brutality. But as his youngest son, Saburo, tells him, this presumption is sheer folly. In a rage, Hidetora banishes Saburo, whose words are nonetheless soon proven true. Jiro and Taro turn against their father, then against each other, and as the dominions of the house of Ichimonji are ravaged by internecine violence, Jiro assassinates Taro. Hidetora, whose retinue has been slaughtered around him, is thrown into the care of his Fool, Kyoami, and one other faithful retainer. In the scenes of exile that follow, Hidetora, like Shakespeare's Lear, is driven mad and restored to temporary sanity and health only through the intervention of his youngest child, who has returned to the realm with military allies. As full-scale war envelops the valley, however, and Saburo is killed by one of Jiro's assassins, Hidetora dies from sorrow, and the destruction of the house of Ichimonji is complete.

Jean-Luc Godard's _King Lear_ (1987) features Molly Ringwald as Cordelia and Burgess Meredith as her father, Don Learo, an elderly gangster. Shakespeare's setting is shifted to a French seaside hotel, where Cordelia and Learo are vacationing. Set in a post-apocalyptic time, Godard's _King Lear_ portrays a world in which all art has been lost, including the plays of Shakespeare. Peter Sellars plays William Shakespeare Jr. the Fifth, a descendant of the bard who attempts to reconstruct Shakespeare's lost work. There are several notable cameos in this production, including Woody Allen as a befuddled film director and Norman Mailer as himself. Godard plays a professor attempting to revive the art of cinema in this disjointed and loose adaptation, which was panned by the critics.

The 1997 film *A Thousand Acres*, based on Jane Smiley's 1991 Pulitzer Prize–winning novel, sets *Lear* in the farming community of Zebulon County, Iowa. The well-respected Larry Cook has three daughters—Ginny, Rose, and Caroline—and a thousand-acre farm. At the beginning of the movie, Larry proposes turning the farm into a family corporation consisting of an equal share for each daughter. Ginny and Rose, who live on the farm with their husbands, agree to the proposal. Caroline, a lawyer in Des Moines, expresses reservations and is immediately shut out of the discussion. The thousand acres are eventually divided between the eldest daughters. But Larry soon begins to behave erratically and Caroline, from a distance, becomes concerned. She confronts Ginny, and when her sister responds evasively, becomes enraged, believing that her sisters are abusing their newfound power and deliberately mistreating their father. But as the family's history of sexual abuse and secrecy is slowly exposed, Ginny and Rose are shown to be "more sinned against than sinning," as Shakespeare's Lear once claimed to be himself. Smiley and the film's director, Jocelyn Moorhouse, produce a powerful story that offers one explanation for the otherwise obscure motives that set Lear's eldest children against him.

Don Boyd's 2001 film *My Kingdom* sets the tragedy among a crime family in modern-day Liverpool. The key figures are Sandeman, the head of Liverpool's violent underworld, his wife Mandy, and his three daughters Kath, Tracy, and Jo. As in *A Thousand Acres*, the Lear-figure is initially presented as an unsympathetic character. Unlike Larry Cook, however, Sandeman is ultimately transformed by his suffering into a figure who attracts our pity. His first and greatest error occurs when he arrogantly confronts a young mugger attempting to steal Mandy's purse. Secure in his fame, Sandeman is certain that the inexperienced thief will not harm them. But Liverpool's new generation of impoverished thugs doesn't understand or recognize Sandeman's importance, and Mandy is shot and killed during the encounter. Grief stricken, Sandeman decides to retire from the crime business. He attempts to hand over the financial assets of the family to his favorite daughter, Jo, so she can act as custodian of his empire. But Jo, tired of the anguish Sandeman's business inflicts on others, rejects her inheritance. Kath and Tracy receive everything instead, and they immediately set about stripping their father of both his home and his respect. Sandeman is cast off to wander the dangerous streets and debris-strewn dockyards of Liverpool. Meanwhile, Kath and Tracy's gangs begin to fight over turf, as each sister seeks to supplant her father in total control of the ravaged city. As Kath and Tracy's feud grinds to its bitter conclusion, Jo alone is spared. Her uncompromising rejection of the corrupt sources of her family's power preserves her to care for her shattered father, who survives at the close of the movie as a senile and harmless old man.

In 2002, Royal Shakespeare Company alumnus Patrick Stewart teamed up with screenwriter Stephen Harrison and executive producer Robert Halmi Jr. to create a made-for-television adaptation of Shakespeare's tragedy. *King of Texas*, which was broadcast on Turner Network Television (TNT) to favorable reviews, sets Shakespeare's tale in the American West of the early 1840s. The all-star cast is lead by Patrick Stewart as the wealthy ranch owner John Lear. Marcia Gay Harden, Lauren Holly, and Julie Cox play Lear's daughters Susanna, Rebecca, and Claudia, respectively. Roy Schneider is Lear's fellow rancher Westover, the Gloucester character. David Alan Grier, as the fool, is Lear's ranch hand Rip. *King of Texas* maintains the majority of Shakespeare's plot while also addressing the prevalent political and racial tensions between Texans, Mexicans, and Tejanos in post-Alamo Texas.

Music

King Lear has inspired some distinguished musical interpretations. First among them is Hector Berlioz's *Ouverture du Roi Lear* (*King Lear Overture* c. 1831). The great Romantic composer noted that, with this piece, he intended to "give voice to" Lear and Cordelia. Berlioz referred to the overture with pride for the rest of his life, yet the piece was born in a painful time for the composer: Berlioz had recently discovered that his intended fiancée was already engaged to another man. The madness and conflict of the Lear story echoes the heartbreak Berlioz suffered while writing his tragic work.

In the twentieth century, the Soviet composer Dmitri Shostakovich produced a score to accompany Grigori Kozintsev's famous 1970 film version of *King Lear*. Shostakovich's compositions were renowned for their forceful melancholy and stark, shocking aural effects, and the incidental music for Kozintsev's movie makes full use of the composer's abilities. In particular, the Shostakovich score is well known for its strong characterization of the Fool, who receives his own disturbing, semi-comic sequence of music.

Several successful operas have been written based upon *King Lear*. German composer Aribert Reimann's 1978 work is a dark piece that uses dissonant harmonies and intense vocals to create an almost ritualistic musical experience. More recently, the accomplished Finnish composer Aulis Sallinen completed his opera *Kuningas Lear* (c. 1999), which received mixed reviews during its first performances at the Finnish National Opera in Helsinki. With its dominant melody line, some critics found the piece overly traditional, while others appreciated the opera's clarity and found it moving and heartfelt.

Visual Arts

Visual artists have responded strongly to King Lear. The old, mad King has come to represent, most commonly, a visual emblem of embattled humanity. In the mid-eighteenth century, a number of artists elaborated on details the editor Nicholas Rowe added to his 1709 edition of Lear. For example, Rowe specifies that Act Three takes place on "a heath," and where the Folio stage directions only indicate "Storm still," Rowe adds thunder and lightning. These details, along with Rowe's insistence that Lear is tearing off his clothes in his mad scenes, inspired the majority of paintings and drawings illustrating Shakespeare's tragedy. These eighteenth-century artworks, including those by Alexander Runciman (King Lear on the Heath, c. 1767) and George Romney (Lear in the Tempest Tearing Off His Robes, 1762), show Lear standing on a heath in some state of undress, his white hair in disarray. These works magnify Lear's internal strife by depicting dark clouds and lightning lingering in the background, suggesting that the natural world rages in concert with Lear. In a more intimate vein, portrait heads of Lear by painters such as Joshua Reynolds (1723–1792) and John Hamilton Mortimer (1740–1779) continue the theme of embattled humanity, emphasizing the wildness of the King's expression and the unruliness of his thick white hair.

Other artists were drawn to the pathos of the play's dramatic trajectory, and in the middle of the nineteenth century, Ford Madox Brown produced an accomplished series of drawings detailing the tragedy from start to finish. But Lear has always been a good subject for idiosyncratic and radical responses, and the English visionary poet and artist William Blake (1757–1827) also produced drawings and watercolors based on Shakespeare's tragedy. In Lear and Cordelia in Prison, c. 1779, Blake places Lear peacefully asleep in Cordelia's lap. This intimate moment is all the more tender when contrasted with Blake's earlier depictions of Lear raging against the storm. In Blake's rendering, the final, tender scenes between Lear and Cordelia seem to represent an idealized state of humanity: reconciled, loving, at peace.

For Further Reading
by Andrew Hadfield

Bradley, A. C. *Shakespearean Tragedy.* London: Macmillan, 1904. One of the key works that has influenced modern interpretations of the play and helped to establish *King Lear* as Shakespeare's greatest play. Bradley tries to explain why Cordelia dies, her death having been the main reason why it was the least popular of the four great tragedies before the twentieth century. Bradley's answer was that Cordelia's death mattered less than her existence as the highest expression of tragic experience.

Brooke, Nicholas. *Shakespeare's "King Lear."* London: Arnold, 1963. A brilliant exposition of a reading of the play as the bleakest expression of human existence. Brooke is a rigorous and often relentless analyst of the implications of *King Lear*'s poetic language and logic.

Colie, Rosalie L. and F. T. Flahiff, eds. *Some Facets of "King Lear": Essays in Prismatic Criticism.* Toronto: University of Toronto Press, 1974. A provocative collection of essays focusing on the play's language and structure. There are valuable essays on the use of commonplaces in the play; *King Lear* in relation to the crisis of aristocratic status in Jacobean England; biblical language; clothing; acting; the relationship of the subplot to the main plot; and other key topics.

Danby, John F. *Shakespeare's Doctrine of Nature: A Study of "King Lear."* London: Faber, 1961. A rigorous reading of the conception of nature in the play, which concludes that *King Lear* is a deeply Christian work.

Dollimore, Jonathan. "*King Lear* and Essentialist Humanism." in *Radical Tragedy: Religion, Ideology and Power in the Drama of Shakespeare and his Contemporaries.* Brighton: Harvester, 1984, pp. 189–203. A ground-breaking reading of *King Lear*, which argues that the play refuses to grant the audience the closure it desires and shows instead the limitations of tragedy read as a genre about individual consciousness and will. Rather, *King Lear* exposes the power structures of Jacobean England and the ways in which the identities of individuals are determined by forces beyond their control.

Foakes, R. A. *"Hamlet" Versus "Lear": Cultural Politics and Shakespeare's Art.* Cambridge: Cambridge University Press, 1993. A comprehensive account of the rival claims of the plays usually considered to be Shakespeare's greatest works. Foakes provides a sensible overview of textual matters, the history of criticism, and the essential features of each play.

Goldberg, Jonathan. *James I and the Politics of Literature.* Stanford: Stanford University Press, 1989. A New Historicist account of the power structures functioning during the rule of King James and the relationship between literature and politics. The work has been criticized for its excessive emphasis on the authority of the King but it remains an often persuasive reading of the literary and political culture out of which *King Lear* emerged.

Greenblatt, Stephen. "Shakespeare and the Exorcists," in *Shakespearean Negotiations.* Oxford: Oxford University Press, 1988, pp. 94–128. Another key New Historicist reading of the play. Greenblatt's essay is an elegant reading of the relationship between *King Lear* and treatises on witchcraft and the supernatural.

Hawkes, Terence. *King Lear*. Plymouth: Northcote House, 1995. A splendid short guide to the play, which is especially strong on the use of the matter of Britain. Hawkes is also thoughtful about the relationship between the play in Shakespeare's time and our own, as well as reading key moments in a characteristically perceptive and provocative manner.

Holland, Peter, ed. *"King Lear* and Its Afterlife." *Shakespeare Survey* 55 (2002). A volume of this distinguished journal that provides an interesting collection of varied essays on the critical, theatrical, and imaginative history of the play.

Ioppolo, Grace, ed. *A Routledge Literary Sourcebook on "King Lear."* London: Routledge, 2003. A useful guide to numerous aspects of *King Lear*. The book contains a collection of sources; a history of criticism; consideration of the work in performance; and an extensive account of key passages with headings and notes. A good place to start.

Jardine, Lisa. "Reading and the Technology of Textual Affect: Erasmus's Familiar Letters and Shakespeare's *King Lear*." in *Reading Shakespeare Historically*. London: Routledge, 1996, pp. 78–97. An important essay on the significance of letters in *King Lear* and in Jacobean England, in a book that makes many startling connections between Shakespeare's plays and historical artifacts and practices.

Kermode, Frank, ed. *Shakespeare, "King Lear": A Selection of Critical Essays*. London: Macmillan, 1969. Now somewhat dated, but still an important collection of essays that contains much of the early commentary on *King Lear*—Nahum Tate, Samuel Johnson, Coleridge, Keats, and others—and landmark essays from the postwar period up to the late 1960s. These include Jan Kott's comparison between *Lear* and Samuel Beckett's *Endgame*, an attempt to read the play as an absurdist drama; G. Wilson Knight's famous essay on the comedy of the grotesque; Enid Welsford's groundbreaking work on the Fool; and Northrop Frye on *Lear* as a tragedy of isolation.

Knight, G. Wilson. *The Wheel of Fire: Interpretations of Shakespearean Tragedy.* London: Routledge, 1989, report of 1930, chs. 8–9. Two important essays on the play that have had a major influence on subsequent interpretations. "The *Lear* Universe" argues that the play represents the universe as "agnostic and somber often, and often beautiful." Even in this bleak world the characters can distinguish good from evil. "*King Lear* and the Comedy of the Grotesque" examines the grim humor of the play.

Ogden, James and Arthur H. Scouten, eds. *"Lear" from Study to Stage: Essays in Criticism.* Cranbury, NJ: Associated Universities Press, 1997. A wide-ranging and varied collection of essays that includes James Ogden's essay on the reality of the heath in the play; R. A. Foakes on textual revision and the Fool; Benedict Nightingale on some recent productions; Anthony Davies on film versions of the play; and two useful essays on the texts by Grace Ioppolo and Richard Knowles.

Ryan, Kiernan, ed. *King Lear.* New Casebook Series. London: Macmillan, 1993. A series of essays informed by contemporary theory and scholarship, including Annabel Patterson on the popular voice; Terry Eagleton on value in the play; Kathleen McLuskie on feminist criticism; Coppélia Kahn on the absence of mothers in the play; Leah Marcus on the context of the first performance; and Leonard Tennenhouse on authority and power.

Taylor, Gary and Michael Warren, eds. *The Division of the Kingdoms: Shakespeare's Two Versions of "King Lear."* Oxford: Clarendon Press, 1983. A pioneering and very influential collection of essays on the two texts of the play. It contains pieces by Gary Taylor on the date and composition of the Folio text; John Kerrigan on the adaptation and revision of the role of the Fool; Thomas Clayton on the revision of Lear's role in the Folio text; Steven Urkowitz on the tradition of editing the play, and others.

Woodford, Donna, ed. *Understanding "King Lear": A Student Casebook to Issues, Sources, and Historical Documents.* Westport, CT: Greenwood Press, 2004. A handy guide to the contexts of the play that contains extracts from the principal sources, Geoffrey of Monmouth, Holinshed, Sidney's *Arcadia*, and others; information on illness, madness, and medicine; documents on kingship and conceptions of the family; adaptations from Nahum Tate to Kurosawa's *Ran*; and a bold section, "Contemporary Application: Treatment of the Elderly."